day trips® series

day trips® from charlotte

second edition

 **getaway ideas for the local traveler**

james l. hoffman

T0015547

Globe
Pequot

Essex, Connecticut

Globe
Pequot

An imprint of Globe Pequot, the trade division of
The Rowman & Littlefield Publishing Group, Inc.
4501 Forbes Blvd., Ste. 200
Lanham, MD 20706
www.rowman.com

Distributed by NATIONAL BOOK NETWORK

British Library Cataloguing in Publication Information available

Library of Congress Cataloging-in-Publication Data available
978-1-4930-7024-4 (paper)
978-1-4930-7025-1 (ebook)

∞™ The paper used in this publication meets the minimum requirements of American National Standard for Information Sciences—Permanence of Paper for Printed Library Materials, ANSI/NISO Z39.48-1992.

For Mom, Dad, and Michael

contents

south

day trip 01

day trip 02

southwest

day trip 01

day trip 02

west

day trip 01

day trip 02

day trip 03

day trip 04

northwest

day trip 01

day trip 02

day trip 03

day trip 04

day trip 05

about the author

James L. Hoffman is a lifelong resident of North Carolina. He's a freelance writer and Executive Director of the Ocean Isle Museum Foundation. Hoffman has also been a newspaper reporter and editor and worked in marketing and public relations at Charlotte's Discovery Place and in several leadership roles at Daniel Stowe Botanical Garden in Belmont. He is the author of *Day Trips from Raleigh-Durham*, *Fun with the Family North Carolina,* and *Day Trips The Carolinas,* all published by Globe Pequot. Hoffman and his wife, Bonnie, raised their family of five in the Piedmont before moving to the coast. They also have one grandchild.

acknowledgments

I would like to gratefully acknowledge all those who contributed their thoughts, ideas, and suggestions that made this work possible. First, thanks to my very patient editors at the Globe Pequot Press for putting up with my questions and uncanny lack of ability to keep style and other guidelines straight. Thanks to all my dear friends in the tourism industry who keep me abreast of the near-constant developments in the world of travel and for their invaluable suggestions: from the NC Department of Tourism, Margo Metzger, Wit Tuttle, Kathy Prickett; local travel PR pros Meara Lyons and Susan Dosier; my good friend the late Jerry Thorton at Visit Charlotte; Tracey Trimble at Hickory Furniture Mart; Harris Prevost at Grandfather Mountain; Amy Phillips at the Spartanburg Visitor Bureau; Dee Grano of the Light Factory; fellow author Jay Ahuja; Dawn Dawson from the South Carolina Department of Parks and Recreation and her extremely responsive partners across the state. A special nod also goes to Sara Pitzer, author of *North Carolina Off the Beaten Path*, for getting me into this mess. I envy your vision and skill as a writer.

Last, but certainly not least, I must thank my family for sharing many of these adventures with me and allowing me the time and space to devote the massive amount of energy a project like this takes. To Melissa, John, and grandson Foster; Michael, Jessie, Michaela, and Kaitlyn, I offer not only my gratitude but my unwavering adoration. And to my wife and soulmate, Bonnie, thanks for always being there; it helps more than you know.

introduction

In the early '70s a Charlotte businessman, inspired by a trip to Disneyland, assembled a group of investors to open a theme park based on experiences in the Carolinas. Partly as novelty, the group plopped it down on the North Carolina/South Carolina state line near Charlotte and called it Carowinds, garnering support on both sides of the border. After a number of changes in ownership by television networks, motion picture studios, and theme park operators, those Carolina themes—a plantation, a frontier outpost, American Indians, country roads, even White Lightning—are a distant memory. The big white line at the park's entrance remains as a symbol of the state line. So it is with Carolina and the places we visit. Plantations of old are gone but provide a window to the past. Frontier outposts are gone, but we can explore their remains. The Catawba and Keyauwee no longer hunt here, but their resilient spirit is still a part of this land. The amount of blacktop is growing to make travel easier, but there is still many a country road to drive. There's not much White Lightning run anymore, but that illicit activity led to one of the region's most prosperous pastimes: stock car racing.

Sharing a border with South Carolina, Charlotteans live in an area of remarkable geographic and cultural diversity. In just over two hours day-trippers can travel through the Piedmont north to Virginia, east to the Sandhills, southwest to the mountains of North Georgia, and west to the mountains of Tennessee.

To the north, in the county of Wilkes, travelers explore the birth of stock car racing and visit a land where tobacco crops have been replaced by vineyards and tobacco barns now accommodate wine tastings and luxurious overnight stays. A place where music is now more important than moonshine. The state's biggest bluegrass festival is here and so is the Bluegrass Hall of Fame. One of the state's favorite sons, Andy Griffith, was born here and so (some say) was the fictional town of Mayberry, known in reality as Mount Airy.

For decades, Charlotteans have heard the roar of modified stock cars that make up much of the entertainment scene and economic climate north of the city. Day-trippers explore fast cars and superstars in the cities of speed: Concord, Kannapolis, and Mooresville. A transportation theme continues with trains at Historic Spencer Shops and in the city of Salisbury, where an unwavering commitment to historic preservation lives. If your car is pointed in this direction, leave home hungry since you'll undoubtedly be directed to the barbecue capital of Carolina: Lexington. The trip to the northeast ends at Winston-Salem, a distinguished city of arts, and in Greensboro, where the gravity of the institution of slavery and racial injustice comes into vivid light.

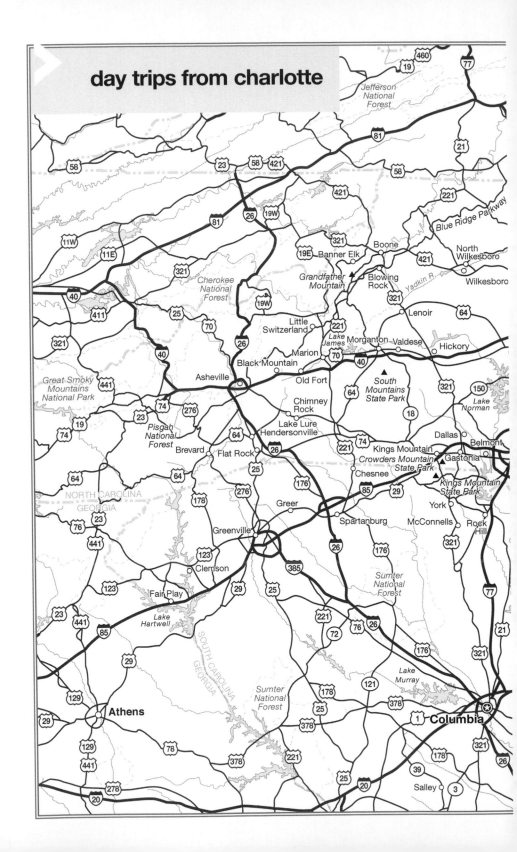

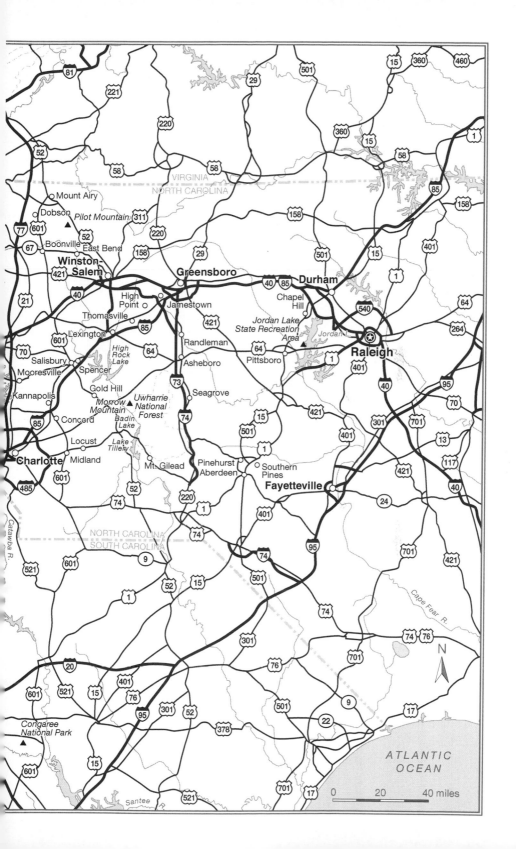

Rolling into the hills of the Uwharrie Mountains, among the oldest on earth, travelers begin to appreciate all that comes from the earth. Two earthy state historic sites and the finest collection of handcrafted pottery in the country are located just east of Charlotte.

The first trip into South Carolina takes travelers to Rock Hill, an area that is busy redis-covering itself in the 21st century. Here day-trippers are asked to "Come See Me" in the state's favorite festival, and can explore life in the time of the Revolutionary and Civil Wars at one of the country's most ambitious antebellum restoration projects. Finally, they end up at this state's zoo and one of upstate South Carolina's centers of recreation, Lake Murray.

The South Carolina foothills of the Blue Ridge Mountains, where North Carolina and Georgia meet the Palmetto State, is known as The Upcountry. It, too, is rife with Revolution-ary War history. More battles were fought in South Carolina than in any other state. And while the agricultural communities here have struggled throughout much of their histories, a new age has realized opportunities in agri-tourism and in the arts. In this region the car fanatic can tour a BMW plant, the baseball fan can visit the home of Shoeless Joe Jackson, and

the carolina thread trail

Throughout the Carolinas, plentiful rivers and rapid development of transportation systems led to the development of the textile industry of the North Carolina Pied-mont and South Carolina Upcountry. The North Carolina Lands Conservancy, in conjunction with local governments and other organizations, is paying homage to that heritage through **The Carolina Thread Trail.** *The trail is a network of green-ways and conserved corridors that link 15 counties in North and South Carolina. As the end of 2022 approached, the conservancy had opened nearly 300 miles of trails that connect to various historical and cultural attractions, points of inter-est, and other trails and natural areas.*

The project, first conceived by Charlotte leadership, began in 2005 and launched two years later. Since then millions in grants have been awarded to support development of trails and to conserve the region's most precious green spaces. Evidence of its success can been seen in areas throughout the Caroli-nas—at Rock Hill's Riverwalk Trail along the Catawba River, at Belmont's Daniel Stowe Botanical Garden, along Bakers Creek Greenway in Kannapolis, and at the Kings Mountain Gateway Trail, to name a few.

Residents and visitors alike are encouraged to hike, bike, and boat to loca-tions along the trail as practical ways of transportation that also reduce pollution and improve their health. Additional points to the trail will be added over the next decade or so, leaving new places and new faces for the day-tripper to discover. For information on how to visit The Thread, see carolinathreadtrail.org.

the military history buff has more than ample selections all along the way. Visual art, theater, music, and more await the more cultured traveler.

Without traveling very far, Charlotteans can find a totally different world that's miles apart from their world of skyscrapers, big league sports, heavy traffic, and all the other good and bad that comes with city life. Just across the Catawba River, day-trippers find the peaceful confines of the town of Belmont with those leading a monastic life just off the interstate. Still dozens of miles from the mountains, travelers find a taste of higher elevations not more than 40 minutes or so from home. The inquisitive traveler will immediately understand the appeal of the North Carolina foothills, and feel the same awe that the 19th-century deep-south elite did. The cooler temperatures and ubiquitous outdoor offerings of Hendersonville, Flat Rock, and beyond are still favorites for miles around. The land of Brevard's waterfalls and the depths and charms of Lake Lure provide some of the most majestic views and reviews in the state.

The drive west is part of the glory of a day trip into the impressive Blue Ridge Mountains. As the traveler ascends its vast slopes, even mundane tasks like shopping for furniture become engaging explorations. The first leg of the Northwest trip takes the traveler to the second of North Carolina's furniture meccas, but that industry brings with it art, history, politics, and religion. Moving onward and upward, the visitor will likely be moved by a people exiled from their homes in the Italian Alps who carved out a new life here. Natural exploits are close at hand as the elevations grow in the cities of Old Fort, Marion, and Morganton, where visitors get to know one of modern-day politics most interesting figures. At an altitude of some 3,500 feet is a mountain city with a curious bohemian flair—the city of Asheville and the location of America's largest residence and the state's most-visited attraction, Biltmore estate.

Rounding out a trip to the northwest is a winter sporter's paradise—the highest points on the Eastern Seaboard and three of North Carolina's ski areas. But it's not all about skiing in Boone, Blowing Rock, and Banner Elk. There's more than a fine restaurant or two. And that view from the car window on the Blue Ridge Parkway can't be beat; it runs along the northernmost parts of day trips in this great range.

Let's hit the road.

using this guide

This guide is divided according to directions on the compass, with all trips originating from the center of Charlotte. It includes the best places to go within about a two-hour drive, but it does not include attractions within Mecklenburg County.

hours of operation

Exact hours of operation are provided where available, but they are subject to change. Attractions often operate seasonally, and that is noted wherever possible. Always remember to call ahead.

pricing key

attractions

Exact pricing for attractions is provided where possible. However, facilities change prices and often charge for special events or may charge more in peak periods. You can assume all establishments listed accept major credit cards, unless otherwise noted. If you have questions, contact the establishments for specifics.

accommodations

The price code reflects the average cost of a double-occupancy room during peak season (not including tax or extras). Always ask if any special discounts are available. Occupancy tax in North Carolina is 6 percent; 7 percent in South Carolina.

$	Less than $100
$$	$100 to $150
$$$	More than $150

restaurants

The price code reflects the average price of dinner entrees for two (excluding cocktails, wine, appetizers, desserts, tax, and tip). You can usually expect to pay less for lunch and/or breakfast.

$	Less than $10
$$	$10 to $20
$$$	More than $20

driving tips

highway designations

Federally maintained highways are designated as US Highway (US 421) or as interstates (I-77). Other highways are roads maintained by the state. North Carolina does not have any county-maintained roadways. Local governments in South Carolina, however, maintain about one-third of its roads statewide.

travel tips

carry a map

This guide includes maps that are intended for reference. Find one of the entire area at the front of each section, and a map for each day trip. "Getting there" directions are also pro-vided from Charlotte to each day trip destination, then from the first destination to the next. Some scenic routes and alternatives are also noted throughout the guide. Typically, a GPS will do nicely in getting travelers from Point A to Point B, but the more skilled, adventurous day-trippers will want to deviate from the beaten path. For that they need a map. The North Carolina Department of Transportation provides a fine map, available by going to visitnc .com, by visiting any one of North Carolina's nine welcome centers, or by calling (800) 847-4862. In South Carolina a road map can be ordered by going to discoversouthcarolina.com or to one of its welcome centers. Also consider purchasing a Delorme *Atlas & Gazetteer* for each state; they are good for back-road travel and hiking.

don't overload your travel itinerary in the mountains

Travel is often slow in the mountains of the Carolinas, so if there is too much on the agenda, you will spend all your time driving and miss all the fun. The maximum speed limit on the Blue Ridge Parkway, for example, is 45 miles per hour. So while it is beautiful, it's not preferred for expeditious travel. In addition, parts of it and other mountain roads are closed during winter or during inclement weather. Also note the parkway uses mileposts, not addresses, to mark specific points. Leaf-lookers come out in droves in autumn, a great time for many day trips, and inevitably slow traffic. Travel information, delays, construction information, and so forth are available at ncsmartlink.org or by dialing 511.

fishing licenses

Fishing licenses are required to fish in any Carolina waters. You can purchase a limited license, an annual license, or a lifetime license by going to ncwildlife.org or dnr.sc.gov. Note that a trout stamp may also be required. Local vendors at bait and tackle shops may also sell licenses and can fill you in on other regulations.

where to get more information

North Carolina Division of Tourism
4324 Mail Service Center
Raleigh, NC 27699
(800) VISITNC
visitnc.com

South Carolina Department of Parks, Recreation & Tourism
1205 Pendleton St.
Columbia, SC 29201
(866) 224-9339
discoversouthcarolina.com

north

>>>

day trip 01

north

moonshine & music:
north wilkesboro, wilkesboro

Daniel Boone and his family lived near here. Tom Dula, the man who became known in musical lore as Tom Dooley, was hanged here. Junior Johnson ran moonshine here. While these historical milestones loom large on the local landscape, it might just be the landscape that draws people to Wilkes County. The eastern slopes of the Blue Ridge, its foothills, and valleys offer a slightly more moderate climate than the higher elevations to the west, but no fewer spectacular views or interesting things to see and do. The area is home to one of the state's most celebrated music festivals, Merlefest.

So close together are these two towns, they almost blend seamlessly into one, and are occasionally referred to as the Wilkesboros.

north wilkesboro

North Wilkesboro was founded on the banks of the Yadkin River just before the start of the 20th century, when the Norfolk and Southern railway ran through here. This was about as far as the trains could chug, so it's called the Key City. Various industries, including mirror producers and Lowe's Home Improvement stores, were founded here and have been important through the city's history. It was known most, however, for its moonshine stills during the days of and following Prohibition. That illegal industry led to the development of the North Wilkesboro Speedway, which stakes significant claims in the development of NASCAR. Races were run here from 1949 to 1996, when Bruton Smith, owner of superspeedways in

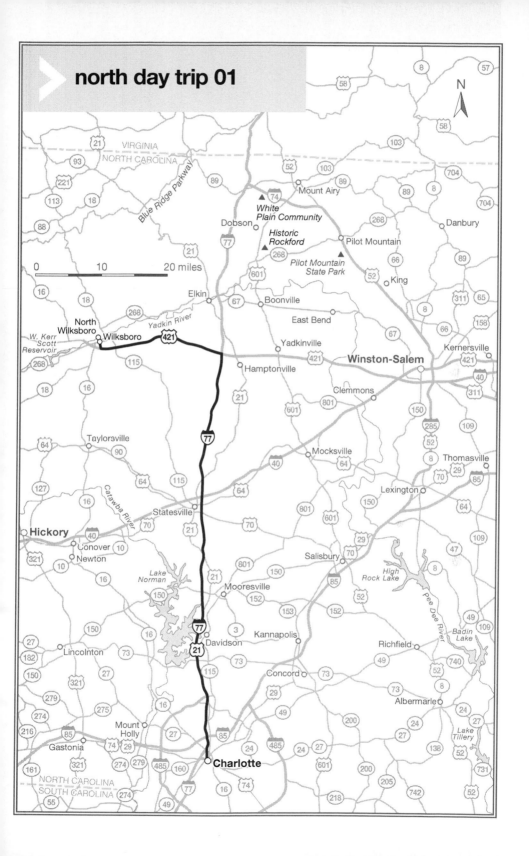

Charlotte and Texas, and a partner bought the facility. Since then, the racetrack's historic fate has been turbulent, but recent investments by NASCAR leaders have given it new life.

getting there

North Wilkesboro is a quick 85 miles from Charlotte, which will take you just about 90 minutes. Head north on I-77 out of Charlotte, then take exit 73B and turn onto scenic US 421 (you'll be traveling west on US 421, but it's labeled north). Follow this into North Wilkesboro.

where to go

North Wilkesboro Speedway. Speedway Lane off Old US 421; (336) 818-9505; northwilkesborospeedway.com. In 1950 a magazine writer called Wilkes County "the moonshine capital of America." It was said that by the middle of the 20th century, 700 bootleggers were running moonshine in cars with modified engines on US 421, the link to Winston-Salem, Greensboro, and Charlotte. Out of this illicit activity grew informal competition among bootleggers and the eventual construction of racetracks throughout the southeast. North Wilkesboro was among the earliest. The speedway fell into disrepair from the time it was closed in 1996 until 2009, when a grassroots organization negotiated a lease from owner Bruton Smith and began developing a schedule of races. It still hasn't returned to its previous glory years, but the owners have begun conducting events here.

Wilkes Art Gallery. 913 C St.; (336) 667-2841; wilkesartgallery.org. Art has been alive in this town for decades, but it wasn't until 2004 when it found a home at the original North Wilkesboro Post Office downtown. The gallery includes 10,000 square feet of exhibition space, working studios for ceramics and painting and drawing, classrooms, and a gift shop. Free. Hours vary seasonally.

The Wilkes Playmakers. Benton Hall, 300 D St.; (336) 838-7529; wilkesplaymakers.com. This active theater group, based at Benton Hall in North Wilkesboro, each summer for years presented a popular play based on the life and death of Tom Dula, a local Civil War veteran who was tried and hanged in 1868 in Statesville for the murder of his fiancée, Laura Foster. In more recent years local theater goers have found more variety in Broadway musicals and interpretations of other dramas. Ticket prices range from $12 to $18.

Yadkin River Greenway. 717 Main St.; (336) 651-8967; yadkinrivergreenway.com. A quick back-to-nature stop is this part of a greenway that runs from North Wilkesboro to Wilkesboro. Here the Yadkin and Reddies Rivers converge. The greenway is part of the North Carolina Birding Trail, and wildlife is abundant along it. Short paved and elevated hiking trails provide a brief respite for travelers.

where to shop

Cook's Sports and Outfitters, 1402 Willow Ln.; (336) 667-4121; cookssports.com. Stop here for camping supplies, the jacket you forgot, and bike and kayak rentals. It's located near the Yadkin River Greenway, where you can hop on the bikes right away. Open Mon through Sat 8:30 to 6 p.m.

Key City Antiques, 502 Main St.; 336-990-0711; keycityantiques.com. Located in a 1930s furniture factory, this antique mall hosts more than 100 vendors in a whopping 28,000 square feet. Locals also sell honey, jellies, jams, repurposed items, and other gift items.

where to eat

The Dispensary. 833 Main St.; 336-818-1152. Its name might be a pretty big clue to the fact this eatery is located in an old drug store—more than 100 years old. Locals meet here for drinks, burgers, Reubens, and the like. Open Tues through Sat beginning at 11 a.m. $$.

Hill Top Restaurant. 1205 2nd St.; 336-667-5564. Located in a red-roofed barn, the Hill Top serves down-home food for breakfast, lunch, and dinner a steady seven days a week. It's open until 8 p.m. $$.

wilkesboro

Situated on the western bank of the Yadkin River opposite North Wilkesboro is the county seat, Wilkesboro. General George Stoneman raided the town in his famous invasion of 1865, but it was after the Civil War that Wilkesboro rose to prominence. Tom Dula (Dooley), a Confederate veteran, was convicted and hanged for the murder of his fiancée, Laura Foster, in a widely publicized and talked-about trial. Many believed he was wrongly convicted and that her killer was one of Dula's jealous ex-girlfriends. The Kingston Trio dredged up the killing in the lyrics of their 1958 song, which went, "Hang Down Your Head Tom Dooley," and Michael Landon (of *Little House on the Prairie* fame) starred as Dula in a 1959 film version of the story.

getting there

From North Wilkesboro, Wilkesboro is about five minutes west on US 421.

where to go

Old Wilkes Heritage Walking Tour. 202 Bridge St.; (336) 667-3171; wilkescountytourism. com/attractions. The 13 buildings on the walking tour of Old Wilkes (and on the National Register of Historic Places) tell the story of the area, from the city's founding in 1800 through the Civil War. On the tour is the city's oldest home, the **Brown-Cowles House** (circa 1830), that still includes several outbuildings, including the slave kitchen and curing house.

Also included on the tour is the **Old Wilkes Jail** (203 N. Bridge St.), constructed in 1859. Tom Dula was held here while he awaited trail, until his lawyer Zebulon B. Vance (who was between stints as governor and whose birthplace is located off the Blue Ridge Parkway near Asheville) had the trial venue changed. Another famous inmate was Otto Wood, one of North Carolina's most notorious criminals, who was born in Wilkesboro and killed by police in a gunfight in Salisbury. The building was restored to its original state using as many of the original materials as possible and is one of the best-preserved examples of 19th-century penal architecture in North Carolina. Of particular note is the survival of its primitive security, including the front door, which contains nails spaced an inch apart so that if a prisoner got hold of an object, he could not saw his way out of the building. The jail is open Mon through Fri.

Among the other buildings on the tour are the Robert Cleveland Log Home, the Federal Building, the Carl Lowe House, St. Paul's Episcopal Church, Wilkes County Courthouse, Old Law Office, the Smithey Hotel, J.T. Ferguson Store, the Johnson-Hubbard House, the Presbyterian Church, and Cowles Law Office. Guided tours of the Old Wilkes Jail and Robert Cleveland Log Home are conducted Tues through Sat 11 a.m., 1 p.m., and 3 p.m. The cost is $6.

St. Paul's Episcopal Church. 200 W. Cowles St.; (336) 667-4231; stpaulwilkesboro .org. Slaves constructed this Gothic chapel in 1848, and it is the city's oldest building. The renowned artist Ben Long painted two frescoes at the church in 2002. Free. Open Mon through Thurs 8 a.m. to 3:30 p.m.

Whippoorwill Academy & Village. 11928 SR 268 West; (336) 973-3237; whippoorwill academy.com. At the heart of this 18th-century village is the one-room schoolhouse known as Whippoorwill Academy, so named because it was built so far back in the woods that not even the whippoorwills could find it. In the cabin's loft are several pieces of art that tell the story of Tom Dula. Of special interest is a replica of the cabin in which Daniel Boone and his family lived. Rocks from the Boone cabin's chimney were used in the replica's construction. Also part of the village are replicas of a chapel, blacksmith shop, and smokehouse. Free. Open Wed through Sat 1 to 5 p.m. Apr through Oct.

Wilkes Heritage Museum. 100 E. Main St.; (336) 667-3171; wilkesheritagemuseum.com. In addition to maintaining the historic properties in Wilkesboro, the Wilkes Heritage Museum also tells the area's tale through exhibits at the 1902 courthouse. On display is one of Junior Johnson's race cars and exhibits that relate to Daniel Boone's history here. The Blue Ridge Music Hall of Fame is also here and includes homage to inductees Emmylou Harris, Arthur Smith, Dolly Parton, Earl Scruggs, and Doc Watson. Admission is $6 per person. Open Mon through Sat 10 a.m. to 4 p.m.

W. Kerr Scott Reservoir Dam & Reservoir Environmental Education Center. 499 Reservoir Rd.; (336) 921-3390; https://www.saw.usace.army.mil/Locations/District-Lakes-and-Dams/W-Kerr-Scott. Fishing, hiking, camping, and other outdoor activities are what the massive lake is all about—on the surface, at least. The US Army Corps of Engineers devised the project in the early 1960s to manage flooding of the area. Now they maintain it for recreational use. Within the area are a handful of boat launch areas and areas designated for swimming and fishing, some requiring a fee. Berry Mountain Park and Boomer Park have beaches where swimming is allowed for $1 per person. Some 30 miles of trails for hiking, biking, and horseback riding weave their way through the park and make up one of the state's best trail systems. Some sections of the trail are designated as part of the Over-mountain Victory National Historic Trail, named in honor of the Patriot Army that marched more than 200 miles to defeat Loyalist forces in Kings Mountain in 1780. Stop by the visitor assistance center to pick up maps and learn about the park before heading out.

where to shop

Wilkes Antique Mall & Emporium. 125 W. Main St.; (336) 667-9809; http://www.buywilkes.com/business_webpage.php?mid=324. A wide, varying range of antiques and collectibles are available at this fun store. Local craftsmen also provide handmade items, including fresh fudge. Open Mon through Sat 10 a.m. to 6 p.m., Sun noon to 6 p.m.

where to eat

Brushy Mountain Smokehouse and Creamery. 201 Wilkesboro Blvd.; (336) 667-9464. The barbecue that comes out of the smoker here has been featured on Bobby Flay's show on the Food Network. The succulent selections are made by a family that was in and out of the restaurant business until they pooled their talents to open this establishment that also serves homemade ice cream. Open Mon, Wed, Thurs, Fri, Sat 11 a.m. to 9 p.m. Eat at the buffet Sun 11 a.m. to 2 p.m. $–$$.

Dooley's Grill and Tavern. 102 E. Main St.; (336) 667-0800; dooleyswilkesboro.com. Clearly one of the area's most popular restaurants, Dooley's uses mostly locally sourced ingredients and offers big and bold flavors.. Pimento cheese is homemade and chili makes its way onto the menu in several ways. Chicken is blackened and roast beef is served rare. $$.

Tipton's Bar-B-Que. 1840 Winkler St.; (336) 667-0669; tiptonsbarbecue.com. Brushy Mountain's competition serves Lexington-style pork barbeque, chicken, and ribs. The menu also sports pizza and burgers. Open daily 11 a.m. to 9 p.m. $.

day trip 02

north

The Yadkin River flows west to east out of the Blue Ridge and runs between Surry and Yadkin Counties before falling off to the south, where it meets the Pee Dee River in the Uwharrie National Forest. The terrain created in the river's valley is filled with rolling hills much like those found in European wine country. The environmental similarities are so strong, in fact, the region has become a center for North Carolina's billion-dollar wine industry. Grape-vines have replaced the tobacco that once filled this and other parts of North Carolina. The industry has thrived in recent years, bringing the number of facilities in North Carolina that produce publicly distributed wine to nearly 200. It is perhaps fitting that this area, once known for its moonshine, would become known for its wine.

The Yadkin Valley was the first of three areas in the state to achieve status as an official American Vitacultural Area; but for the day-tripper, wineries produce more than wine and inviting tasting rooms. Many have restaurants, intriguing histories, and of course those stunning, rolling landscapes. Yadkin Valley's US 601 and US 421 offer scenic drives and other interesting places to visit. For more information, the North Carolina Department of Tourism has a website dedicated to North Carolina wines and related attractions at visitnc.com/wine.

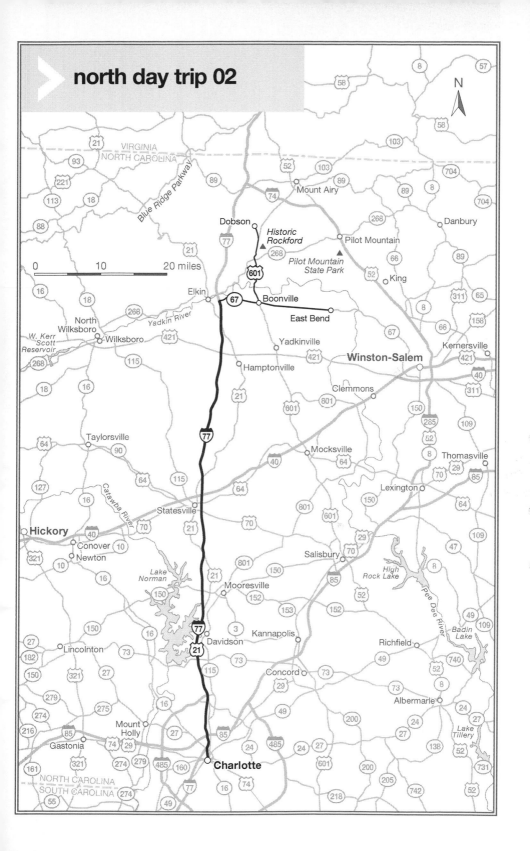

boonville

Local legend says that Daniel Boone camped and hunted in this area around 1768, sleeping in a hollowed-out tree. When the post office was located here in 1857, it was named after him, and so was the incorporated area in 1895. The small town of a few more than 1,000 people has undoubtedly benefited from the tourism of the wine industry.

getting there

I-77 north takes you quickly out of the city and into the Yadkin River Valley. To get to Boonville, drive about 70 miles and take the exit for SR 67 east. The other towns in this day trip are equidistant from Boonville, so it makes little difference driving-wise, which is the second leg of the trip.

where to go

RagApple Lassie Vineyards. 3724 RagApple Lassie Ln.; (336) 367-6000; ragapplelassie .com. Frank and Lenna Hobson named their vineyard after a calf that Frank had as a boy and took to the North Carolina State Calf Show, where it won grand champion. A black and white Holstein sitting in a crescent moon adorns all bottles from the vineyard. RagApple Lassie offers Chardonnay, Viognier, Merlot, Syrah, Cabernet Sauvignon, Zinfandel, and Pinot Gris. Open daily noon to 6 p.m.

Sanders Ridge. 3200 Round Hill Rd.; (336) 677-1700; sandersridge.com. Located on a bucolic 150 acres with a small lake, nature trails, and restaurant with organic offerings, this vineyard has been in the family for more than 150 years. Among the offerings are Cabernets, Chardonnays, Merlots, and Muscadine wines. Charcuterie boards, salads, and sandwiches are also available for purchase. Open daily noon to 6 p.m.

worth more time

More than two dozen wineries are located in this area, so travel here is worth as much time as you can afford. Try the vineyards of Elkin, Yadkinville, or Hamptonville or allow yourself to be diverted by other interests. **Shallowford Popcorn Farm** (3732 Hartman Rd., Yadkinville; 336-463-5938), produces concoctions such as grape- or green-apple-flavored popcorn. There might even be a kernel that pairs well with North Carolina wine. Tours of the plant are also offered. The **Yadkin Arts Council** (226 E. Main St.; 336-679-2941; yadkinarts.org) is housed in a stunning, renovated contemporary facility with studios, shops, and a cafe.

In most parts of North Carolina it would be surprising to see Amish buggies on area farm roads. Not here. A small Amish community has settled here. In fact, the Hallmark film

The Shunning, set in Pennsylvania Amish Country, was shot in the area in late 2010. For a glimpse of Amish life, visit Hamptonville's **Shiloh General Store & Bakery** (5520 St. Paul Church Rd.; 336-468-4789; shilohgeneralstorenc.com).

east bend

East Bend was named for its location in the east bend of the Yadkin River and was incorporated in 1887. With fewer than 700 residents, it has few claims to fame but still is a nice place to visit. More and more people are discovering East Bend because of its burgeoning wine business.

getting there

East Bend is about 15 minutes from Boonville on SR 67.

where to go

Carolina Balloon Adventures. 3028 Black Diamond Ln.; (336) 699-3332; usaballoon .com. Take a two- or three-hour flight over hills, trees, rivers, and farms in Yadkin Valley. Flights start at $225 per person and include a champagne toast and light food.

Divine Llamas Vineyards & Farm. 4126 Divine Llama Lane; (336) 699-2525; divinellama vineyards.com. Like a little llama companionship with your wine? This is the place to get it. Offered are Chardonel, Traminette, Merlot, and Cabernet Franc. The llamas are typically for aesthetics, but they are available for treks in the summer. Open Thurs through Sat noon to 6 p.m., Sun 1 to 6 p.m.

Flint Hill Vineyards. 2133 Flint Hill Rd.; (336) 699-4455; flinthillvineyards.com. This century-old farm has been a vineyard since 2005, making it one of the oldest in the state. Its tasting room is open by appointment and for frequent events featuring live music and local restaurants.

where to eat

Kitchen Roselli. 105 E. Main St.; (336) 699-4898; kitchenroselli.com. Located in what was the historic Davis Brothers Store, this restaurant seamlessly blends Italian recipes with fresh local foods they turn into fresh pasta and other dishes. The menu often features shrimp scampi and filet mignon. Open Thurs though Sun 5 to 9 p.m. $$–$$$.

O. Henry's Restaurant. 10227 NC Highway 67; (336) 699-8693. This mom-and-pop restaurant serves good American staples and regularly schedules music. $

dobson

If Yadkin Valley is at the heart of North Carolina's wine industry, Dobson has a finger on its pulse. The North Carolina Center for Viticulture and Enology is located on the campus of Surry Community College in Dobson. The center educates future generations in the art of winemaking by offering a two-year degree in Viticulture and Enology. It is also the only campus with a working vineyard and bonded winery east of the Rocky Mountains. Just to the south of Dobson is the unincorporated Village of Rockford that takes visitors back to the 1700s.

getting there

Access to Dobson is through the town of Boonville via US 601 North. Day-trippers opting to head to East Bend first will need to return to Boonville via SR 67 West before proceeding to Dobson.

where to go

Shelton Vineyards. 286 Cabernet Ln.; (336) 366-4724; sheltonvineyards.com. Among the most prominent of wineries is this, the state's largest family-owned vineyard, located on a picturesque hillside. Docents offer tastings as the story of the winery is told on a tour of the facility. Have a picnic by the lake or have lunch at The Harvest Grill, which offers Merlot, Syrah, Cabernet, Chardonnay, and more. Open Mon through Sat 10 a.m. to 5 p.m., Sun 1 to 5 p.m.

where to shop

The Rockford General Store. 5174 Rockford Rd.; (336) 374-5317; rockfordgeneralstore .com. Jars of candy—a selection of more than 200, the owner says—line several counters at the Rockford General Store. That might be surprising, were it not for the old metal signs that cover the outside of the building. They are for sale, too. In fact it might be easier to list items not for sale at this general store, which has been the heart of the community since the 1920s—except for the years between 2003 and 2010, after original owner Annie Gray Seats Barnett, died and before the new owners took over. Open Wed through Sat 10 a.m. to 5 p.m. and Sun noon to 5 p.m.

where to eat

The Depot Restaurant. 112 Old Depot Ln.; (336) 386-8222; codycreek.org. A functional water wheel, a display of stuffed game, and a waterfall decorate the entrance of the depot.

Steaks, chops, and seafood are the stars of the menu, served in a down-home atmosphere. Open Wed and Thurs 5 to 9 p.m., Fri 4 to 10 p.m., Sat 3:30 to 10 p.m., Sun 11:30 a.m. to 8 p.m. $$.

The Harvest Grill. 286 Cabernet Ln.; (336) 366-3590; sheltonvineyards.com. Located at Shelton Vineyards, this spectacular restaurant offers bistro-style dining in a handsome dining room or on a bright, enclosed patio at the base of the vineyard. Outstanding selections include pulled barbecue duck, sautéed rainbow trout, and blackened dishes. $$$.

where to stay

The Rockford Inn Bed & Breakfast. 4872 Rockford Rd.; (336) 469-4601. rockfordinn.com. Located in the Rockford community and surrounded by huge old trees, the Rockford Inn dates to about 1850. The rooms overflow with country charm. All three have fireplaces. $$.

day trip 03

north

>>> **mayberry memories:**
mount airy, pilot mountain

Just short of the Virginia state line is a day trip that offers a bit of southern television culture. Both Mount Airy and Pilot Mountain were cast into the national spotlight when the *Andy Griffith Show* first aired on CBS in 1960. The show's star, who went on to become TV's *Matlock* and other characters, grew up here, and the fictional towns of Mayberry and Mount Pilot were based on the real-life towns. Today that much-heralded history is preserved, as are the Snappy Lunch, Floyd's Barbershop, a museum, and other attractions that pay homage to the show.

Other well-known celebrities, including country music singer Donna Fargo and bluegrass legend Tommy Jarrell, are natives of Mount Airy. The original Siamese twins, Eng and Chang Bunker, lived in the nearby White Plains community. For more information, contact the **Mount Airy Visitor Center** (200 N. Main St.; 800-948-0949, 336-786-6116; visitmayberry.com).

mount airy

getting there

Mount Airy is a straight shot out of Charlotte north on I-77, almost exactly 100 miles and just more than 90 minutes away. SR 89 at exit 100 leads to this TV town.

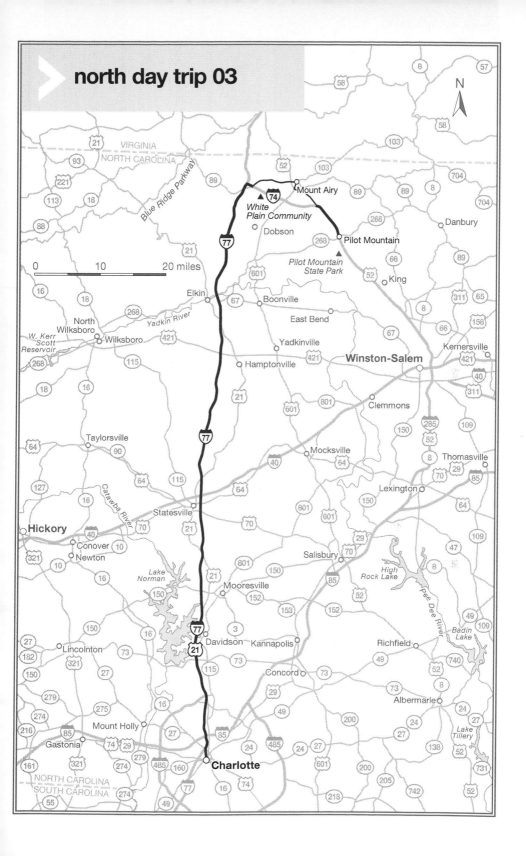

where to go

Andy Griffith Museum. 218 Rockford St.; (336) 786-1604; www.surryarts.org/agmuseum. Of course, the first stop for any Andy Griffith fan is going to be this museum, home of the world's largest collection of Andy Griffith memorabilia. Griffith's childhood friend and Mount Airy resident Emmett Forrest put the display together with the help of actors from the show, including Betty Lynn, who until her death in 2021 lived in Mount Airy and made regular appearances at the museum. The collection contains everything from the chair Andy was rocked in as a baby to the seersucker suit he wore on *Matlock*. The adjacent Andy Griffith Playhouse was built in 1920 as the first known site of a public school in Mount Airy. This is where Griffith attended elementary school and first performed on stage. Named for Griffith in the early 1970s, it now houses the Surry Arts Council's exhibits and performance venue. Admission is $8 for adults and $6 for children. Open Mon through Sat 9 a.m. to 5 p.m. and Sun 1 to 5 p.m.

Mount Airy Museum of Regional History. 301 N. Main St.; (336) 786-4478; northcarolinamuseum.org. More than 35,000 square feet of exhibits include a wall-size mural of the surrounding mountains, and displays and exhibitions on the natural history of the area, the Saura tribe, and Siamese Twins Eng and Chang Bunker. The story of the area's culture, of the settlers who came to the area, and the history of the world's largest open-face granite quarry are revealed here. Included is an authentic reproduction of a log cabin, a turn-of-the-20th-century general store, a train room with a 70-foot scale model train exhibit, and a gallery on firefighters that features 1916, 1926, and 1946 fire trucks. Rotating exhibits on the second floor focus on the early 1900s. Admission is $6. Open Tues through Sat 10 a.m. to 4 p.m.

Siamese Twins Burial Site. 506 Old US Hwy. 601; (336) 786-6116, (800) 948-0949; www.visitnc.com/listing/Wbca/siamese-twins-burial-site. Eng and Chang Bunker, born in Siam, became circus performers who fathered 22 children. Known as "the original Siamese twins," they are buried outside the Mount Airy city limits in the White Plains Church community. To get there take SR 601 south from Mount Airy past a Walmart on the left. Turn left onto Old US Highway 601, then travel two miles to pass over I-74 to White Plains Baptist Church on the right. The cemetery is behind the church.

Wally's Service & Squad Car Tours. 625 S. Main St.; (336) 786-6066; wallysinmayberry.com. Departing from this 1937 service station that was restored in 2007 are 30-minute tours around town (Squad Car Tours; 336-789-OPIE; tourmayberry.com). It's named for the filling station on the *Andy Griffith Show*. Also located here is a replica of the courthouse and jail featured on the show. A store with Mayberry souvenirs, collectibles, apparel, coffee, and more is also on site. The cost is $30 for as many people as you can load in the squad car. Call for reservations. Open Mon through Sat 9 a.m. to 5 p.m. and Sun 10 a.m. to 4 p.m.

where to eat

Snappy Lunch. 125 N. Main St.; (336) 786-4931; thesnappylunch.com. In an episode of the *Andy Griffith Show,* Andy suggested to Barney that they go to the Snappy Lunch to get a bite to eat. In a television news interview, Griffith talked about getting a hot dog and a bottle of pop for 15 cents at the Snappy Lunch when he was a boy. Mount Airy's oldest restaurant, circa 1923, is famous for the pork chop sandwich, which was created by owner Charles Dowell, who has been at Snappy Lunch for more than 50 years. Try it if you must, but it's not recommended for calorie and cholesterol watchers. Open Mon through Sat 6 a.m. to 1:45 p.m. $.

where to stay

Andy's Homeplace. 711 E. Haymore St.; (336) 783-6282; https://andygriffithhome.com. Spend the night in the home where Andy lived with his mother and father until he graduated from high school. Furnished with all the comforts of home, it has two bedrooms, a kitchen, a living room, and one bath. Andy's Homeplace is located near the Andy Griffith Playhouse and Historic Downtown Mount Airy. Enjoy a continental breakfast provided by your host or have breakfast at Snappy Lunch. $$$.

Cousin Emma's Bed and Breakfast. 501 S. Main St.; (336) 756-5656; cousinemmas. weebly.com. Dating to before the Civil War, this is one of the oldest homes in Mount Airy. It's been renovated in recent years with modern conveniences and now offers three rooms and a historic cabin for nightly rental. Located in the heart of downtown, it's become a gathering place for small local events. $$.

The Mayberry Motor Inn. 501 Andy Griffith Pkwy. North; (336) 786-4109; mayberry motorinn.com. A gazebo off Fife Street (named for the famed TV deputy Barney Fife) gives a great view of Pilot Mountain. Guests can walk along Thelma Lou's trail or check out the Andy Griffith and Donna Fargo memorabilia that adorns the inn's office. A 1963 Ford squad car and Emmet's fix-it truck sit in the driveway of the inn. $.

pilot mountain

Twelve miles south of Mount Airy and 26 miles north of Winston-Salem on US 52, Pilot Mountain offers views of the Winston-Salem skyline and the Blue Ridge Mountains. Stop here on the way to or from Mount Airy to get a feel for the High Country.

getting there

Pilot Mountain is a 20-minute drive south from Mount Airy on US 52.

where to go

Pilot Mountain State Park. 1721 Pilot Knob Park Rd., Pinnacle; (336) 325-2355; https://www.ncparks.gov/state-parks/pilot-mountain-state-park. Pilot Mountain's solitary peak, rising more than 1,400 feet above the rolling countryside of the upper Piedmont plateau, is the centerpiece of the state park. Divided into two sections, with 1,000 acres on the Yadkin River, the park offers hiking trails, scenic overlooks, picnicking, family and group camping, and a climbing area. It's an excellent place to observe wildlife, including the fall migration of raptors. Pilot Mountain was named a National Natural Landmark in 1976. Admission is free, but some events require permits and fees are charged. Typically open during daylight hours.

where to stay

Flippin's Bed & Breakfast. 203 W. Main St.; (336) 368-1183. Situated in the picturesque setting of Pilot Mountain State Park, this Victorian-style bed-and-breakfast is lavishly furnished with antiques, beautiful chandeliers, and hand-carved Mahogany beds. It was built in 1896 by the town's Dr. Flippin. $$–$$$.

Pilot Knob Inn Bed & Breakfast. 361 New Pilot Knob Ln.; (336) 325-2502; pilotknobinn.com. Three suites in the main lodge and cabins with rustic exteriors (converted from tobacco barns) and lavish interiors offer a peaceful, private retreat at Pilot Mountain. Most have whirlpools and fireplaces. $$–$$$.

northeast

>>>

day trip 01

northeast

>>>

cities of speed:
concord, kannapolis, mooresville

Most Charlotteans are well aware of Concord's reputation as a city of speed. The opening of the NASCAR Hall of Fame in downtown Charlotte in 2009 inextricably linked the two cities. At one time Concord called itself "The Jewel in the Queen City's Crown," but has since taken advantage of the wild popularity explosion in the sport of NASCAR racing and developed experiences the city to the north can claim all its own. Almost an extension of the county seat of Concord, the city of Kannapolis is also deeply rooted in the business of racing, but with the addition of the North Carolina Research Campus spearheaded by entrepreneur David Murdoch, who in the past decade or so brought part of his Dole Food Company operations from Hawaii to cities in North Carolina. The biotechnology research center is a public-private venture involving state universities and industry to research better ways to produce food. It was built at the former site of the bankrupt Pillowtex, a textile center once called Canon Village that employed 25,000 people.

Also linked to the rich heritage of stock car racing is the city of Mooresville, home of more than 60 NASCAR teams and related companies. This probably isn't news to the legions of NASCAR fans in the area, but there are still surprises to be discovered in these cities of speed, even for the most studied among them. Those who aren't fans of the smell of burning rubber and gasoline will be floored by the massive number of racing teams, shops, and other race-related activities in these cities. Everyone might be surprised by the diversity of offerings sprinkled among the checkered flags.

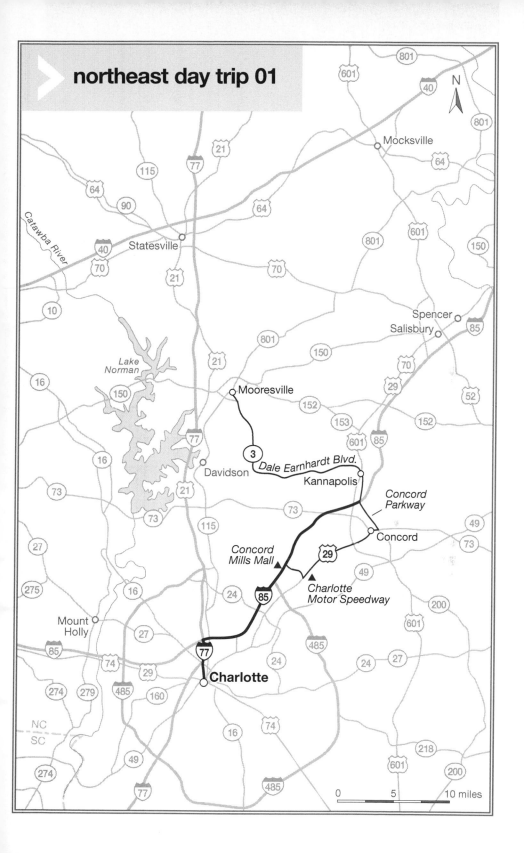

N

801
601
40
801

Mocksville

601
21
77
64
115

64
90
64

801
601
150

40
Statesville
70
21
70

Spencer
Salisbury
85

10

801
150
70

Lake
Norman
21
29

16
150

52

Mooresville

152
153
152

77

601
85

3
Dale Earnhardt Blvd.

16
Davidson
Kannapolis

Concord
Parkway

73
73

115
49
73

27
Concord

Concord
Mills Mall
29

16
24

49

85
Charlotte
Motor Speedway

200

275

Mount
Holly

601

85
27

77
485
24
27

74
29
24

274
279
485
160

NC
SC

16
74

218

49

200

274
77

601

0   5   10 miles

Charlotte

Catawba River

concord

Cabarrus County has grown by leaps and bounds over the past several decades, and its seat, the city of Concord, has grown to be the second largest city in the Charlotte metropolitan area with more than 80,000 people. Its biggest draw, Charlotte Motor Speedway, built in 1960, also includes a newer dirt track and dragway attracting visitors year-round. More recent years brought the opening of the sprawling Concord Mills Mall, which claims to be the most-attended tourist attraction in the Carolinas, and a Big Wolf Lodge, a massive indoor water park and resort. The contemporary atmosphere from the mall at I-85 to the speedway is in stark contrast to the small-town aura of downtown Concord, where small businesses appear to thrive.

getting there

Parts of Concord are bedroom communities for Charlotte, so traffic in and out of Concord can be heavy at rush hour. At other times it's an easy drive north on I-85, which delivers you to a point between Concord Mills Mall and the Charlotte Motor Speedway. At the speedway, a left turn on US 29 takes you to downtown Concord.

where to go

Bost Grist Mill. 4701 SR 200; (704) 782-1600; bostgristmill.com. On the National Register of Historic Places and located on the banks of the Rocky River, this mill was built in the early part of the 19th century and produced flour and cornmeal for much of the region. The original building was reconstructed in the 1870s and suffered significant damage in a storm in 1908. At that point the owners moved it back about 200 yards from the river. Still it grinds corn to grits and meal just like it did 200 years ago. Admission is free. Hours are erratic and are based largely around a few annual celebrations. The owners say they'll be glad to open any time, even if it's just to sell a bag of grits.

Camp TN Spencer Park. 3155 Foxford Rd.; (704) 920-3350; cabarruscounty.us/parks/Camp-T.N.-Spencer-Park. Run by the county and the local Boys and Girls Club is this big park and campground. Outdoor enthusiasts will find room to stretch their legs on a 1.5-mile nature trail, to fish in one of three lakes, or to hop on a paddleboat. The campground has cabins as well as a number of tent sites. Daytime admission is $4 for adults and $2 for children ages 5 to 12. Open daily 10 a.m. to 8 p.m. Tent sites are $15 per night. Cabins are $65 per night.

Charlotte Motor Speedway. 5555 Concord Pkwy. South; (704) 455-3209; charlotte motorspeedway.com. NASCAR Cup, and Truck Series racing is conducted on this major 1.5-mile track throughout the year. Its biggest events, however, are the May and October races that feature events that go on for two weeks at a time. The Memorial Day Coca-Cola

600 is known as one of the longest and most brutal races in the championship series. In October is the Bank of America Roval 400, also part of the championship series, which runs a close second. When the 167,000-seat track isn't used for racing, it hosts car shows, Legends Car, Bandolero, and Thunder Roadster Racing. Stock car driving schools are also conducted here. Tours are offered when big events aren't scheduled.

The Dirt Track at Charlotte Motor Speedway seats another 14,500 people around a half-mile track and offers dirt car racing and monster trucks. The zMAX Dragway hosts National Hot Rod Association events on a track that is four wide instead of the traditional two. While the cars at the big track might flirt with 200 miles per hour, these roaring monsters head down a straight strip topping 300 miles per hour.

Davis Theatre. 65 Union St. South; (704) 920-2787; cabarrusartscouncil.org. The Davis Theatre is the 227-seat performance venue in the beautifully restored Cabarrus County Courthouse. The building, which dates back to the 19th century and is built in a Greek Revival style with Italianate and Second Empire influences, is operated by the Cabarrus Arts Council and houses several art galleries on the lower floors.

Frank Liske Park. 4001 Stough Rd.; (704) 920-2701; cabarruscounty.us/parks/Frank -Liske-Park. A 10-acre lake for fishing and paddleboats is at the center of this county park that also hosts concerts and other events throughout the year. Play a round of miniature golf or get your legs pumping on the walking trails. Free. Typically open during daylight hours.

Garage Pass Shop Tours. 810 Treva Anne Dr.; (704) 455-2819; garagepassshoptours .com. Stan at Garage Pass Tours can spin a racing yarn with the best of them. After a long career working for race teams, he's taking a step back from the sport so he can pass along his love for it to others. In fact, all guides have backgrounds in the sport to give tourists an insider's view of some of the biggest names in motorsports. Included on the tours are Hendrick Motorsports, Stewart-Haas Racing, Roush-Fenway Racing, Gibbs Racing, Penske South, Richard Childress Racing, Dale Earnhardt Inc., museums, and motorsports galleries. Guides vary tours to give participants the best chance of catching action or even spying a NASCAR superstar. Tours start at $60 per person plus meals and entry fees.

Hendrick Motorsports. 4400 Papa Joe Hendrick Blvd.; (877) 467-4890; hendrickmotor sports.com. Over 25 years, Rick Hendrick has turned his racing business into a racing dynasty with nine championships and dozens of major victories. As a tribute to those who made it happen, he opened the Hendrick Motorsports Museum with famous stock cars, sports cars, and championship hardware. On display are Jeff Gordon's Daytona 500 winning car, the Chevy Lumina driven by Tom Cruise in the film *Days of Thunder*, video, and items depicting technology from the sport. Get a peek at the shop from numerous viewing windows. Open Mon through Fri 8:30 a.m. to 5:30 p.m. and Sat 10 a.m. to 3 p.m.

Memorial Garden. 36 Spring St. Southwest; (704) 786-8009; https://firstpresconcord. org/about/memorial-garden. The gentler, sweeter-smelling side of Concord is found at this 200-year-old garden that's not much bigger than half a city block. The highlight of the year is spring's offering of daffodils and tulips. Other times guests can enjoy a stroll through hardwood trees and crepe myrtles. Free. Open Tues through Sat 9 a.m. to 4 p.m. and Sun 1 to 5:30 p.m.

Racing Schools. 5555 Concord Pkwy. South; (704) 866-2400; charlottemotorspeedway/ expereinces/racingschools. A handful of former NASCAR drivers lend their names to driving schools that offer slightly varying experiences on the Charlotte Motor Speedway track. Full experiences include a meeting with the crew chief, training, and instruction before heading out onto the track, where passing is allowed. The schedule varies according to the NAS-CAR schedule here and at speedways across the country. A three-lap ride-along starts at $129.99, and driving experiences begin at $449.

Morrison Motor Car Museum. 4545 Concord Pkwy. South; (704) 788-9500; https:// morrisonmotorcarmuseum.com. Renamed for the Morrison Motor Company, which also sells classic and late model used cars, Backing Up Classics was in operation next door to the Charlotte Motor Speedway even before operating a stock car was cool. The museum has 50 classic, antique, 1950s, 1960s, and muscle cars on display. It also carries a wide selection of NASCAR merchandise representing a number of drivers and teams. Admission is $8 for adults and $6 for students or seniors. Hours are Mon through Fri (except Wed) 10 a.m. to 5 p.m., Sat 9 a.m. to 5 p.m., and Sun noon to 5 p.m.

RFK Racing Museum. 4600 Roush Place Northwest; (704) 720-4600; rfkracing.com. Take a self-guided tour through a museum dedicated to one of the most storied owners in NAS-CAR history. Its dozens of championships include five in the top cup races. At the museum is a wall graphic with a timeline of the organization, trophies, and team vehicles. Free. Open Mon through Thurs 9 a.m. to 4 p.m. and Fri 9 a.m. to 12:30 p.m.

SEA LIFE Aquarium. 8111 Concord Mills Blvd.; (855) 450-0512; visitsealife.com. Walk beneath the sea to get face to face with sea turtles, sharks, rays, and more in a tunnel that spans a 117,000-gallon aquarium. A half-dozen exhibits include a touch pool, stingray bay, jellyfish, and more. Tickets are $22.99 for adults and $19.99 for children. Hours vary.

where to shop

Afton Village. 360 Exchange St. Northwest; (704) 721-5337; www.aftonvillage. The modern, upscale ambience at Afton Village combines with new but friendly streets, homes, and storefronts to form a progressive community all its own. A village green and pergola are surrounded by a handful of shops and restaurants.

Concord Mills. 8111 Concord Mills Blvd.; (704) 886-5000; www.simon.com/mall/concord-mills. More than 200 stores, anchored at one end by a Bass Pro Shops Outdoor World, are arranged in (you guessed it) a speedway pattern. In addition to specialty stores are a variety of brand outlet stores from Adidas to Zumiez. Lionel, the maker of popular model trains, operated its only retail store here.

Depot at Gibson Mill. 325 McGill Ave. Northwest; (704) 787-9351; depotgibsonmill.com; Operating as a mill in 700,000 square feet on a 58-acre campus, the Depot now claims to be the largest antique mall in the South. We can't confirm that, but it is big and bustling. It includes Ellie's Diner and a fabric center in addition to hundreds of vendors. Open Mon through Sat 10 a.m. to 7 p.m. and Sun 1 to 6 p.m.

Wild Birds Unlimited. 8609 Concord Mills Blvd.; (704) 979-3443; concord.wbu.com. Do you want to talk birding? This is the place to do it. WBU offers advice, birdhouses, birdseed, and everything else you need to turn a backyard into a winged haven. Open Mon through Fri 10 a.m. to 6 p.m., Sat 9 a.m. to 5 p.m. and Sun noon to 5 p.m.

where to eat

44 Mills Kitchen and Tap. 6189 Bayfield Parkway; (704) 787-9655; 44mills.com. With the development of Concord Mills, chain restaurants flooded Concord, but this locally owned spot provides a diversion. An ever-changing menu provides ahi tuna poke bowls as well as braised pork chops. $$.

Louis' Grill. 5062 SR 49 South; (980) 258-0075. Meat and veggie dishes are offered in this popular breakfast and lunchtime destination. Many race teams visit the diner, which is decorated in a race motif. Open Mon through Fri 6 a.m. to 3 p.m., Sat 8 a.m. to 2 p.m. $$.

where to stay

Great Wolf Lodge. 10175 Weddington Rd.; (866) 925-9653; greatwolf.com. Take a trip to the Great Northwoods in only a day at this lodge situated between Concord Mills and the Charlotte Motor Speedway. The resort includes wide-ranging overnight accommodations and a massive 80,000-square-foot indoor water park with 84-degree water year-round. A MagiQuest live fantasy adventure game, miniature golf course, arcade, and other amenities make this a day trip unto itself. $$$.

kannapolis

At one time Cannon Mills employed nearly 25,000 people in the Kannapolis area. The company built a village around its manufacturing facility, including homes for line workers and executives alike. The textile giant began hitting rocky waters at the end of the 20th century. After a series of takeovers and changes in ownership, parent company Pillowtex abruptly closed the plant in 2003. It sent the town into a tailspin. Enter David Murdock. He had already purchased part of the downtown area in 1982, but now the owner of Dole Food Company and a Hawaiian island spearheaded talks with the state's university system to redevelop the site as a biotechnology research center. The mill village homes are now more desirable, privately owned by families finding a new way of life in Kannapolis. Downtown reflects Williamsburg-style architecture and provides a vibrant shopping experience.

getting there

From the Concord Mills area, use I-85 North for the quickest route into Kannapolis. From downtown Concord, use Concord Parkway (US 29 North), which crosses I-85 and becomes Cannon Boulevard and leads to Dale Earnhardt Boulevard (SR 3). Take Dale Earnhardt Boulevard into Kannapolis.

where to go

Curb Motorsport Museum. 600 Dale Earnhardt Blvd.; (704) 938-6121; mikecurb.com. The name Mike Curb might be more synonymous with country music than with NASCAR. Curb, whose country music label includes artists such as Tim McGraw, LeeAnn Rimes, and Hank Williams Jr., is also a NASCAR and Indy car owner. He blends his passion for the two industries at this museum. Featured are NASCAR and Indy cars and other exhibits combined with gold records and autographed items from country and pop music icons. Open Mon through Fri 9 a.m. to 5 p.m.

Dale Earnhardt Plaza. S. Main and W. B Streets at Cannon Village; (704) 938-3200. When Dale Earnhardt died tragically at Daytona in 2001, people all over the Carolinas called in sick the following day. Instead of going to work, they created temporary memorials for the man in the black Number 3 car. Today in the heart of Cannon Village in Earnhardt's hometown is a permanent tribute to his life and career. The plaza includes a nine-foot bronze statue and a granite monument sent by fans in Vermont and New York. The Cannon Village Visitor Center also has a series of works by Sam Bass on Earnhardt's legendary career.

The Dale Trail. 3003 Dale Earnhardt Blvd.; (800) 848-3740; daletrail.com. Pick just about any spot in Kannapolis, and it's a starting point for the Dale Trail. Even the minor league baseball team, the Intimidators, is named for Earnhardt. The Dale Trail map can be downloaded from the website and takes fans to a dozen or so spots that were important to the legendary race driver, including Idiot Circle where he cruised in the 1960s and other hangouts such as his favorite restaurant. From Kannapolis the Dale Trail leads to other sites in Mooresville and Concord.

North Carolina Music Hall of Fame. 600 Dale Earnhardt Boulevard; (704) 934-2320; northcarolinamusichalloffame.org. Donna Fargo, Doc Watson, Arthur Smith, and Maurice Williams are among the best-known names honored at the North Carolina Music Hall of Fame. It opened in 2009, so the number of inductees and exhibits is growing and now includes Ben Folds, the Avett Brothers, and James Taylor. Exhibits include items and memorabilia from the state's music history as well as personal items from the musicians. Free. Open Mon through Fri 10 a.m. to 4 p.m.

where to shop

Karriker Farms. 7933 Karriker Rd.; (704) 938-9863. Pick-your-own fruits and vegetables are offered here on a seasonal basis. Karriker also specializes in a selection of flowering plants, including iris, peony, and daylilies that you can purchase when the time is right.

Stewart-Haas Racing. 6001 Haas Way; (704) 652-4227; stewarthaasracing.com. Find apparel and keepsakes from Tony Stewart and Ryan Newman at this shop that has garage viewing windows, too. Open Mon through Fri 8 a.m. to 4:30 p.m.

mooresville

Mooresville can be accessed by traveling north on I-77, but it also easily connects to the Concord-Kannapolis area to the northeast. That's why it has become such a hot location for the racing industry. While there are fewer public locations, businesses on which race teams depend are economic staples of this community.

getting there

From Kannapolis take SR 3, also known as Dale Earnhardt Boulevard, north into Mooresville.

where to go

Dale Earnhardt, Inc. 1675 Dale Earnhardt Hwy. 3; (704) 662-8000; daleearnhardtinc.com. DEI was once one of the largest teams on the NASCAR circuit, but now its companies focus on racing technologies. Its facility here is the area industry's largest and includes both a showroom and a retail store. As a corporation, the organization's contributions to racing are far-reaching, from technological advances to philanthropy. Open Mon through Fri 9 a.m. to 5 p.m., Sat 10 a.m. to 4 p.m.

Kyle Busch Motorsports. 351 Mezeppa Rd.; kylebuschmotorsports.com. Nicknamed Rowdy for his driving style, Kyle is the younger brother of retired driver, Kurt Busch. The 77,000-square-foot corporate headquarters includes a museum from Busch's career as well as a retail shop. Open 10 a.m. to 4:30 p.m. Mon through Fri.

Lazy 5 Ranch. 15100 SR 150 East; (704) 663-5100; thelazy5ranch.com. This drive-through animal park includes views of kangaroo, zebra, giraffe, watusi, and other exotic animals. Founder Henry Hampton says he has more than 750 animals from six different continents along just 3.5 miles. Guests can either drive through in their own vehicles or catch a ride on horse-drawn wagons. Lazy 5 also has a petting zoo, barn, and playground. Admission is $15 for adults and $11 for children and seniors. Open Mon through Sat 9 a.m. to an hour before sunset, Sun 1 p.m. to an hour before sunset.

Memory Lane Motorsports Museum. 769 River Hwy.; (704) 662-3673; memorylaneauto museum.com. Of all the race shops and museums in the area, this is the one that should not be missed. More than 150 vintage cars and retired NASCAR vehicles are on display to tell the story of auto racing, from buggies to the moonshine runners that led to the founding of today's popular sport. Also here is the car driven by Will Ferrell in the movie *Talladega Nights: The Legend of Ricky Bobby* along with other cars of film and fame. Admission is $12 for adults and $6 for children ages 6 to 12. Open Mon through Sat 10 a.m. to 5 p.m. Winter hours may vary.

North Carolina Auto Racing Hall of Fame. 119 Knob Hill Rd.; (704) 663-5331; ncarhof .com. This should not be confused with Charlotte's NASCAR Hall of Fame. This is a much smaller facility that acts as a visitor center for tourists seeking all things racing. It includes a display of several dozen cars, a theater that shows a film on the history of racing in North Carolina, and an art gallery. Admission is $6 for adults, $4 for children ages 6 to 12 and for seniors. Open Mon through Fri 10 a.m. to 5 p.m., Sat 10 a.m. to 3 p.m.

where to shop

JR Motorsports. 349 Cayuga Dr.; (704) 799-4800; www.jrmracing.com. This is Dale Earn-hardt Jr.'s operation that also owns cars driven by Danica Patrick and Kelly Bires. The retail store here sells Jr.'s personal brand.

Penske Racing. 200 Penske Way; (704) 799-7178; www.teampenske.com/about/index .cfm/52655/team_penske_retail_store. In addition to checking out the retail operation for drivers Kurt Busch, Brad Keselowski, Sam Hornish, Justin Allgaier, and Parker Kligerman, visitors can walk a catwalk over the garage area. Open Mon through Fri 8 a.m. to 5 p.m.

day trip 02

northeast

life on the rails:
salisbury, spencer, lexington

Elizabeth Dole, who served as director of the American Red Cross, secretary of transportation, secretary of labor, the state's US Senator for six years, and Republican presidential nominee Bob Dole's wife for more than 35 years, was born here. Cheerwine, a North Carolina soda, was invented here in 1917 in the basement of L.D. Peeler's wholesale grocery store. But what Salisbury has become is thanks to Southern Railway's location of its steam locomotive operation in the town of Spencer, north of Salisbury, in 1896. There now is the North Carolina Transportation Museum, where kids and railroad enthusiasts can get their fill of life on the rails. The site also presents exhibits on the development of various other modes of transportation. An Amtrak stop is located in Salisbury as are the operations and headquarters for the regional supermarket chain Food Lion, one of the city's largest employers. There are other historic sites here, too, including one of the Civil War's largest Confederate prisons.

salisbury

Daniel Boone once roamed the Salisbury region, and Andrew Jackson practiced law here. During the Civil War Salisbury was home to the only Confederate prison camp in North Carolina. In addition, 5,000 Union troops were buried nearby in a plot of land now designated a National Cemetery, making this one of this region's richest areas in which to examine the war between the states.

29

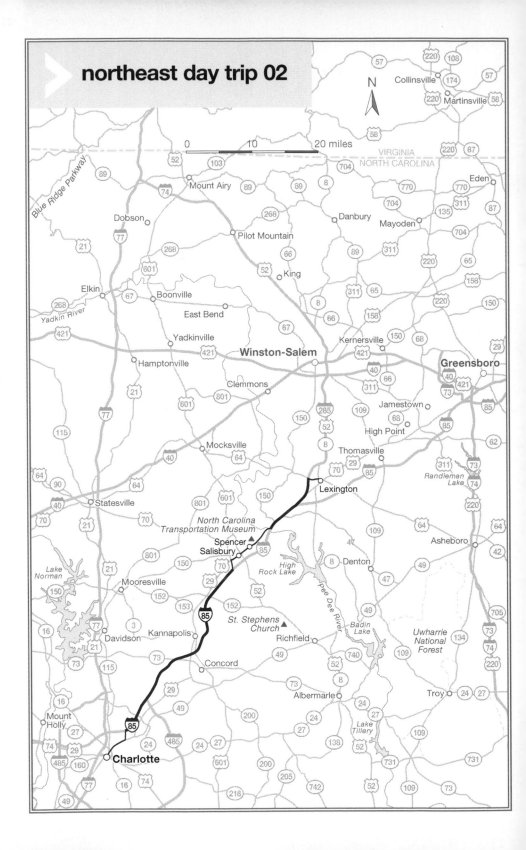

northeast day trip 02

The 30-square-block historic district consists of downtown Salisbury and the West Square residential district. Listed on the National Register of Historic Places, this area includes the Dr. Josephus Hall House, which was built in 1820 as the Salisbury Female Academy and later became the home of physician Josephus Hall. Also in the historic district is the Utzman-Chambers House, an 1819 Federal town house constructed by master builder Jacob Stirewalt. If you want more information on the historic district, visit the **Rowan County Convention & Visitor Bureau** at 204 E. Innes St. in person, call (800) 332-2343 or (704) 638-3100, or visit virtually at visitrowancounty.com. Get walking maps and other information through any option.

getting there

Salisbury is less than an hour north on I-85. Take the Jake Alexander Boulevard (SR 601) exit to Old Concord Road. Take a left on Old Concord Road, and it leads into Salisbury.

where to go

Dan Nicholas Park & Campground. 6800 Bringle Ferry Rd.; (704) 216-7800; dannicholas .net. This park's huge variety of activities makes it a popular stop for schools and families alike. At its center is a 10-acre lake where visitors can cast a line or rent a paddle boat. There are also a small water park, miniature golf, a carousel, gem mining, and a small nature center with native species. Rowan Wildlife Adventures allows visitors to view bears, bald eagles, and other animals from the region. Admission is free, but various attractions require a fee. The park is typically open during daylight hours, but attraction hours vary.

Dr. Josephus Hall House. 226 S. Jackson St.; (704) 636-0103; historicsalisbury.org. Dr. Josephus Hall was chief surgeon at the Salisbury Confederate Prison during the Civil War, and his impressive Federal-style home has been preserved as a window into that era. Built in 1820, the house was renovated significantly in 1859 and again in 1900 with Greek Revival and Victorian features. The interior has painted ceilings and original fixtures, and is filled with an impressive collection of mid-Victorian furnishings and other items that belonged to the Hall family. Docents in period costume conduct guided tours of the home that sits in what is now almost a parklike setting. Admission is $5 for adults and $3 for children ages 6 to 12. Open Sat 1 to 4 p.m.

Historic National Cemetery & Confederate Prison Site. 501 Statesville Blvd.; (800) 332-2343, (704) 636-2661; visitrowamcountync.com. Nothing remains of the Salisbury prison but three monuments erected by the State of Maine, the Commonwealth of Pennsylvania, and the US government. Find those at the Salisbury Historic National Cemetery, a tribute to the 11,700 Union soldiers who died while at the prison. Union General George Stoneman and his men burned the prison, which had already been abandoned, in April 1865 just before the war ended. A nearby log house, the former garrison for the prison, remains and houses various antiques and artifacts. CDs to accompany the driving tour are available from the Rowan County Convention & Visitors Bureau (204 E. Innes St.) for $5 each.

Meroney Theatre. 213 S. Main St.; (704) 633-5471; piedmontplayers.com. The Piedmont Players present their work in this renovated 361-seat theater, built in 1906. The Meroney's history is impressive, to say the least. Sarah Bernhardt, Lillian Russell, John Philip Sousa, William Howard Taft, Cary Nation, and the New York Symphony Orchestra have all made appearances here. Now it's the home to classics such as *The Sound of Music* and *A Christmas Carol* plus Broadway hits such as *Kinky Boats.*

Old Stone House.   770 Stone House Road, Salisbury; (704) 633-5946; rowanmuseum .org. German immigrant Michael Braun built this two-story Georgian-style house in 1766, making it the oldest structure in Rowan County. Braun was a merchant, a wheelwright, and a farmer who owned about 2,000 acres in this area, and his home was a veritable mansion at the time he built it in a virtual wilderness. Today Braun's house is operated by the Rowan Museum. Free. Open Sat 1 to 4 p.m.

Rowan Museum. 202 N. Main St.; (704) 633-5946; rowanmuseum.org. The 1856 court-house, which survived Stoneman's Raid, is one of the finest examples of pre–Civil War architecture in the state. The well curated artifacts and displays depict the life and history of Rowan County, including artifacts from the Civil War and documents and artifacts that trace the community's commerce. Among the displays are tools and modes of transportation from the 19th century. Free. Open Mon through Fri 10 a.m. to 4 p.m., Sat and Sun 1 to 4 p.m.

Utzman-Chambers House. 116 S. Jackson St.; (704) 633-5946; rowanmuseum.org. Constructed by Jacob Stirewalt for cabinetmaker Lewis Ultzman, this 1815 Federal town house is maintained as a museum that reflects the lifestyle of the more affluent citizens of the early 1800s. That lavish lifestyle is evident in the Chippendale and Hepplewhite furniture that is still part of the home. With an unusual curved staircase and intricate interior moldings and details, it is one of the few surviving Federal period town houses in Piedmont. Free. The house and gardens are open Thurs through Sun 1 to 4 p.m.

Waterworks Visual Arts Center. 123 E. Liberty St.; (704) 638-1882; waterworks.org. Originally located in the city's first waterworks building, the center is now located across the street from the police station in another refurbished building. The center offers regional and national gallery exhibitions, studio classes, workshops, and lectures. The sculpture gallery invites visitors to participate in the art experience through touch, sound, fragrance, and sight. Free. Open Mon through Fri 10 a.m. to 4 p.m.

where to shop

Eagle's Farm. 2924 Old Mocksville Rd.; (704) 647-0063. Visitors can pick their own strawberries, cucumbers, squash, or tomatoes depending on the season. Those more interested in eating than gathering can just stop at the roadside market. Open Mon through Sat 8 a.m. to 6 p.m.

Rail Walk Studios & Galleries. 409 Lee St.; (704) 469-2781; railwalkstudioandgalleries.com. All week long the artists of Rail Walk work hard on their pieces and unveil them to the public on Saturdays. Painters, fiber artists, and others are still there working on Saturday and happy to chat, but hey hope you'll buy a piece as well. Hours are 10 a.m. to 2 p.m.

The Salisbury Emporium. 230 E. Kerr St.; (704) 642-0039; https://salisburyemporium.com. The Salisbury Emporium is a collection of 85 shops and galleries located in a renovated historic landmark adjacent to the architecturally acclaimed Salisbury Train Station. The emporium contains more than 15,000 square feet of gifts, antiques, home accessories, Christmas items, fine art, handcrafts, and more. Open Tues through Sat 10 a.m. to 6 p.m. and Sun 1 to 5 p.m.

Spice and Tea Exchange. 115 N. Main St.; (980) 432-8287; spiceandtea.com/salisbury. As advertised, you'll find a variety of fine spices and loose-leaf teas, but also available are salts, sugars, and a selection of gifts sets. Open 10 a.m. to 6 p.m. Mon through Sat and 2 to 5 p.m. on Sun.

Stitchin' Post & Gifts. 104 S. Main St.; (704) 637-0708; spgifts.com. This historic 1879 shop has high ceilings, original wood floors, and exposed brick walls. The renovated storefront casts the warm feeling of walking into history. Unusual gifts for every season can be found here in the heart of downtown Salisbury just off the square. Open Mon through Sat 10 a.m. to 5:30 p.m. Also open Sun afternoons between Thanksgiving and Christmas.

where to eat

Haps Grill. 1161/2 N. Main St.; (704) 633-5872. Often attracting a crowd during the workweek, this lunch counter restaurant offers some of the best hot dogs and burgers for miles around. They come most often topped with homemade chili and a local offering of Cheerwine in a glass bottle. Seating is limited, so plan to enjoy your dog elsewhere if you see a line outside the door. $.

Mabo Grill and Tapas. 122 E. Fisher St.; (704) 637-0192; mambogrillandtapas.com. With the exception of French fries and a few local beers, find all that's Cuban, including cocktails, dessert, and everything in between. The menu is varying from soups to salads to salmon all with a tropical flair. $$

Sweet Meadow Cafe. 105 E. Fisher St.; (704) 637-8715. This quaint cafe serves contemporary cuisine with a twist. An eclectic menu includes crab cakes, red beans and rice, and other items, typically locally sourced. Fresh breads are made daily. Works by local artists are on display. $–$$.

where to stay

Across the Pond B&B. 324 N. Fulton St.; (866) 296-7965; acrossthepondbandb.com. Andrew and Mary Walker really came across the Atlantic Ocean to open this B&B, pausing to raise a family in Pittsburgh along the way. Built for a local surgeon in 1919, the house features leaded glass, cedar closets, and quarter-sawn oak floors. Three rooms are available for nightly stays. $$

Turn of the Century Victorian Bed & Breakfast. 529 S. Fulton St.; (704) 642-1660; turnofthecenturybb.com. Historical hospitality meets contemporary comfort in this inn. The home was built in 1905 and offers four rooms for overnight stays or longer. Like many area homes, it has an inviting wraparound front porch. $$$.

spencer

Spencer was chosen as Southern Railway's repair facility because of its location between Atlanta and Washington, D.C., and was named for Southern Railway's first president, Samuel Spencer, who coincidentally died in a train accident.

getting there

Spencer is two miles north of Salisbury on Salisbury Avenue, an extension of Main Street.

where to go

North Carolina Transportation Museum. 411 S. Salisbury Ave.; (704) 636-2889; nctrans.org. This massive facility defies the typical connotation of a museum. It is located on the site of what was once Southern Railway Company's largest steam locomotive repair facility and comprises 13 buildings, including a restored roundhouse, on 57 acres. While the highlights of the museum are related to trains, exhibits on other early transportation include automobiles at the Bumper to Bumper exhibit. Trace the history of transportation in Wagons, Wheels, & Wings. The highlight is the restored 1924 Robert Julian roundhouse, what was an innovative working railroad repair shop. Visitors actually get an opportunity to ride on the turntable that once dealt out cars needing repair work to the roundhouse. But a trip to this museum would not be complete without a train ride around the facility. Admission is $6 for adults, $5 for seniors and $4 for children. There is an additional charge for train rides, turntable rides, and guided tours. Open Tues through Sat 9 a.m. to 5 p.m. and Sun noon to 5 p.m.

Spencer Historic District. (704) 633-2231. Adjacent to the North Carolina Transportation Museum, the Spencer Historic District was built between 1905 and 1920 as housing for the families of those who operated the repair facility. With 322 residential and commercial buildings, it is the largest contiguous historic district in North Carolina.

where to shop

The Little Choo Choo Shop. 500 S. Salisbury Ave.; (704) 637-8717; littlechoochooshop .com. Across the street from the North Carolina Transportation Museum, this well-stocked model-railroad shop is for serious model railroaders, but it is a must-see for any train enthusiast. Open Tues through Sat 10 a.m. to 5:30 p.m.

where to eat

Hendrix Barbecue. 615 N. Salisbury Ave.; (704) 638-0542. In a locale with more than a couple of choices for barbecue, Hendrix consistently gets rave reviews. In addition to traditional barbecue selections, there are some diversions like barbecue salad and funnel cake fries and even breakfast. Open 7 a.m. to 9 p.m. Mon through Sat and 8 a.m. to 2 p.m. on Sun.

Pinocchio's. 518 S. Salisbury Ave.; (704) 636-8891; pinocchiosofspencer.com. Home-style Italian fare, made to order from scratch, includes seafood, pasta, pizza, and home-made gelato. Live music is scheduled periodically. Open for lunch Mon through Fri and dinner Tues through Sat. $$.

worth more time

Complete the historic leg of this day trip by heading to the site of the richest gold mining property east of the Mississippi in the aptly named town of **Gold Hill.** Once a thriving, rough, and rowdy mining town in the eastern part of Rowan County, Gold Hill is now a quaint, restored village of homes and stores. With boardwalks and narrow streets connecting places that were here as early as the 1840s, Gold Hill feels like the set of a Western movie. There are few formal attractions, but there is ample opportunity to hike, picnic, and visit a time gone by. It's only about 20 minutes south on US 52.

 E.H. Montgomery Store (770 Saint Stephens Church Rd.; (704) 267-9439), aside from being a general store open since 1850, serves hot dogs, milkshakes, and soft drinks. You might also find some candy you haven't seen in years, like Zagnuts and Bit-o-Honey.

Locals listen to other locals play bluegrass on Friday nights. **Mauney's** (775 Saint Stephens Church; 704-279-1632) opened a decade earlier and was the first store in Gold Hill. Today it offers Victorian-era antiques for sale, but doubles as a museum that displays photos from the days when Gold Hill was emerging as a mining town.

Grab a bite at **Mama T's** (840 Saint Stephens Church; 704-209-6049). Downhome cooking is the staple at Mama T's. with stick-to-your-ribs meals such as country-style steak, and meatloaf. You'll also find a selection of salads and sandwiches. $$.

lexington

Bob Timberlake, one of the state's great wineries, and what some say is the best barbecue available *anywhere* can all be found in the city of Lexington. Settled in 1775 and incorporated in 1828, Lexington was named in honor of the Revolutionary War battle in Massachusetts. Uptown is listed on the National Register of Historic Places. Access to the railroad gave the area an upper hand early on in producing furniture and textiles, but the textile jobs have since traveled overseas and furniture capitals nearby have taken Lexington's share of the furniture industry. Now perhaps the city's greatest contemporary claim to fame is as home to Bob Timberlake, the internationally renowned artist and home furnishings designer, and the Bob Timberlake Gallery. Lexington's pork barbecue is a close second, if not the outright winner.

getting there

Lexington is in the middle of Day Trips 02 and 03, so great barbecue is close at hand for travelers on either journey. From Spencer, however, Lexington is accessed most easily via I-85 north, which at this point converges with US 52. Be aware that this route also combines with US 29 and 70, but don't let that make the drive more complex than it is. Simply follow the signs for US 52. Lexington is only 15 miles, or about 20 minutes, away.

where to go

Historic Uptown Lexington Walking Tour. 114 E. Center St.; (336) 236-4218, (866) 604-2389; lexpublib.org/walkingtours. Begin one of several themed walking tours of the historic downtown at the local visitor center. Maps and audio tours are available for downloading on the local library website. On one tour are 11 historic properties in a five-block area on the National Register of Historic Places, plus fringe sites dating from 1824 to 1948. You will also want to stop at The Candy Factory, best known for Red Bird Peppermint Puff, and listen to the player piano, then browse Lanier Hardware. Plus, see how many pigs you can count along the way. The fiberglass porkers are pieces of art to promote barbecue and other businesses in town.

Childress Vineyards. 1000 Childress Vineyards Rd.; (336) 236-9463; childressvineyards .com. NASCAR got its start from early drivers running illegal liquor, so it seems appropriate that a race team owner is involved in the wine business. The striking Italian Renaissance building and the beautiful rolling hills of this world-class vineyard are more than welcoming. *Wine Enthusiast* magazine has named the tasting room here one of the top 25 in America. Take a tour, have a spectacular meal, and—most important—taste the wine. The tasting room is open daily 10 a.m. to 5 p.m. Winery tours are Mon through Fri at noon, and 3 p.m. and on Sat and Sun at 11 a.m., 1, and 3 p.m.

Davidson County Historical Museum. 2 S. Main St.; (336) 242-2035; davidsoncountyhis toricalmuseum.com. Permanent and changing exhibits in the old Davidson County Courthouse spotlight the history of the area. Artifacts include clothing, books, furniture, and more that help tell the story of the area. Perhaps as interesting is the Greek Revival architecture of the building completed in 1858 and damaged in an 1865 fire during Union General Judson Kilpatrick's occupation. Admission is free. Open Tues through Fri 10 a.m. to 4 p.m. and Sat 10 a.m. to 3 p.m.

Richard Childress Racing Museum. 180 Industrial Dr., Welcome; (336) 731-3389, (800) 476-3389; rcrracing.com. This has become somewhat of a shrine and tribute to the late Dale Earnhardt, who died in a tragic wreck in Daytona in 2001. Visitors can tour behind the scenes of some of RCR's successful NASCAR teams. Located just 10 minutes north of Lexington, the museum and gift shop display a variety of race cars, trophies, photos, and videos of RCR's 30-plus years in the sport. The museum includes 28 cars and other items from the career of the late, great Dale Earnhardt. Hours are Mon through Fri 10 a.m. to 5 p.m. and Sat 9 a.m. to 3 p.m. Admission is $12 for adults, $8 for seniors, and $5 for children ages 7 and older; free for children 6 and younger.

where to shop

The Bob Timberlake Gallery. 1714 E. Center St.; (336) 249-4428; bobtimberlake.com. This gallery, retail store, and museum features the art, home furnishings, and accessories of Bob Timberlake. A coffee shop is located in the courtyard garden. Special events throughout the year highlight Timberlake and other North Carolina artists. Open Wed through Sat 10 a.m. to 3 p.m.

Historic Uptown Lexington. 13 E. 1st Ave.; (336) 249-0383; uptownlexingtonnc.com. Historic Uptown Lexington has antiques stores, the state's largest True Value hardware store (Lanier's), bridal shops, a dress fabric store, an old-fashioned candy store, bakeries, consignment shops, an old-fashioned grocery store known for homemade pimento cheese and chicken salad, a toy store, restaurants, and more.

where to eat

Cafe 35. 103 S. Main St.; (336) 238-3535; cafe35menu.com. While you can get great home-style cooking here, diners are advised to stray from the ordinary and try items such as grilled redfish. Although in the historic district, the dining room is sleek and contemporary. $$.

Lexington Area Barbecue Restaurants. While you can get a good plate of barbecue in a lot of North Carolina cities, you just can't get Lexington barbecue on every corner. It's known far and wide for slow-cooked pork shoulders left to linger over hot hickory coals. Hungry travelers will find no less than a dozen barbecue restaurants in and around the city of Lexington. Here barbecue is offered sliced or chopped with a tomato-vinegar sauce sans mayonnaise along with hush puppies and sweet tea. Included are a few favorites along with a comprehensive list. All of the following are easily accessible from Lexington, but may be located in other towns as noted. $–$$.

> **The Barbecue Center.** 900 N. Main St.; (336) 248-4633; barbecuecenter.net. The Barbecue Center is known for more than cooked pig. Banana splits and banana pudding are big here, too. Open Mon through Sat 11 a.m. to 9 p.m.

> **Speedy's Barbecue.** 1317 Winston Rd.; (336) 248-2410; speedysbbqinc.com. Speedy's is one of the oldest barbecue joints in town. It opened in the 1930s as Tussey's, but the owner changed the name in the early 1960s. It has been in the Dunn family since about that time. Speedy's is known for big portions and curbside service. Open Mon through Sat. 10:30 a.m. to 9 p.m.

> **Speedy Lohr's BBQ.** 3664 Highway 8; (336) 242-9195. Not to be confused with Speedy's, Speedy Lohr operated for a number of years in nearby Arcadia before moving to its current location. It's known for skin sandwiches, not for the faint of heart. Ribs are served on Wed nights. Open Mon through Thurs and Sat from 7 a.m. to 8:30 p.m. and Sun 7 a.m. to 9 p.m.

Other recommended stops to satisfy your BBQ fix include:

Backcountry Barbecue. 4014 Linwood-Southmont Rd.; (336) 956-1696

Cook's Barbecue. 366 Valient Dr.; (336) 798-1928

Kerley's Barbecue. 5114 Old US 52, Welcome; (336) 731-8245

Lexington Barbecue. 100 Smokehouse Ln.; (336) 249-9814; lexbbq.com

Smiley's Barbecue. 917 Winston Rd.; (336) 248-4528;

Smokey Joe's Barbecue. 1101 S. Main St.; (336) 249-0315; smokeyjoes bbqlexington.com

Stamey's Barbecue of Tyro. 4524 S. SR 150, Tyro; (336) 853-6426

Tarheel Q. 6835 W. US 64; (336) 787-4550; theqsoflexington.com

Troutman's Barbecue. 18466 S. SR 109, Denton; (336) 859-2206

where to stay

High Rock Lake Campground. 1013 Wafford Circle; (336) 798-1196; highrocklakecamp ground.com. A pine and hardwood forest surrounds this part of the beautiful High Rock Lake. In addition to RV camping sites, cabins that accommodate four to six people are available starting at $80 per night.

day trip 03

northeast

North Carolina State Senator John W. Thomas was instrumental in getting $3 million in state money with which to build a railroad system, so when he settled in an area near the proposed route and built a depot, general store, and home, the area became known as "Thomas's Depot." In 1852 the area officially took the name Thomasville. High Point would stand to benefit more in the long run, establishing a strong and resilient furniture manufacturing industry. It straddles four different counties and is home to more than 100,000 people, making it one of the 10 largest cities in the state.

Long before the railroad located here, the Pennsylvania Quakers settled in the area in search of religious freedom. Here they found fertile land and a good climate. But in later years the city was more inclined to accept industrialists and carpetbaggers of the early 20th century. Thus, a variety of industries, mainly tobacco and textiles, won out, and their owners built large, architecturally interesting homes.

thomasville

The small city of Thomasville claims fame as the location of the world's largest chair and the state's oldest railroad depot. Thomasville Furniture Company started here in 1904 before expanding into Lenoir. A Thomasville showroom, however, is still located in Thomasville.

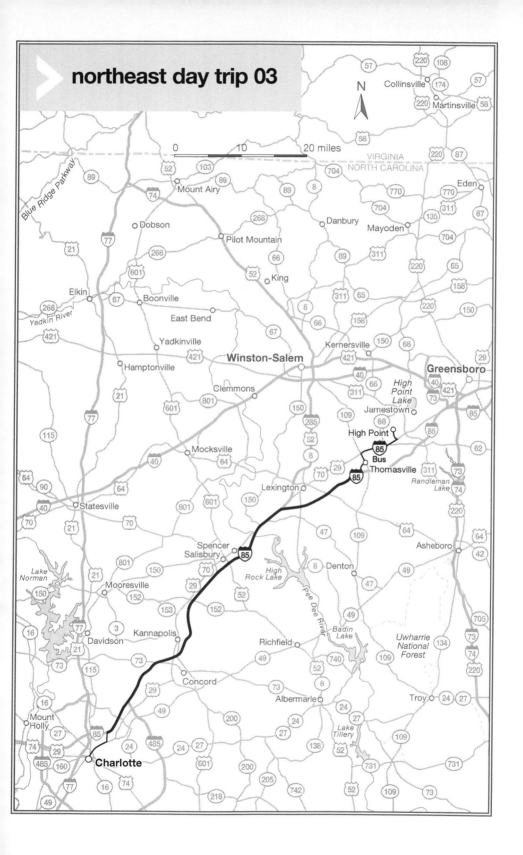

getting there

Thomasville is about 69 miles, or just over an hour, from Charlotte. Take I-85 north to exit 102. Turn right onto Lake Road, which will become Baptist Children's Home Road. Turn right onto W. Main Street and follow it into the center of Thomasville.

where to go

North Carolina's Oldest Railroad Depot. 44 W. Main St.; (336) 472-4422; visitthomas villenc.com. The oldest remaining railroad depot in North Carolina, built in 1870, houses the Thomasville Visitor Center. Pick up brochures and get a glimpse of some locally made furniture or see other rotating exhibits. The restored structure is on the National Register of Historic Places. Open Mon through Fri 9 a.m. to 5 p.m.

World's Largest Chair. Intersection of Main Street and SR 109. Standing 30 feet tall is a symbol of Thomasville's furniture heritage in the heart of downtown. The first "big chair," a real wood chair, was built in 1922 for the Thomasville Chair Company. In 1936 the old wood chair was scrapped, and in 1951 ground was broken for a new chair. Refurbished, the present structure is a mix of cement, granite dust, and iron, but it appears to be a wood Duncan Phyfe with a fabric seat. Still, after so much effort, there are challenges from other cities around the world regarding its record height. There is no debate that the 10-foot-tall seat has accommodated President Lyndon B. Johnson, Miss America, and other celebrities.

where to eat

Sixty-six Grill and Tap House. 1037 Randolph St.; (336) 476-6666; sixtysixgrillandtap house.com. The wide-ranging menu at this eatery includes flatbread pizza, burgers, pasta, and even family-style meals served for four. $$

T'Ville Diner. 132 W. Main St.; (336) 472-3322. Opened in 1936 in the dining car of the railroad, T'Ville Diner moved into its current building to accommodate larger crowds, but the brass lights, shelving, and other fixtures moved, too. Any day of the week you can get a meat and two veggies for only $6.99. $

high point

In 1859, when High Point was named for being the "highest point" on the North Carolina Railroad, city founders knew that its central location would attract industry and commerce. It did. Today High Point draws visitors from around the globe for the biannual International Home Furnishings Market, the largest event of its kind in the world. The show is typically attended by pros looking for deals, so the April and October periods when the show is going on might not be the best times for the casual visitor. At other times, day-trippers can explore the region's rich history, distinctive cultural events, and diverse shopping selection.

Even for casual furniture shoppers throughout the year, High Point offers more than 100 retail furniture stores and outlets.

getting there

High Point is about 15 minutes from Thomasville. Follow I-85 Business Route, also known as US 29/70, to the US 311/S. Main Street exit. Turn right onto US 311 and take it into High Point.

where to go

All A-Flutter Farms. 7850 Clinard Farms Rd.; (336) 454-5651; all-a-flutter.com. The migration of the monarchs, the mystery of metamorphosis, and more are covered at this fun attraction. Here you can visit a butterfly house where you feed the occupants by hand while learning about the butterfly's lifecycle. The farm is only open for school groups during the week, so visit the website to learn about weekend family day tickets, which are $10 per person.

High Point Museum & Historical Park. 1859 E. Lexington Ave.; (336) 885-1859; high pointnc.gov/2329/Museum. Telling the story of High Point's growth from a small Quaker village to the furniture capital of the world, the High Point Museum preserves the **Hoggatt House** (1754), the **Haley House** (1786), and a working blacksmith shop. Collections include tools, vehicles, photos, and other items that showcase developing commerce in the area. Admission is free. Open Tues through Sat 10 a.m. to 4:30 p.m.

Piedmont Environmental Center. 1220 Penny Rd.; (336) 883-8531; highpointnc.gov. These 375 glorious acres on High Point City Lake include hiking trails, a nature preserve, a nature store, small animal exhibits, and the North Carolina Mapscape. Free. Open Mon through Fri 9 a.m. to 5 p.m. More than 6 miles of hiking trails are open daily, sunrise to sunset.

World's Largest Chest of Drawers. 508 N. Hamilton St. This unusual but beautiful 19th-century-style dresser is now a roadside attraction, but was known as the Bureau of Information in 1926 when it was built. It also once housed the local Jaycees and later the chamber of commerce. Originally 20 feet tall, it was renovated in 1996 to 38 feet, with two socks sloppily hanging out of one drawer. Don't be misguided by the dresser at Furnitureland off the interstate; it's simply an attachment to the storefront.

where to shop

Furniture Shopping. High Point Convention & Visitor Bureau; (336) 884-5255; visit highpoint.com. In addition to the furniture markets held in April and October, there are more than 50 discount outlets here. The High Point Convention & Visitor Bureau has a complete list on its website of everything from rugs to art to sofas. Names include Boyles, Ashley, and Drexel Heritage.

High Point Farmers Market. 901 N. Main St.; (336) 689-4463; highpointnc.gov/1753 /High-Point-Farmers-Market. Fresh fruit and vegetables, baked goods, flowers, and plants are available every Wed and Sat April through mid-Oct.

where to eat

The Dog House. 668 N. Main St.; (336) 886-4953; A local favorite since the 1950s, the Dog House features lunch-counter dining for hot dogs and hamburgers served with awesome chili. Open for lunch only, Mon through Sat. $.

Kepley's Barbecue. 1304 N. Main St.; (336) 884-1021; kepleysbarbecue.com. Proclaimed by some as the best barbecue north of Lexington, Kepley's serves barbecue sandwiches, plates, trays, hush puppies, and vinegar-based barbecue slaw. Open Mon through Sat 8:30 a.m. to 8:30 p.m., $–$$.

Magnolia Blue. 1807 N. Main St.; (336) 885-2583; magnoliabluehighpoint.com. Start with pimento cheese dip or the house specialty Magnolia dip, which leads in nicely to a selection of steaks, chops, and a few more entrées. Open for dinner at 5 p.m. Tues through Sat and for brunch Sat and Sun 11 a.m. to 4 p.m. $$.

Steak Street. 3915 Sedgebrook St.; (336) 841-0222; steakstreet.com. The wrought-iron furniture, outdoor lighting, and brick inlays on the main dining room floor give this restaurant a street-side cafe feel. The restaurant's Cajun-Creole menu features select cuts of meat, as well as pasta, seafood, and large salads. Open Mon through Fri 11 a.m. to 9 p.m., Sat 4 to 9:30 p.m. $$–$$$.

where to stay

JH Adams Inn. 1108 N. Main St.; (336) 882-3267; jhadamsinn.com. John Hampton Adams of Adams-Mills Hosiery Corporation built this posh Italian Renaissance–style inn as his residence in 1918. Today the inn serves as a stately reminder of a bygone era and is every bit as posh. Located in the heart of downtown High Point, the restored home is now a 30-room property with Jacuzzi tubs, fireplaces, and king-size beds in many rooms. A full breakfast buffet is served. $$$.

Pandora's Manor. 407 W. High Ave.; (336) 886-4253; pandorasmanor.com. Local designers were invited to decorate the six unique rooms offered at Pandora's Manor. Bult In 1905 it doesn't lack any of the modern luxurious conveniences. Complimentary breakfast, pajamas, and even wine come with each stay. $$$

day trip 04

northeast

>>> **schooled in the arts:**
winston-salem

winston-salem

Winston-Salem was once more prominent for its smokes than for its culture. Once known for the cigarette factory Richard Joshua Reynolds established in 1874, today it is more famous for its art and cultural opportunities. More than a century before R.J. Reynolds Tobacco Company was established here, the region was home to German-speaking Moravians, members of the persecuted Protestant sect that came from Germany by way of Pennsylvania. They settled in an area they called Die Wachau, Latin for Wachovia (the bank once based here), where they established the villages of Bethabara and Bethania. You still can see how these thrifty people lived at historic Bethabara Park, site of the area's first Moravian settlement, and at Old Salem, founded as a town and backcountry trading center in 1766. While Old Salem has long been lauded as one of the most authentic restorations, there are other good reasons to visit this city of nearly a quarter million residents.

The city's emergence as Winston-Salem began in the 1840s, when Forsythe County bought a parcel of land from the Moravians and merged it with the county seat called Winston in 1913. At the time it was the largest city in North Carolina with vigorous and healthy tobacco and textiles industries. Since the tobacco market withered and textiles jobs went overseas, the cultural legacy left by the Moravians and by philanthropists such as Reynolds and executives from the banking industry has remained healthy and strong. In the the 1960s the city began to bill itself as the "City of the Arts." City leaders formed the nation's first arts

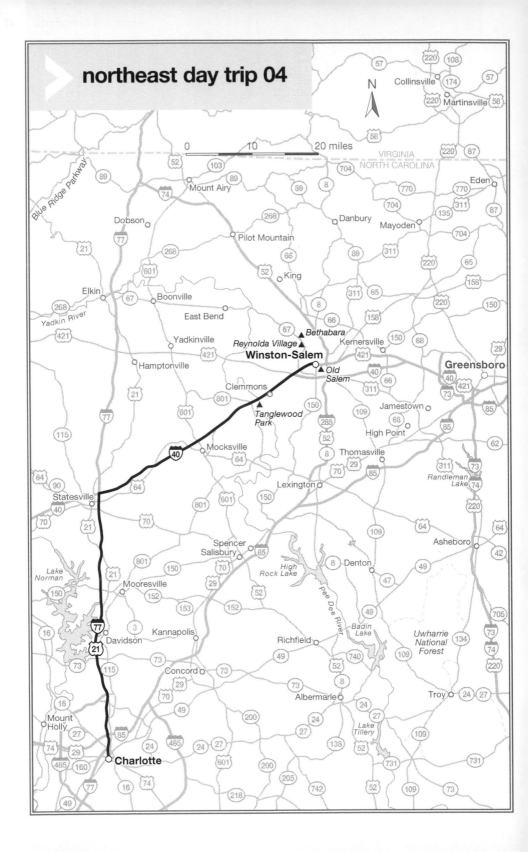

tanglewood park

*Traveling east on I-40 from I-77, before you arrive in Winston-Salem are the town of **Clemmons** and **Tanglewood Park,** one of the area's best parks that includes horseback riding, a lakefront beach, a manor house, and acres and acres of space in which to stretch your legs. The **Arboretum at Tanglewood** is maintained by the North Carolina Agricultural Extension Service and local master gardeners. Within it is the **1959 Manor House Bed & Breakfast,** once owned by the brother of R.J. Reynolds. Hayrides, pony rides, and more serious guided trail rides originate at **Tanglewood Stables.** Spring and summer feature a variety of scheduled nature programs, and the holiday season brings one of the state's biggest drive-through lights experiences. The park, now maintained by the county parks and recreation department, is located at 4061 Clemmons Rd. (336-703-6400; www.forsyth.cc).*

council here, which has been used as a model in much larger cities. Winston-Salem ranks first nationally in per capita contributions to the arts and boasts impressive art galleries, museums, and performance centers. The renowned North Carolina School of the Arts is here. So is one of the nation's finest collections of American art at Reynolda House, as well as a fine symphony and opera company. For more information, contact the **Winston-Salem Visitor Center** (200 Brookstown Ave.; 866-728-4200; visitwinstonsalem.com).

getting there

To get to Winston-Salem from Charlotte, take I-77 north to I-40 east; it's about 84 miles or close to 90 minutes away. (An alternative and slightly shorter route, but not recommended if you're coming from northwest Charlotte, would be to take I-85 north to US 52.)

where to go

Old Salem. 900 Old Salem Rd.; (336) 721-7350; oldsalem.org. Founded in 1766 as a Moravian church town and backcountry trading center, Salem is frequently praised as one of America's most authentic and well-documented Colonial sites. Costumed interpreters demonstrate daily activities and trades that were part of the lives of people, including Moravian, Black, and Indigenous peoples, in Salem in the late 18th and early 19th centuries. The cobblestone streets of Old Salem are lined with homes, shops, gardens, and other examples of how the Moravians lived and worshipped. St. Philips Moravian Church, one of the nation's oldest Black churches, is also located here along with several museum shops, and the famous Winkler Bakery, where shoppers can still get Moravian cookies and other goodies. In all, this self-guided tour features about 100 restored and reconstructed buildings where costumed staff demonstrate various tasks or give abbreviated tours of specific buildings. Among them are the T. Vogler Gunsmith Shop, Shultz Shoemaker Shop, Single Brothers' House, and Salem Tavern.

Visitors are welcome to roam the streets of Old Salem as in any other small town and view a number of structures, but admission is required for the formal tours that include the Museum of Early Southern Decorative Arts and the Toy Museum, with an option of a one-day ticket or a two-day ticket. Old Salem's all-in-one tickets are $20 for adults and $12 for children and college students; two-stop tickets are $12 for adults and $10 for children and college students. Old Salem is open Feb through Dec, generally Wed through Sat 10 a.m. to 4 p.m., but check the website for varying hours of attractions. Staff may close tour buildings periodically for maintenance.

The Gallery at Old Salem. 924 S. Main St.; (888) 348-5420; oldsalem.org. Located in the MESDA building, the Gallery at Old Salem provides additional space for art and historical exhibits throughout the year. Some exhibits come from MESDA collections, while other exhibits feature other artists or collections from other museums.

Museum of Early Southern Decorative Art (MESDA). 924 S. Main St.; (888) 348-5420; oldsalem.org. MESDA is the only museum dedicated to exhibiting and researching the regional decorative arts of the early South. With its 24 period rooms and seven galleries, MESDA showcases the furniture, paintings, textiles, ceramics, silver, and other metalware made and used in Maryland, Virginia, the Carolinas, Georgia, Kentucky, and Tennessee through 1820.

Salem Tavern. 800 S. Main St. Salem Tavern was built first across the street in 1771 and was one of the first public buildings constructed in Salem. Fire destroyed it in 1784, but it was quickly rebuilt. The tavern included two front rooms for gathering and a gentlemen's room for private dining. Guests could rent rooms upstairs for overnight stays. Believe it or not, President George Washington stayed here from May 31 to June 2, 1791.

Single Brothers' House. 600 S. Main St. This example of a Germanic half-timbered construction (1768–1786) in the Moravian planned community of Salem was used as a trade school for Moravian boys beginning at around age 14. It also served as a dormitory for master craftsmen, journeymen, and apprentices. The first building of the Single Brothers' House (the half-timbered part) was built in 1769; the brick structure was added in 1786. The building has been restored to its original condition.

Delta Arts Center. 2611 New Walkertown Rd.; (336) 722-2625; deltaartscenter.org. Exhibits, events, and activities held here emphasize the contributions of minorities to the arts and humanities. The center presents regularly changing exhibits by Hispanic and Black artists. Open Tues through Fri 10 a.m. to 5 p.m. and Sat 11 a.m. to 3 p.m.

Historic Bethabara Park. 2147 Bethabara Rd.; (336) 924-8191; https://historicbethabara.org. Bethabara was the first Colonial townsite established in the Carolina Piedmont. At the beautiful 175-acre park is the only "house of passage" built by the Moravians at any of their Colonial settlements in the New World. Archaeological remains have contributed to a significant understanding of the Moravian culture, in particular the manufacture of Moravian pottery. A National Historic Landmark, this 1753 site of the first Moravian settlement in North Carolina was the area's frontier trade and religious center until 1772. Guests can tour the 1788 congregation house known as the Gemeinhaus, view the archaeological remains in the reconstructed palisade fort, and stroll through the historic gardens. Exhibit buildings are open for guided tours Apr 1 through Dec 15, except for Thanksgiving Day, Tues through Sat 10:30 a.m. to 4:30 p.m. and Sun 1:30 to 4:30 p.m. Admission is $4 for adults and $1 for children. Grounds, gardens, and trails are open free of charge, all day, all year.

Reynolda House, Museum of American Art. 2250 Reynolda Rd.; (888) 663-1149; https://reynolda.org. An impressive collection of American masterpieces span the gracious 64-room estate of R.J. and Katherine Reynolds, which is much like it was when they lived here beginning in 1917. The architecture, furnishings, costume collection of some 700 pieces, and artwork reflect their elegant and extravagant tastes. Visitors can view three centuries of major American paintings, prints, and sculptures by the likes of Jacob Lawrence, Jasper Johns, Stuart Davis, and Georgia O'Keeffe, one of the finest collections of American art in North America. A National Historic Property, Reynolda House also offers tours of the formal gardens and the estate's support buildings, now converted to specialty shops, offices, and restaurants. Admission is $18 for adults, free for students and children. Open Tues through Sat 9:30 a.m. to 4:30 p.m., Sun 1:30 to 4:30 p.m. Closed Mon, Thanksgiving, Christmas, and New Year's Day.

Kaladium North. 400 Hanes Mill Rd.; (336) 767-6730; north.kaladium.org. Formerly Sci-Works, which opened here in 1974, this science center has been a national leader among science museums, and its hands-on exhibits continue to engage visitors of all ages. Kaladium features permanent and traveling exhibitions on a variety of physical, natural, and life sciences. Exhibits take visitors from the Mountains to the Sea and teach about how sound works, how physics works, and how health works. The Coastal Encounters lab tank allows guests to touch horseshoe crabs and other coastal species while chemicals fizz, pop, and react in dazzling science shows, and models of dinosaurs open a window to the world as it was millions of years ago. A 120-seat planetarium allows audiences to tour the constellations and learn about the night sky over the Carolinas. Outdoor exhibits with live animals and other hands-on displays on 15 acres blend seamlessly with picnic areas and nature trails. Admission is $10 for adults, $9 for seniors and students ages 3 to 19, and free for children ages 2 and under. Open Tues through Fri 10 a.m. to 4 p.m., Sat 10 a.m. to 5 p.m., and Sun noon to 5 p.m. The park and barnyard close 30 minutes before the museum.

Southeastern Center for Contemporary Art (SECCA). 750 Marguerite Dr.; (336) 725-1904; secca.org. SECCA comprises impressive and open series galleries in the 1929 English hunting lodge, home of the late industrialist James G. Hanes. The lodge has been enhanced with 20,000 square feet of exhibit space, where temporary exhibits change several times a year and represent the finest contemporary art both regionally and nationally. Shoppers can buy handcrafted jewelry, home decor, toys, and other items at the Centershop. Admission is $5 for adults, $3 for students and seniors, children under 12 get in free. Open Wed through Sat 10 a.m. to 5 p.m., Sun 2 to 5 p.m.; closed national holidays.

Stevens Center. 405 W. 4th St.; (336) 721-1945; www.uncsa.edu/stevenscenter. The restored 1929 silent movie theater in downtown Winston-Salem is part of the acclaimed North Carolina School of the Arts and regularly showcases student and faculty work, as well as a host of feature performances that include chamber music, jazz, ballet, the symphony, and films. Extensive renovations are planned for late 2023, so call ahead for information.

where to shop

Downtown Arts District. Meander along Trade and 6th Streets near the Marriott Hotel for the eclectic mix of shops and galleries that make up the resurgent arts district. Some examples follow:

Artworks Gallery. 564 Trade St. Northwest; (336) 723-5890; www.artworks-gallery .org. Established in 1984, the artist-run cooperative exhibits members' works. Open Tues through Fri 10 a.m. to 5 p.m., Sat 10 a.m. to 4 p.m.

Earth Sage. 608 Trade St. Northwest, Suite A; (336) 800-2565; earth-sage.com. Customers are asked to bring their own refillable containers to this store that helps them on a journey to leading a plastic-free lifestyle. It offers a variety of personal care items.

Fiber Company. 600 N. Trade St. (336) 725-5277. A collective of fiber artists and designers established in 1987 has a working studio complemented by a shop and gallery that offer the works of member artists as well as those of other craftsmen. Open Tues through Fri 10 a.m. to 5 p.m., Sat 11 a.m. to 3 p.m.

Piedmont Craftsmen Gallery. 601 N. Trade St.; (336) 725-1516; piedmont craftsmen.org. The gallery showcases the works of more than 350 of the Southeast's finest craft artists. It's open Tues through Fri from 10:30 a.m. to 5 p.m. and Sat from 10 a.m. to 5 p.m.

Hanes Mall. 3320 Silas Creek Pkwy.; (336) 765-8321; shophanesmall.com. This is one of the largest malls between Washington, D.C., and Atlanta, with more than 200 stores.

Historic Reynolda Village. 2201 Reynolda Rd.; (336) 758-5584. On the former estate of R.J. Reynolds, this shopping plaza has more than 30 upscale shops, including restaurants, art galleries, jewelry and antiques, fine gifts, and specialty items. Open Mon through Sat 10 a.m. to 5 p.m.

where to eat

Foothills Brewing. 638 W. 4th St.; (336) 777-3348; foothillsbrewing.com. One of the biggest craft brewers in the state also operates one of the best restaurants in Winston-Salem. Wings, hot chicken, and other pub food gets high marks as does its wide selection of beer. Open daily 11 a.m. to midnight. $$.

Krispy Kreme. 259 S. Stratford Rd.; (336) 724-2484. Krispy Kreme is found around the country, but Winston-Salem is home to this doughnut giant. Look for the HOT DOUGHNUTS NOW sign flashing, and you can watch as these sugary delights come off the conveyor belt. Get them glazed, cream-filled, frosted, or with sprinkles. $.

Old Fourth Street Filling Station. 871 W. 4th St.; (336) 724-7600. Originally a gas station, this restaurant offers the best patio dining in town, with a fireplace inside for chilly nights. Menu choices range from salads to filet mignon. Try popular broiled mahimahi with crab stuffing or the shrimp and grits. Open 11 a.m. to 11 p.m. Mon through Thurs, to midnight on Fri and Sat. Sunday brunch 10 a.m. to 3 p.m. $$–$$$.

Sweet Potatoes. 607 N. Trade St., (336) 727-4844; sweetpotatoes.ws. Virginia Joiner and Stephanie Tyson opened their award-winning restaurant in 2003. Forged in the great southern tradition, this arts district restaurant serves classics like fried okra, fried green tomatoes, and sweet potatoes—fried, baked, or just about any other way you would like. Sure you can get a good burger or spectacular meat loaf here, but the fried bologna sandwich comes highly recommended. Open Tues through Sat 11 a.m. to 3 p.m. and 5 to 10 p.m.; 10:30 a.m. to 3 p.m. Sun. $–$$.

Village Tavern. 221 Reynolda Village; (336) 748-0221; villagetavern.com. Enjoy delicious entrees in a warm, casual atmosphere. Treat yourself to a meal on the outdoor patio. Try the hot crab dip appetizer, which was created by the owner and hasn't changed in years. The Carolina burger, with homemade chili, is also another popular menu item. Open 11 a.m. to 11 p.m. Mon through Thurs, to midnight Fri and Sat, and 9 a.m. to 10 p.m. Sun. $$–$$$.

WestEnd Cafe. 926 W. 4th St.; (336) 723-4774; westendcafe.com. A trendy local favorite, the cafe serves salads, grinders, Reubens, and other sandwiches. Open Mon through Fri 11 a.m. to 10 p.m., Sat noon to 10 p.m. $.

where to stay

The Zevely Inn. 803 S. Main St.; (336) 748-9299; https:// zeveleyinn.com. This 12-room bed-and-breakfast, situated in the heart of Old Salem, has been meticulously and accurately restored to its mid-19th-century appearance. A continental breakfast of Moravian baked goods is served during the week and a full buffet breakfast on weekends. Complimentary wine and cheese are served in the evening. $$–$$$.

The Historic Brookstown Inn. 200 Brookstown Ave.; (336) 701-3904; brookstowninn .com. Built in 1837 and on the National Register of Historic Places, the inn was once a warehouse and Winston-Salem's oldest factory. Brookstown's guest rooms typically have exposed brick and original beams with extra-tall ceilings. Rates include a complimentary wine and cheese reception every evening from 5 to 7 p.m., milk and cookies before bed, and a complimentary continental breakfast each morning. $$$.

The Shaffner Inn. 150 Marshall St. Southwest; (336) 293-6875; theshaffner.com. Built in 1907 by one of the co-founders of Wachovia Loan and Trust Company, the Victorian-style Henry F. Shaffner House is now a restaurant and bed-and-breakfast. Located just blocks from historic Old Salem and downtown Winston-Salem, The Shaffner Inn offers evening wine and cheese and a complimentary breakfast. Lunch is available Mon through Fri 11 a.m. to 2 p.m., and dinner daily 6:30 to 8 p.m. $$–$$$.

day trip 05

northeast

>>> **redemption song:**
greensboro

greensboro

Nowhere else in North Carolina is the struggle for racial equity told better than it is in Greensboro. While the area's history dates to the Saura and Keyauwee people, the earliest known inhabitants of the region, Greensboro had a unique role in American history from the Revolutionary War to the Underground Railroad and to the sit-ins that helped launch the national civil rights movement. As a result, the city is uniquely diversified, refreshingly cultural, and simply special.

Germans, Quakers of Welsh and English descent, and Scotch-Irish from the northern colonies were the first European settlers in the Greensboro area. Permanent settlement began around 1740. In 1774 a log courthouse and jail were built in a place called Guilford Courthouse, the site of a fierce battle on March 15, 1781. That day, American Major General Nathanael Greene deployed 4,400 rebels at the Battle of Guilford Courthouse to thwart a redcoat invasion of North Carolina under Lord Cornwallis. Though Cornwallis held the site, he lost a quarter of his army, leading to defeat at Yorktown seven months later. Early in the next century, the city would be named Greensborough in honor of General Greene with its spelling simplified in 1895. Decades before the Civil War, Quaker anti-slave advocate Vestal Coffin and his cousin Levi operated an underground railroad here to move slaves out of the state. Guilford College is built on the site of the Underground Railroad depot that operated through the war. During the Civil War, Greensboro was both a storehouse and a railroad

53

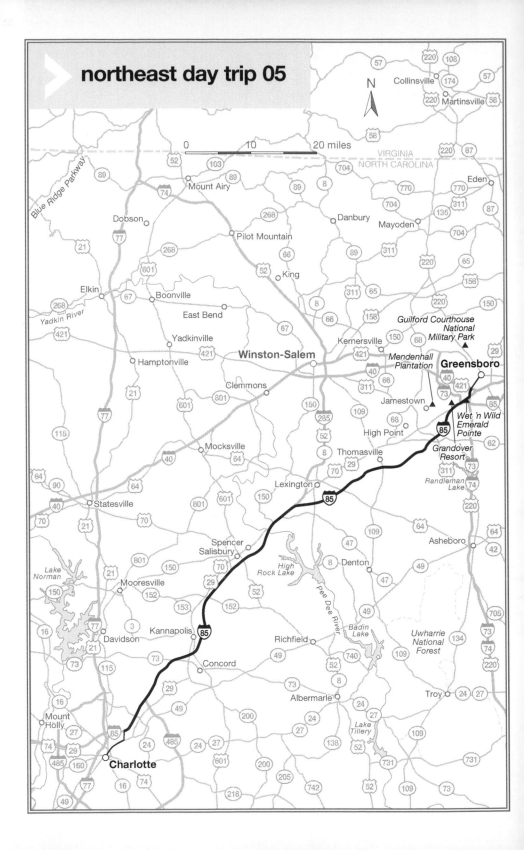

northeast day trip 05

center for the Confederacy, a vital source of supplies and troops for Robert E. Lee's Army of Northern Virginia. Civilian refugees and wounded soldiers were transported and sheltered here. Greensboro became the seat of the Confederacy on April 11, 1865, when Confederate President Jefferson Davis arrived here after Lee's surrender at Appomattox, to discuss the military situation of General Joseph E. Johnston and the weakened Army of Tennessee. Here Johnston advised Davis to enter into surrender negotiations with William Tecumseh Sherman. These negotiations led to Johnston's surrender to Sherman on April 26, 1865, at Bennett Place outside Durham. Later, all Confederate forces in North Carolina were mustered out and paroled in Greensboro.

In the early 1900s, Dr. Charlotte Hawkins Brown founded a preparatory school for African Americans that would operate for nearly 70 years. It is now a historic site and memorial. The most significance, however, comes from the simple act of four Black students, who ordered lunch at a Woolworth lunch counter and started a national movement. The International Civil Rights Center and Museum is located on that spot. Other contributions of Black Americans—including Jessie Jackson, who attended college at North Carolina A&T, Challenger astronaut Ron McNair, and Martin Luther King—are evident in cultural experiences throughout the region. To get a jump on the Greensboro experience, contact the **Greensboro Area Convention & Visitor Bureau** (2411 W. Gate City Blvd.; 336-274-2282; visitgreensboronc.com).

getting there

Heading north on I-85, take exit 35B and follow US 220 north into Greensboro. It is an easy 90-minute drive from Charlotte.

where to go

Blandwood Mansion & Carriage House. 447 W. Washington St.; (336) 272-5003; preser vationgreensboro.org. This elegant 19th-century farmhouse with Italian villa addition was home to prominent one-time North Carolina Governor John Motley Morehead. The 1844 addition by renowned architect Alexander Jackson Davis contributed to Blandwood's designation as a National Historic Landmark. Today it displays many original furnishings and is operated as a museum by Preservation Greensboro Inc. and the Blandwood Guild. Admission is $8 for adults, $7 for seniors, and free for students. Open Tues through Sat 11 a.m. to 4 p.m., Sun 2 to 5 p.m.

Community Theatre of Greensboro. 520 S. Elm St.; (336) 333-7470; ctgso.org. One of the state's most active community theatre companies offers a full season of performances for adults and children in the heart of the Old Greensboro Historic District in this theater originally built in 1927 as the Salvation Army. The adult season runs Feb through July and Sept through Dec. Children's performances run Sept through June.

Carolina Theatre. 310 S. Greene St.; (336) 333-2605; carolinatheatre.com. First opened in 1927, this restored vaudeville theater listed on the National Register of Historic Places was the first commercial building in the state equipped with air conditioning. It once served as one of Greensboro's principal performing arts centers, showcasing the city's ballet, community theater, opera, and even film festivals.

Charlotte Hawkins Brown Museum & State Historic Site. 6136 Burlington Rd., Gibsonville; (336) 449-4846; https://historicsites.nc.gov/all-sites/charlotte-hawkins-brown-museum. Located just outside Greensboro, this is North Carolina's first official historic site to honor an African American and a woman. The site is the former location of the Palmer Institute, a preparatory school for African Americans established by Brown in 1902. It operated until the Supreme Court's decision in *Brown vs. the Board of Education* forced busing of students in an effort to balance the racial mix in public schools. Exhibits, both archival and audiovisual, tell the story of education of African Americans. Free. Open Mon through Sat 9 a.m. to 5 p.m.

The Greensboro Arboretum. 401 Ashland Dr.; (336) 373-4334; greensborobeautiful.org. Fourteen labeled plant collections, special garden displays, and distinctive features are contained within a 17-acre portion of Lindley Park. An interesting combination of conifers, wetland plants, shrubs, and small trees provide year-round interest. Free. Open daily sunrise to sunset.

Miriam P. Brenner Children's Museum. 220 N. Church St.; (336) 574-2898; mbcmuseum.com. Elementary school students get their hands full at one of the state's first and best children's museums. Young guests can fly in an airplane, dig for buried treasure, or get wrapped up in a gigantic bubble. "Our Town" is complete with a grocery store, bank, and theater, and there are also early childhood exhibit areas. Admission is $10 for anyone over age 1. Open Tues through Sat 9 a.m. to 5 p.m., Fri to 8 p.m., Sat to 6 p.m. and Sun 1 to 5 p.m. Open Mon in the summer.

Greensboro Cultural Center at Festival Park. 200 N. Davie St.; (336) 373-2547; greensboro-nc.gov. Located in and around a four-story building adjacent to this city-maintained park is a showplace with 12 visual and performing arts organizations, four art galleries, rehearsal halls, a sculpture garden, a privately operated restaurant with outdoor cafe-style seating, and an outdoor amphitheater. Open Mon through Fri 8 a.m. to 10 p.m., Sat 9 a.m. to 6:30 p.m., and Sun 1 to 6:30 p.m.

Greensboro History Museum. 130 Summit Ave.; (336) 373-2043; greensborohistory.org. Stories of Piedmont people and events come alive in 12 galleries and two restored houses. Accounts told include the 1960 Greensboro civil rights sit-ins, Guilford native Dolley Madison's lasting legacy as first lady, and the popular short stories written by O. Henry. Displayed are 20th-century photography, a Model T, a world-class collection of Civil War firearms, and furniture created by Piedmont craftsmen. Stroll through a historic cemetery and check out the merchandise of an old-fashioned general store. Free. Open Tues through Sat 10 a.m. to 5 p.m., Sun 2 to 5 p.m.

Guilford Courthouse National Military Park. 2332 New Garden Rd.; (336) 288-1776; nps.gov/guco. More than 200 acres are dedicated to the March 15, 1781, battle that occurred here. Twenty-eight monuments of soldiers, statesmen, and patriots of the American Revolution are here in memorial to those who gave their lives for American freedom. Park activities include cell phone–guided walking and driving tours. In the visitor center are a dramatic 30-minute live-action film, an animated battle map program, and information-packed museum exhibits featuring original Revolutionary War weaponry and artifacts. The park also provides paved walking trails and a bookstore. Free. Open daily 9 a.m. to 5 p.m. Closed New Year's Day, Thanksgiving, and Christmas.

The International Civil Rights Center & Museum. 134 S. Elm St.; (336) 274-9199; sitin movement.org. The four Black students from North Carolina A&T State University couldn't have imagined the impact their walking into the Greensboro Woolworth and ordering lunch would have on American history. It started a national sit-in movement that literally changed the country. Today that store has been converted into a center and museum dedicated to telling the story of the civil rights movement. Central among archival displays is the lunch counter where those students and their classmates sat in peaceful protest over segregation, which was a way of life in the 1960s South. Through one-and-a-half-hour guided tours, visitors begin to understand the history and the effects of segregation from 18th- and 19th-century slavery to the Jim Crow South. Three levels of exhibits document the efforts of those students and others who contributed to change a society. Admission is $15 for adults, $10 for students,. There is an additional charge for tour options. Open Mon through Sat 10 a.m. to 6 p.m.

Mattye Reed African Heritage Center. 202 University Circle; (336) 334-3209; ncat.edu. Located in the Dudley Building on the North Carolina A&T State University campus, the Mattye Reed African Heritage Center houses one of the best collections of African culture in the country. More than 6,000 art and craft items that originated from more than 30 African nations, New Guinea, and Haiti are on display. Free. Open Mon through Fri 10 a.m. to 5 p.m.

Greensboro Science Center. 4301 Lawndale Dr.; (336) 288-3769; greensboroscience. org. Roam through the Dinosaur Gallery and learn about gems and minerals at this hands-on museum, zoo, and planetarium. Visit snakes and amphibians in the Jaycee Herpetarium and explore Kids Alley. The science museum also has space for national touring exhibits. A small zoo with tigers, crocodiles, primates, a farm petting zoo, and many other animals is also open for visiting. Admission is $19.50 for adults, $18.50 for seniors, and $17.50 for children. Open daily 9 a.m. to 4 p.m.,

O. Henry Statues. Corner of North Elm and Bellemeade Streets; (336) 373-2043. This three-piece outdoor sculpture group honors Greensboro's best-known writer, William

mendenhall homeplace

*A bottomless wagon, used to transport slaves on the Underground Railroad, is housed and on exhibit in the barn at Jamestown's **Mendenhall Homeplace,** which in the 19th century became a symbolic opposition to slavery from an otherwise quiet people. The 1811 house is central to the complex of buildings that was the home of Quaker Richard Mendenhall. Much of the house, including the kitchen, remains as it was when the Mendenhalls lived here, with an obvious absence of slave quarters. One addition was made in 1840 to accommodate the growing family. While the only evidence that the wagon was used in transporting slaves from North Carolina to Ohio are the stories passed down from generation to generation, there is other evidence that Mendenhall also hid slaves in the basement of the home. Tours are conducted Tues through Fri 11 a.m. to 3 p.m., Sat 1 to 4 p.m., and Sun 2 to 4 p.m. and cost $5 for adults, $3 for seniors, and $2 for children. The plantation is located south of Greensboro at 603 W. Main St. in Jamestown. Find it by traveling US 70/29 to the town of Jamestown. For information call (336) 454-3819.*

Sydney Porter, better known as O. Henry. It features a bronze likeness of the author, a 7-foot by 14-foot open book of his renowned short stories, and a statue of his small dog, Lovey. O. Henry was an eyewitness to the Union occupation of Greensboro and recounted these experiences in some of his short stories. Porter's uncle ran a successful town drugstore in the 1890s. Lunsford Richardson, one of the store's investors, later developed a line of Vick's Family Remedies. Vicks VapoRub was one of his successful creations.

Old Greensborough & the Downtown Historic District. 532 S. Elm St.; (336) 379-0060; downtowngreensboro.org. Mixed into this revitalized, century-old commercial, residential, and industrial district are more than a dozen antiques, art, and other shops and restaurants. Many of Greensboro's most popular attractions are located here; an mp3 file of the walking tour is available from the Greensboro History Museum. A free downtown shopping guide is available at most merchant locations, the Greensboro Area Convention & Visitor Bureau, the Greensboro History Museum, and the Downtown Greensboro Incorporated office. The district is located in and around S. Elm Street from Market Street to Lee Street.

Tanger Center for Performing Arts. 300 N. Elm St.; (336) 333-6500; tangercenter .com. The 3,000-seat, $93 million Tanger Center opened in downtown Greensboro in 2021. It became the home for the city's performing arts groups, Broadway Lights plays, and big-name performers such as Sting, Josh Groban, and Little Big Town.

Tanger Family Bicentennial Garden and **David Caldwell Historic Park.** 1105 Hobbs Rd., just north of Friendly Avenue; (336) 373-4544; greensborobeautiful.org. This beautiful garden features flowering trees, shrubs, annual displays, and the Bog Garden, a marsh of ferns, bamboo, and other plants. The adjacent park is named in honor of Caldwell, who served as a local minister and educator and owned much of this land.

Tannenbaum Historic Park. 2200 New Garden Rd.; (336) 288-1776. Operated by the City of Greensboro's Parks and Recreation Department, this eight-acre park was the 18th-century farmstead of Joseph Hoskins, who served the Guilford County community as constable, tax collector, and sheriff. During the Revolutionary War Battle of Guilford Courthouse, Hoskins's land served as a staging area for British troops. The site also features a 19th-century barn, moved from a southeastern part of Guilford County and restored and located within the park. A reconstructed kitchen, blacksmith shop, farm exhibit, and gardens provide visitors with the opportunity to experience what daily life was like for the Colonial settlers of Piedmont. Free. Open Fri through Sun 8:30 a.m. to 5 p.m.

Triad Stage. 232 S. Elm St.; (336) 272-0160; triadstage.org. Classic, contemporary, and new theatrical works, both drama and comedy, are presented in this 300-seat live performance theater with two spacious lobbies and many other amenities in the former Montgomery Ward store in Greensboro's downtown historic district. No performances in Aug and Sept.

Walkway of History. S. Elm Street at February One Plaza; (336) 274-2282. Sidewalk markers chronicle six chapters in local African-American history, ranging from the first fugitive slave on the Underground Railroad to the first Black state Supreme Court justice. The walkway was unveiled on the 34th anniversary of the Woolworth civil rights sit-ins by the Greensboro Four.

Weatherspoon Art Museum. 500 Tate Street; (336) 334-5770; weatherspoonart.org. This fine museum on the campus of UNC-Greensboro houses a nationally recognized collection. Within six galleries of open dramatic space and a sculpture courtyard, the museum has a collection of more than 5,000 paintings, sculptures, drawings, prints and photographs, and objects in miscellaneous media. Highlights include the Dillard Collection of art on paper and the Cone Collection of prints and bronzes by Henri Matisse, Picasso, and others. Free. Open Tues, Wed, Fri, and Sat 10 a.m. to 5 p.m., Thurs 5 to 8 p.m.

Wet 'n Wild Emerald Pointe Water Park. 3910 S. Holden Rd., I-85 exit 121; (336) 852-9721, (800) 555-5900; emeraldpointe.com. The largest water park in the Carolinas and one of the top 12 in the US offers more than 35 rides and attractions. Thunder Bay, one of only four tsunami pools in the country, makes massive, perfect waves. Dr. Von Dark's Tunnel of Terror drops 40 feet, spinning riders 360 degrees in total darkness. Enclosed slides, drop slides, tube rides, and cable glides provide thrills for all ages and sizes. Two great children's areas and a drifting lazy river complete the fun for everyone. Tickets start at $29. Call or check the website for seasonal hours of operation.

where to shop

Four Seasons Town Centre. I-40 at High Point Road/Koury Boulevard; (336) 299-9230; shopfourseasons.com. The center's three levels include more than 200 specialty stores and eateries, as well as anchors Dillard's and JCPenney. Stop by for a bite to eat in the food court, or enjoy free and regularly scheduled entertainment in the performing arts amphitheater. Open Mon through Sat 10 a.m. to 9 p.m., Sun 12 to 7 p.m.

Friendly Center. 3110 Kathleen Ave.; (336) 299-9802; friendlycenter.com. This open-air shopping center, originally established in 1957, isn't as slick as modern malls, but it has a steady list of tenants and customers. Shops include Loft, Chico's, Old Navy, Banana Republic, Victoria's Secret, and anchors such as Belk, Macy's, and Sears. Also located here is a multiplex theater, the Grande. Friendly Center boasts several restaurants, including Harpers and the ever-popular Jay's Deli. Open Mon through Sat 10 a.m. to 9 p.m. and Sun 1 to 6 p.m.

Greensboro Farmers Curb Market. 501 Yanceyville St.; (336) 373-2402. Homegrown vegetables, fruits, and other produce are only half the story of this farmers' market; fresh-cut herbs and flowers, baked goods, pottery, and crafts also are available. Open year-round, Sat 7:30 a.m. to noon.

Piedmont Triad Farmers Market. 2914 Sandy Ridge Rd.; (336) 605-9157; ncagr.gov/mar kets. Get to know some of the South's friendliest people while shopping for local Piedmont fruits, vegetables, flowers, baked goods, jams, honey, crafts, and more. Make sure you visit the garden center and Moose Cafe while you're there. Open daily 7 a.m. to 6 p.m.

Replacements, Ltd. Knox Road off I-85/40 exit 132 at Mt. Hope Church Road; (336) 697-3000, (800) REPLACE; replacements.com. Replacements claims to be the world's largest retailer of old and new china, crystal, flatware, and collectibles and to have more than 13 million pieces of inventory in 300,000-plus patterns. During the free daily tours of the showrooms, museum, warehouse, and restoration facility, patrons can inquire about patterns and shop Replacements' 13,000-square-foot showroom for giftware, dinnerware, one-of-a-kind items, antiques, and collectibles. Open daily 9 a.m. to 7 p.m.; closed Christmas Day.

State Street Station. Between North Elm and Church Streets, just north of Wendover Avenue; (336) 383-5917; visitgreensboronc.com. This historic area of downtown features three dozen or so unique shops, restaurants, and boutiques housed in buildings that date to the 1920s.

where to eat

913 Whiskey Bar & Southern Kitchen. 913 S. Chapman St.; (336) 617-4291; 913whis keybar.com. No fewer than eight versions of old-fashioned cocktails are on the menu at this cozy corner bar and restaurant. On the food menu find their signature mac and cheese, sliders, and flatbreads. $$

Barn Dinner Theatre. 120 Stage Coach Trail; (336) 292-2211; barndinner.com. This is one of Greensboro's oldest entertainment traditions. Since the 1960s it has produced popular Broadway-style plays, musical shows and traditional buffets. Performances are Wed through Sun evenings year-round. Matinees are offered Sun through Tues. $$$.

DiValletta Restaurant. Grandover Resort and Conference Center, 1000 Club Rd.; (336) 834-4877; grandoverresort.com/dining. As the most elegant dining room in the area, this AAA four-diamond restaurant overlooks a golf course and offers unique Mediterranean dishes to suit all tastes. Outdoor dining is available. Open daily for breakfast, lunch, and dinner. $$-$$$.

Europa Bar & Cafe. Greensboro Cultural Center at Festival Park, 200 N. Davie St.; (336) 389-1010; https://europagso.com. Enjoy a full menu or dine lightly on a variety of hors d'oeuvres or appetizers at this informal but stylish cafe. It has an extensive list of wines from around the world, reasonably priced by the bottle or glass. Outdoor dining is available. Open Mon through Sat for lunch and dinner, Sun for brunch and dinner. $-$$.

The Green Valley Grill. 622 Green Valley Rd.; (336) 854-2015; greenvalleygrill.com. The owners refer to this grill, adjacent to the O. Henry Hotel, as "informally elegant fine dining." Patrons enjoy internationally elegant dining with an Old World influence. Changing menus feature regional European recipes that may be from Provence one month and Tuscany the next. $$-$$$.

Liberty Oak. 100 W. Washington St.; (336) 273-7057; libertyoakgso.com. Liberty Oak offers casual elegance, a changing menu, extensive wines by the glass, and outdoor dining. Open Tues through Sat 11 a.m. to 9 p.m. $-$$.

Lucky 32. 1421 Westover Ter.; (336) 370-0707; lucky32.com. Changing menus every month or so, Lucky 32 offers regional American cuisine focused largely on Southern tastes with locally available foods such as collard greens and heirloom tomatoes. Open daily for lunch and dinner, Sun for brunch. $$-$$$.

Natty Greene's Pub & Brewing Company. 345 S. Elm St.; (336) 274-1373; nattygreens .com. Philly cheesesteak is made all over, but this is the only place you can find an Elm Street Philly. Grinders, burgers, crab cakes, and the like fill up this filling menu. Twelve hand-crafted brews are also available for sampling. Open daily 11 a.m. to midnight. $$.

Scrambled Southern Diner. 2417 Spring Garden St.; (336) 285-6590; scrambledgreens boro.com. Located in the heart of the historic district, Scrambled has become a much-beloved staple in the Gate City. Here local produce finds its way into Bloody Marys as well as the eclectic breakfast and lunch plates. $$

Yum Yum Better Ice Cream Co. 1219 Spring Garden St.; (336) 272-8284. This 100-year-old Greensboro institution located near the UNC campus serves ice cream and hot dogs, all the way with chili, slaw, and onions if you like. Open Mon through Sat. $.

where to stay

Biltmore Greensboro Hotel. 111 W. Washington St.; (336) 272-3474, (800) 332-0303; thebiltmoregreensboro.com. Accommodations at this unique European boutique hotel, conveniently located in the heart of Greensboro, include a complimentary deluxe continental breakfast. The interior is warm, decorated with historic portraits and furnishings. $$$.

Grandover Resort & Conference Center. 1000 Club Rd.; (336) 294-1800, (800) 472-6301; grandoverresort.com. Located on 1,500 spectacular acres just off I-85 is this top-rated resort with 247 guest rooms in an 11-story tower. Though built in the last century and contemporary by design, it is intended to represent an old world European castle. It features tons of amenities that include men's and women's spa facilities, a four-court tennis complex, two racquetball courts, an indoor/outdoor swimming pool, five food and beverage outlets, and lush gardens, as well as the rolling terrain of the resort's top-rated golf courses. The resort has a spa with five treatment rooms and an 1,800-square-foot fitness center. $$$.

Greenwood Bed & Breakfast. 205 N. Park Dr.; (336) 763-1941; greenwoodbnb.com. "Dollhouse" might come to mind when describing this turn-of-the-20th-century "chalet on the park." Its culinary delights are memorable—guests enjoy a fine-dining breakfast by candlelight. Located in Greensboro's finest historic district, Greenwood serves upscale traditional American dishes with European touches and offers private baths and an in-ground pool. $$.

O. Henry Hotel. 624 Green Valley Rd.; (336) 854-2000, (800) 965-8259; ohenryhotel .com. Located near Friendly Center, this stately AAA four-diamond hotel evokes the grandeur of the original O. Henry, which stood in downtown Greensboro from 1919 to 1978. The new hotel was designed, as were hotels at the turn of the 20th century, to be a part of the community and blend into its surroundings. A great restaurant and lounge are on the premises. $$$.

The Proximity Hotel. 704 Green Valley Rd.; (336) 379-8200, (800) 379-8200; proximity hotel.com. A day trip to Greensboro can help the planet, too. The Proximity was the country's first LEED Platinum hotel—the US Green Building Council's highest recognition in the Leadership in Energy and Environmental Design (LEED) rating system, the nationally accepted benchmark for the design, construction, and operation of high-performance green buildings. The hotel received a four-diamond AAA rating because of its custom furnishings and detail, commissioned art, and innovative, stylish design complemented by abundant natural light and carefully selected, green construction materials. $$$.

day trip 06

northeast

king of the jungle:
asheboro

asheboro

Once upon a time, travelers to Randolph County went to the zoo and then went home. Today the experience among these rolling hills is royally different. This area to the north and just beyond Uwharrie National Forest is called the Heart of Carolina; Murphy in the North Carolina Mountains is 280 miles to the west, and Manteo on the coast is 260 miles to the east. The area has benefited largely from the resurgence in popularity of Seagrove pottery that can be found near here. (More details are in East Day Trip 01.) Better access provided by I-74, which bisects the region north to south, has also made this a more desirable place to live and to visit.

The rolling hills of the Uwharrie National Forest were once hunting grounds for the Keyauwee, who settled here and along the Pee Dee and Yadkin Rivers about 300 years ago. Celebrated explorer John Lawson encountered these natives in 1701. The visitor is likely to be impressed with the feel of Asheboro's mountainous geography. It's technically on a plateau more than 100 miles from mountains; thus when its warmer climate is added, it equals a perfect environment for the state's Zoological Park. This attraction prides itself on allowing exotic animals to roam as if in the wild.

The 1,450-acre park could be a day trip unto itself, but the county seat of Randolph offers more. Not only is it home to the king of the jungle, but it's also where the King of NAS-CAR, Richard Petty, grew up. In addition to new restaurants and other recreational opportunities, found here are one of the finest collections of vintage Harley-Davidson motorcycles and the North Carolina Aviation Museum, home to vintage military aircraft.

63

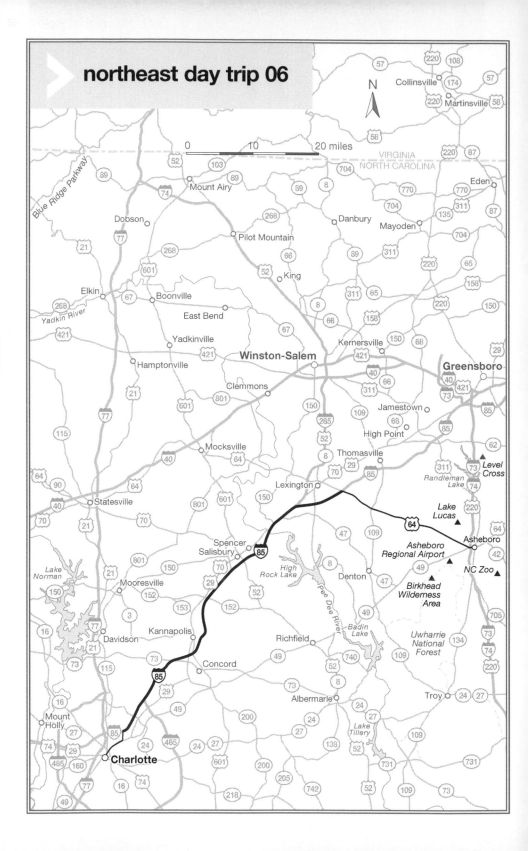

getting there

Asheboro is about 90 minutes from Charlotte. I-85 North to US 64 East is likely a few minutes faster, but SR 49 North is a more direct and more scenic route. Choose the SR 49 route, too, to combine a trip to Asheboro with adventures in East Day Trip 01.

where to go

American Classic Motorcycle Museum. 1170 US 64 West; (336) 629-9564. Not only is this a museum; it's a working repair shop. One of the South's finest collections of antique and classic Harley-Davidson motorcycles, the museum has more than 30 bikes dating from 1936 to 1972, and an authentic 1948 Harley dealership and repair shop. Free. Open Mon 6 a.m. to 2 p.m., Tues through Fri 6 a.m. to 5:30 p.m., and Sat 6 a.m. to 4 p.m.

Birkhead Wilderness Area. Access areas located at 3977 Lassiter Mill Rd. and 3091 Tot Hill Farm Rd.; (828) 257-4200. These 5,160 acres in the Uwharrie National Forest are the only ones in the Piedmont designated as a federal wilderness area. Formed by ancient volcanoes, the Uwharries are among the oldest mountains in the world. Centuries of erosion have left rock outcroppings scattered throughout the old-growth hardwood forest. Leading from the access areas are trailheads through the forest. From the trails along sparkling streams, hikers can spot foundations, chimneys, walls, abandoned mines, and other archeological evidence of historic homesteads and even American Indian settlements.

Lake Lucas. 3158 Old Lexington Rd.; (336) 629-1639;. Operated by the local parks and rec department is this small lake, where visitors can fish, picnic, and rent a johnboat or canoe. There are also a short walking trail and playground. Free; fees are charged for some activities. Typically open during daylight hours. Closed Wed.

North Carolina Aviation Museum & Hall of Fame. 2222 Pilots View Rd., Asheboro Regional Airport; (336) 625-0170; ncamhof.com. This museum, created for the preservation of military aircraft, is home to an impressive collection of airworthy vintage military aircraft. Featured is a 1941 Piper Flitfire flown by Orville Wright. The museum also houses exhibits of World War II military uniforms and a collection of World War II–era newspaper features. Admission is $10 for adults and $5 for students. Open Thurs through Sun 11 a.m. to 5 p.m.

North Carolina Zoological Park. 4401 Zoo Pkwy.; (336) 879-7000, (800) 488-0444; nczoo.org. When this zoo was created at a temporary facility in 1974, its founders knew it would be a facility largely free of the obvious bars and fences that separate humans from exhibits. It would be one of the first American zoos within which horticulturalists, zoologists, and designers would work together closely to develop exhibits that leave animals free to roam as they might be on the American Plains or African desert. Its first permanent exhibit was the Forest Edge, home to zebra, ostrich, and giraffe, which opened in 1979 and exists today much as it did then.

Today the zoo allows guests to travel from African habitats through North America, zoologically speaking, in just a few hours. Big animals such as elephants and rhinos highlight the African exhibits, not to be outdone by lions, gorillas, and other primates. As guests travel through North America, polar bears and playful otters aim to please the crowd as alligators linger in a swamp. Other exhibits allow visitors to get up close and personal with snakes and other reptiles or to do a little bird watching in the aviary.

The best way to see the zoo is on foot, so you can explore the exhibits and trails. An internal tram is available to transport visitors between exhibit areas, but most animals are not visible from the trams. You can enter or exit by either the North American or African gate; a shuttle bus transports visitors to the parking areas. Zoo officials recommend taking a minimum of five hours to explore all that the park offers at a comfortable pace.

The zoo is open daily 9 a.m. to 5 p.m. Apr 1 to Oct 31, daily 9 a.m. to 4 p.m. Nov 1 to Mar 31, and closed Christmas Day. There are additional hours during special events and reduced hours during inclement weather. Admission is $15 for adults, $13 for seniors, and $11 for children.

Pisgah Covered Bridge. Take exit 49, just south of Asheboro off US 220 Business. Look for the historical markers that will direct you to the covered bridge, one of only two in North Carolina, which was built around 1910 at a cost of $40. Hiking trails, picnic tables, and parking are available.

Richland Creek Zip Line & Canopy Tours. 2728 Fairview Farm Rd.; (336) 736-5623; richlandcreekzipline.com. If the animals at the zoo bring to mind Johnny Weissmuller flying through the jungle from vine to vine, then head to this next attraction just four miles away. Though zip lines are popping up throughout the Carolinas, this is one of the more authentic canopy tours along Richland Creek, Mendenhall Falls and . . . wait for it . . . Purgatory Mountain. Two skywalks and 15 zip lines make up this wild ride. Cost is $40 for adults, $25 for children ages 12 and under. Open daily 9 a.m. to 6 p.m.

where to shop

Circa Gallery. 150 Sunset Ave.; (336) 736-8015. Located next to the local farmers' market is this eclectic art gallery that has everything from prints and original paintings to handblown glass. Monthly exhibits feature emerging local artists. Open Tues through Sat 11 a.m. to 6 p.m.

Collector's Antique Mall. 211 Sunset Ave.; (336) 629-8105; collectorsantiquemall.com. More than 125 dealers offer antiques and collectibles in more than 35,000 square feet of retail space in the downtown antiques district of Asheboro. Open Mon, Fri, and Sat 10 a.m. to 8 p.m., Tues through Thurs 10 a.m. to 6 p.m., Sun 1 to 5 p.m.

where to eat

Flying Pig. 208 Sunset Ave.; (336) 610-3737. The Flying Pig has quickly become the place to go in Asheboro for evening fun. The pub also serves sandwiches and wood-fired pizza. Give the spicy, fried angry okra (really fried jalapenos) a try. Open Mon, Thurs, and Fri 5 p.m. to 1 a.m., Sat and Sun noon to 1 a.m. $$.

Sir Pizza. 813 E. Dixie Dr.; (336) 629-2874. Sir Pizza has been an Asheboro favorite for pizza, pasta, and sandwiches since 1969. The locals tell us that when people who have moved from Asheboro return home, this is the first place they want to return to. Open daily. $$.

Something Different Restaurant & Catering. 1512 Zoo Pkwy.; (336) 626-5707; eat-somethingdifferentrestaurant.com. Located near the North Carolina Zoological Park, this restaurant is a fusion of Greek, Italian, American, and other cuisines. It all comes together with an offering of a full, varied menu that includes, pasta, quesadillas, kabobs, and other surprises. Open Thurs through Sun 11 a.m. to 9 p.m. $$

The Table. 139 S. Church St.; (336) 736-8628; thetablefarmbakery.com. Being located in a 1925 office building just feels right for this market and breakfast and lunch bakery and restaurant. Pastries and sandwiches made with fresh-baked breads have become hallmarks here. Open Tues through Sat 7:30 to 2:30 p.m., and until 8 p.m. Thurs and Fri. $$

where to stay

Getaway Cabins. 2846 Old Cox Rd., (617) 914-0211; getaway.house. While this company operates a couple dozen "outposts" throughout the US, this is the only one in North Carolina. Offered here are 32 modest but comfortable cabins. You'll find a small stove and cookware, a small shower, and other limited amenities. $$

worth more time

Before visiting the king of the jungle at North Carolina Zoological Park, head north on US 220 to Level Cross in **Randleman** to learn about a different kind of king. Long known as "The King," NASCAR legend **Richard Petty** and his Petty Racing Team make their home here. The Petty family is recognized as one of the greatest philanthropic families in racing; they founded Victory Junction Gang Camp for terminally and chronically ill children, which is also located here.

Visit the **Richard Petty Museum** (309 Branson Mill Rd., Randleman; (336) 495-1143; https://rpmuseum.com). Race cars, awards, and photos honor the seven-time NASCAR champion. See highlights of The King's 35-year career in a full-length movie in the mini theater, and take home gifts for a favorite race fan. Admission is $8 for adults, $5 for children ages 7 and up, and free for children 6 and under. Open Wed through Sat 9 a.m. to 5 p.m. The Petty Compound, where his garage is located, is in Randleman, too.

day trip 07

northeast

tar heel country:
pittsboro, chapel hill

Pushing the limits of a Charlotte day trip is a journey to the idyllic, picturesque college town that's home to the University of North Carolina. Chapel Hill is a place students and alum will tell unknowing travelers is just south of heaven. The flagship of the state's 16-school system is consistently ranked among the country's top colleges, even among private and more costly schools of higher learning. Its athletic programs, particularly basketball, baseball, football, and women's soccer, rank among the country's best.

This day trip east of Charlotte starts in Pittsboro, long known for the unusual placement of its courthouse in the middle of town with traffic from US 64 and US 15/501 routed around it. A fire in 2010 came just short of destroying the historic 1881 building.

Plan to stop at Fearrington Village while traveling between Chapel Hill and Pittsboro on US 15/501. Tucked away on farmland dating to the 1700s, Fearrington Village is the anchor to a bustling center of shops and services that serve the 2,000 residents of this special community.

pittsboro

Located in the heart of North Carolina, Pittsboro offers beautiful rolling landscape, quaint antiques stores, pottery shops, and more than 50 art studios and galleries. Local leaders once lobbied to have the university located in Pittsboro, first established in 1785. Legislators also briefly considered it as the state capitol. Instead it ended up as the seat of Chatham County with a population of fewer than 2,500 people.

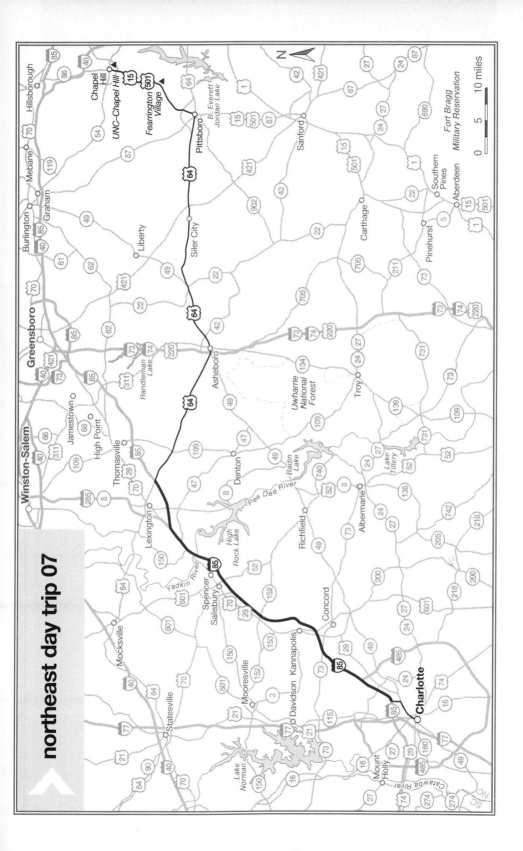

getting there

Much like Asheboro, Pittsboro is accessible from Charlotte via I-85 to US 64. You could choose the more scenic route of SR 49, which merges with US 64 in Asheboro, then leads to Pittsboro. Either way the trip is about two hours with the interstate route being 20 miles longer than the 100-mile country road drive.

where to go

Carolina Tiger Rescue. 1940 Hanks Chapel Rd.; (919) 542-4684; carolinatigerrescue.org. On this tour are some of the world's most endangered species, such as caracals, servals, ocelots, binturongs, and kinkajous. Tours of the compound, developed as a home for injured and displaced cats, take about 90 minutes and are available by reservation only. Cost is $18 for adults and $12.50 for children ages 4 to 12.

Chatham County Courthouse & Historical Museum. Historic Traffic Circle at the intersection of US 15/501 and US 64; (919) 542-6222; chathamhistory.org. Built in 1881 and designed by a local lawyer after the roof blew off an earlier building during a trial, this is the fourth courthouse built in the county since 1771. Listed on the National Register of Historic Places, it was extensively renovated in 1959 and again in the late 1980s. In March 2010 fire devastated the building, its clock tower, and the third level, and damaged the museum and its contents. A new judicial center was already slated for Chatham County prior to the fire, but following repairs and renovations, the museum's holdings returned to the courthouse. Among the exhibits are geology collections as well as items the tell Chatham's history.

Fearrington Gardens. 2000 Fearrington Village Center; (919) 542-2121; fearrington.com. Gardens and walking paths weave through the bucolic Fearrington Village, a retreat-style community located on a historic farm. The more than 50 beds of annuals, perennials, and shrubs provide color and horticultural interest throughout the year. The Belted Galloways—the black-and-white "Oreo" cows—a rare breed of Scottish beef cattle, are hard to miss standing sentinel over the farm's rolling grassy land. Open daily. For more, see the entries that follow on where to eat and where to shop at Fearrington Village.

Jordan Lake Educational State Forest. 2832 Big Woods Rd.; (919) 542-1154; ncesf .org/jordanlake.html. Jordan Lake Educational State Forest is the newest of North Carolina's educational state forests. A variety of wildlife can be found here, including birds of prey, deer, songbirds, flying squirrels, and beavers. The three-quarter-mile Talking Tree Trail features—you guessed it—"talking trees," each with a recorded message about its history and surroundings. The center of life at the park is a 14,000-acre lake that meanders from Pittsboro east to Apex and north almost to Chapel Hill.

Pittsboro Historic District. Listed on the National Register of Historic Places, the district stretches beyond the original four-block town center to include Chatham Mills, the Patrick

St. Lawrence House, the Pittsboro Community House, the County Courthouse, and other homes and buildings erected between the 1780s and 1949. Among the historic buildings are **Hall-London House** (128 Hillsboro St.; 919-542-2400), built by Henry Armand London, a lawyer, state senator, and founder-editor of the *Chatham Record,* a local newspaper that has been in continuous publication since 1878; **Manly Law Office** (Masonic Street, US 15/501; https://chathamhistory.org/Preservation-Manly-Law-Office), built by Charles Manly, governor of North Carolina from 1849 to 1850; and the 1850 **Pittsboro Presbyterian Church** (95 East St.; 919-542-4702). Visitors may request a Pittsboro Historic District brochure and a complete visitor information packet from Chatham County Tourism (visitpittsboro.com).

where to shop

Mays Pottery. 4762 US 15/501 North; (984) 298-6011 (Nathan) or (919) 858-6264 (Martha); mayspottery.com. Home to hand-thrown pottery, dinnerware, and one-of-a-kind art pottery for more than 25 years, the Mays studio and gallery are located on the banks of the Haw River. Seven cabins and kiln houses built on 10 acres contain the production and retail gallery. The pottery is marked by traditional Japanese bamboo brushwork not likely found elsewhere in this area.

Fearrington Farmers' Market. 2000 Fearrington Village Center; (919) 923-6262; https://fearringtonfarmersmarket.com/. Residents of Fearrington Village shop here all the time, but it's also a good stop for baked goods, eggs, cut flowers, orchids, honey, jams, jellies, soaps, plants of all kinds, poultry, and other meats. Open Tues 4 p.m. to dusk Apr to Thanksgiving.

Historic Downtown Pittsboro. (919) 542-5722; shoppittsboro.com. Visit 12 great antiques shops, breweries, a distillery, and other locally-owned businesses in this quaint downtown.

where to eat

The City Tap. 89 Hillsboro St.; (919) 545-0562; thecitytap.com; With indoor and outdoor seating, The City Tap has a solid selection of local craft beers. On the menu find Reubens, hoagies, salads, and flatbread pizzas. Open daily at 11:30 a.m. $$

Fearrington House Restaurant. 2000 Fearrington Village Center; (919) 542-2121; fearrington.com. The Fearrington House is one of only a handful of AAA five-diamond award winners and Mobil five-star recipients in the nation. Carolina staples like trout are combined with gnocchi beets and English peas to create exotic dishes alongside more recognizable options such as beef tenderloin. Enjoy gourmet dining Tues through Sat 6 to 9 p.m., Sun to 8 p.m. $$$.

Postal Fish Company. 75 W. Salisbury St.; (919) 704-8612; postalfishcompany.com. Located in a big open space with expansive windows, this fish restaurant brings diners a little closer to the coast. Oysters, scallops, shrimp, and the catch of the day are all prepared fried or in varied creative fashions. $$$

S & T's Soda Shoppe. 85 Hillsboro St.; (919) 545-0007; sandtsodashoppe.com. Enjoy good food and reminisce about the past in this nostalgic soda shop. Restored woodwork, a marble counter with bar stools, and several pieces from the past make this place a great stop while shopping. Open Mon through Sat 11 a.m. to 7:30 p.m. $$.

where to stay

Fearrington House Inn. 2000 Fearrington Village Center; (919) 542-2121; fearrington.com. Everything about Farrington House is elegant and luxurious from the gardens to the linens. Rates include gourmet breakfast and afternoon tea. A spa, fitness center, and first-class service make this one of North Carolina's premier getaways. $$$.

The Rosemary House. 76 West St.; rosemary-bb.com. This 1912 Colonial Revival home in the heart of Pittsboro offers five guest rooms with private baths, telephones, ceiling fans, fireplaces, two-person whirlpools, and a full gourmet breakfast. $$–$$$.

chapel hill

Chapel Hill was named after the New Hope Chapel, which stood on a hill at the crossing of two primary roads in the late 1700s. Town lots were auctioned in 1793 when construction of the Old East building began at the University of North Carolina. Delayed by the Revolutionary War, the university was chartered in 1789. Still, it would be six more years before Hinton James would arrive from a 170-mile walk to become the first student to enroll in this country's first state university.

Today part of the 16-campus University of North Carolina system, UNC–Chapel Hill is ranked among the great institutions of higher education in the nation. The campus covers 740 acres and provides education to more than 24,000 undergraduate, graduate, and professional students. The town, incorporated in 1851, has a population of about 49,000. The famous Franklin Street, which borders the campus, is packed with shops, boutiques, restaurants, cafes, coffee shops, movie theaters, and houses of worship. The town has historic districts, museums, performing and visual arts activities, a library, parks, malls, and many recreational facilities. While its offerings are typical of a college town, it's also a small town where you can sit at the soda fountain at Sutton's Drug Store or gaze at the stars of Morehead Planetarium. Visit the university, browse the shops, and have lunch or dinner at one of the many "institutions" that are now Chapel Hill landmarks, such as Spanky's, Breadmen's, the famous bar He's Not Here, and Carolina Coffee Shop.

Chapel Hill and neighboring Carrboro are extremely bike-friendly towns with handy dedicated bike paths between and in each of the two towns and good signage. Planning ahead? Contact the **Chapel Hill & Orange County Welcome Center** at 38 W. Franklin

St.; (919) 245-4320; visitchapelhill.org. The **UNC Visitor Center** is located at 134 E. Frank-lin St. Contact folks there at (919) 962-1630; unc.edu/visitors.

getting there

From Pittsboro, Chapel Hill is an easy 30-minute drive on US 15/501.

where to go

Ackland Art Museum. 101 S. Columbia Street (101 S. Columbia St. on the university cam-pus); (919) 966-5736; ackland.org. The permanent collection of more than 20,000 objects includes art from around the world and throughout the ages. The museum holds the most significant collection of Asian art in the state and one of the largest collections of works on paper in the Southeast. Long known for its strength in European painting and sculpture, the Ackland in recent years has focused on collecting contemporary art. Free. Open Wed through Sat 10 a.m. to 5 p.m. and Sun 1 to 5 p.m. It is also open the second Fri of the month until 9 p.m.

Carolina Basketball Museum. 450 Skipper Bowles Dr.; (919) 962-6000; goheels.com. Adjacent to the Dean E. Smith Center where the Tarheels play hoops in the Ernie Williamson Athletic Center is the Carolina Basketball Museum with artifacts and highlight tapes of some of the greatest moments in the university's storied basketball program. Championship tro-phies, audiovisual displays, and exhibits are found throughout the facility. Free. Open Mon through Fri 10 a.m. to 4 p.m. and Sat 9 a.m. to 1 p.m.

Charles Kuralt Learning Center. 281 Carroll Hall, Hussman School of Journalism and Mass Media; (919) 962-1204; hussman.unc.edu. The Kuralt Center is on the second floor of Carroll Hall on the UNC campus. Much of Kuralt's TV works, including the famous CBS News "On the Road" episodes, have been digitized so visitors can watch the programs using touch-screen technology. The contents of Kuralt's three-room office suite on W. 57th Street in midtown Manhattan have also been re-created here. It's open during classroom hours for student study and for visitors.

Horace Williams House. 610 E. Rosemary St.; (919) 942-7818; preservationchapelhill.org. As the only historic house in Chapel Hill open to the public, the facility features changing art exhibits in its octagon wing and throughout the house and hosts chamber music concerts on a regular basis. It is also the starting point for a self-guided tour that leads to a number of Chapel Hill's historic homes, as well as to the oldest church in town. Free. Open Tues through Fri 10 a.m. to 4 p.m., Sun 1 to 4 p.m., closed on major holidays and the first two weeks in Aug.

Morehead Planetarium & Science Center. 250 E. Franklin St.; (919) 962-1236; more headplanetarium.org. The first planetarium in the South and a one-time training center for NASA astronauts, Morehead Planetarium has been teaching space sciences education since 1950. The planetarium features public shows in the Star Theater, digital theater, educational exhibits, the Rotunda Portrait Gallery, the Infinity gift shop, and a giant sundial rose garden. Star Theater admission is $14.95 for adults; $12.95 for children, senior citizens, and students. Building hours are Wed through Fri 10 a.m. to 4:30 p.m., Sat.10 a.m. to 6 p.m., and Sun 1 to 6 p.m.

North Carolina Botanical Garden. 100 Old Mason Farm Rd.; (919) 962-0522; ncbg .unc.edu. The largest natural botanical garden in the Southeast, the North Carolina Botanical Garden consists of 600 acres of preserved land, including nature trails, carnivorous plant collections, and aquatic and herb gardens. Collections of plants indigenous to North Carolina and the Southeast are arranged by habitat in simulated natural settings. Playwright and Pulitzer Prize winner Paul Green's restored cabin, moved here from a site nearby, is also at the garden. A LEED-certified visitor center constructed of wood from the property hosts temporary exhibits of paintings, quilts, and other media. Free. Open year-round, Tues through Sat 10 a.m. to 5 p.m. and Sun 1 to 5 p.m.

North Carolina Collection Gallery. UNC–Chapel Hill Louis Round Wilson Library, 200 South Road; (919) 962-3765; library.unc.edu/wilson/ncc. The world's largest collection of resource materials related to Sir Walter Raleigh is here, including a document signed by Queen Elizabeth I in 1570. Be sure to visit the North Carolina Collection, a treasure trove of historical material related to the state, and the Southern Manuscripts Department. There are even obscure objects, such as a plaster death mask of Napoleon Bonaparte. Open Mon through Fri 9 a.m. to 5 p.m., Sat 9 a.m. to 1 p.m., Sun 1 to 5 p.m. Free.

University Lake. 130 University Lake Rd.; (919) 942-8007; www.owasa.org/recreation. This 213-acre lake was created in 1932 as a source of drinking water for the university and the communities of Chapel Hill and Carrboro, and also as an outdoor recreation facility. The lake has fishing, picnic, and sunbathing areas; rowboats, canoes, motorboats, and paddleboats are available for rent. It's typically open during daylight hours.

where to shop

Carr Mill Mall. 200 N. Greensboro St., Carrboro; (919) 942-8669; carrmillmall.com. Located just beyond walking distance from campus, Carr Mill Mall is a beautifully restored textile mill, built in 1899 and listed on the National Register of Historic Places. It houses many specialty stores, restaurants, a chocolate shop, boutiques, and galleries.

Chapel Hill Downtown. Running East and West on Franklin Street from Columbia Street you will find a wealth of mostly family-owned and independent shops and restaurants. From

Johnny T-shirt to Julian's, founded by the famous designer's father in 1942, you'll find just the right gift or piece of Carolina memorabilia.

where to eat

Breadmen's Restaurant. 261 S. Ellott Rd.; (919) 967-7110; breadmens.com. This Chapel Hill institution is the place to get breakfast anytime, day or night, including specialty omelets. It's also a good place to get a big burger, sandwiches, fresh salads, and homemade soups and desserts. Open daily 7 a.m. to 8 p.m. $–$$.

Carolina Brewery. 460 W. Franklin St.; (919) 942-1800; carolinabrewery.com. Chapel Hill's first microbrewery and restaurant serves contemporary American cuisine and handcrafted beers, which serve as ingredients in many dishes. Live music is presented every Thurs. Open Mon through Thurs 11:30 a.m. to midnight, Fri and Sat 11:30 a.m. to 1 a.m., Sun 11 a.m. to 11 p.m. $$.

Carolina Coffee Shop. 138 E. Franklin St.; (919) 942-6875; carolinacoffeeshop.com. A Chapel Hill landmark established in 1922, this dim pub has wooden church-pew booths where you can order a cup of coffee or a brew as well as a meal. Open daily 8 a.m. to 3 p.m. $$.

Crossroads Chapel Hill. 211 Pittsboro St.; (919) 918-2777; www.destinationhotels.com/carolina-inn/crossroads-chapel-hill. Located on the UNC campus in the historic Carolina Inn, this AAA four-star restaurant serves elegant American cuisine that melds world-class cooking with North Carolina seasonal specialties. It also has an award-winning wine list. British tea service daily at 2 p.m. Patio dining is available. Open daily for breakfast 6:30 to 11 a.m.; for lunch 11 a.m. to 2 p.m.; for dinner 5:30 to 10 p.m. $$–$$$.

Crook's Corner. 610 W. Franklin St.; (919) 929-7643; crookscorner.com. Fine, seasonal southern dining and fresh seafood specialties are served inside and on the patio. The menu changes daily at this home of shrimp and grits and vegetarian jambalaya. Crook's closed at the peak of the Covid-19 pandemic but appeared to be headed toward reopening in 2023. Open daily 5:30 to 10 p.m.; Sunday brunch 10:30 a.m. to 2 p.m. $$–$$$.

Il Palio Ristorante. The Siena Hotel, 1505 E. Franklin St.; (919) 918-2545; ilpalio.com. Enjoy classic Italian cuisine in one of North Carolina's best Italian restaurants. The chef prepares memorable Tuscan cuisine with an emphasis on flavorful infused oils and healthy alternatives, paired with fine Italian wines. Open for breakfast Mon through Fri 6:30 to 10 a.m., Sat and Sun 7 to 10 a.m., for lunch daily 11:30 a.m. to 2 p.m., and for dinner nightly 5:30 to 10 p.m. $$$.

Mama Dip's Kitchen. 408 W. Rosemary St.; (919) 942-5837; mamadips.com. Cookbook author Mama Dip has been preparing down-home Southern food since she was nine. She's been serving in Chapel Hill since the 1980s. Her restaurant offers an abundance of traditional

American food, especially vegetables, and the most popular menu item: fried chicken that can't be beat. Open Mon through Sat 8 a.m. to 10 p.m., Sun 8 a.m. to 9 p.m. $$.

Top of the Hill Restaurant & Brewery. 100 E. Franklin St.; (919) 929-8676; thetop ofthehill.com. Overlooking downtown Chapel Hill from a large third-floor outdoor patio, Top of the Hill offers casual, upscale dining and is a favorite among students and alumni alike. The restaurant continually wins "Best of Triangle" awards, including Best Restaurant in Chapel Hill, Best Microbrew, and Best Outdoor Deck. There's live music Thurs evenings. Open daily except Tuesday noon to 9:30 p.m. $$–$$$.

where to stay

The Carolina Inn. 211 Pittsboro St.; (919) 933-2001; https://www.hyatt.com. A historic 184-room hotel, the Carolina Inn is the epitome of gracious southern hospitality and elegance. Located on the campus of UNC, one block from charming downtown shops and restaurants, the inn has many amenities, including a fitness center, on-demand video, room service, nightly turndown service, antiques, and a self-guided history tour. The Carolina Inn is listed on the National Register of Historic Places. $$$.

Graduate Chapel Hill. 311 W. Franklin St.; (929) 442-9000; graduatehotels.com/chapel -hill. The former Franklin Hotel was completely renovated as a Graduate Hotel, a brand being introduced in college towns across the country. Rooms are decorated In Carolina Blue and/ or pay homage to some of the university's most famous students, including Michael Jordan and Mia Hamm as well as campus landmarks like Old Well. $$.

The Siena Hotel. 1505 E. Franklin St.; (919) 929-4000; www.marriott.com/en-us/hotels /rduak-the-siena-hotel-autograph-collection. This boutique hotel offers exceptional service amid fine antique furnishings. Classic Italian cuisine is served in Il Palio, the state's only AAA four-diamond Italian restaurant. Rates include a full buffet breakfast, nightly turndown service, local phone calls, and daily newspaper. On-site services: restaurant, lounge, fitness center, business center, room service, and airport shuttle. $$$.

east

>>>

day trip 0 i

east

Any Piedmont gardener (or construction worker, for that matter) knows about the red clay that can occur in parts of North Carolina, but there is something special in the earth tracking east out of Charlotte. First it spurred the nation's first gold rush. Then it developed into the nation's premier destination for world-class pottery. Much earlier than either of those events, American Indians in Mount Gilead recognized the importance of the earth, too.

The Yadkin River flows through this central portion of North Carolina, where the rolling hills of the Uwharrie National Forest lie and the Keyauwee once lived. On the Charlotte side of the forest, in Midland at the end of the 18th century, young Conrad Reed discovered a big hunk of yellow rock. His family used it as a doorstop for years, but when they figured out it was gold, it started the country's first gold rush, preceding the more famous rush of 1849 on the West Coast. Just beyond the forest along SR 705 lies one of the state's most distinctive arts districts. Seagrove, a town of just under 300, invites day-trippers to discover one of the finest sources of decorative pottery on the East Coast.

midland

Midland began as a railroad town around 1913 with the arrival of rail service, and was named so because it was midway between Charlotte and Oakboro on the line. Midland wasn't incorporated until 2000, but now is becoming an extended bedroom community for those working in Concord and North Charlotte. It is the site of the first documented gold rush in America.

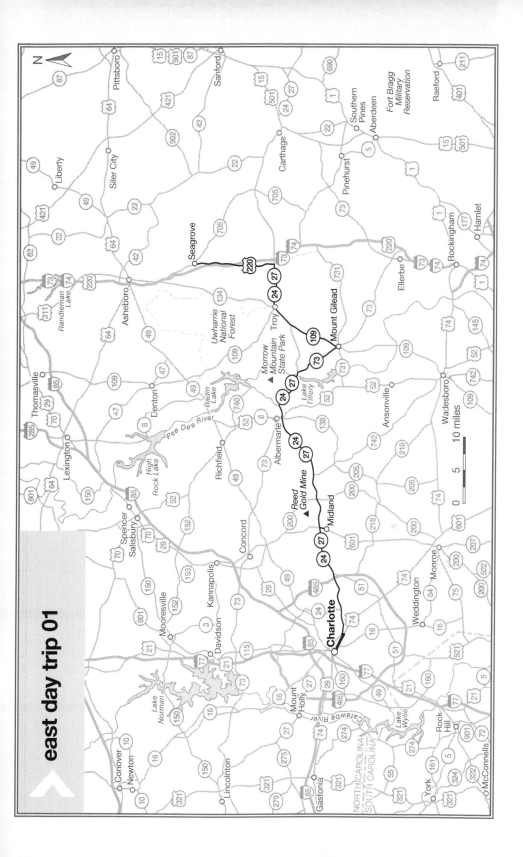

getting there

Midland is about 30 minutes from the center of Charlotte—a straight shot on SR 27, which most Charlotteans might know better as Albemarle Road. Staying on this highway, you will eventually come to Albemarle, but this trip requires a detour left on Reed Mine Road, just a few miles past Midland.

where to go

Reed Gold Mine. 9621 Reed Mine Rd.; (704) 721-4653; historicsites.nc.gov. Twelve-year-old Conrad Reed didn't know what he was getting into in 1799 when he pulled a 17-pound gold nugget out of a special fishing hole in Little Meadow Creek. His family used it as a doorstop for three years before his unsuspecting father, John Reed, sold the nugget for $3.50 to a jeweler in Fayetteville without realizing its value of some $3,000. After realizing his error, Reed and three friends established a gold mining operation that is now a state historic site. It effectively started the nation's first gold rush, about 50 years before the more famous one in California. Today it is the only underground gold mine in North Carolina open to the public. Visitors can experience the mine's history by panning for gold, exploring restored portions of underground tunnels as part of a guided tour, and viewing exhibits of gold and historic mining equipment. Several trails cross lode and placer mining areas and archaeological sites. The Lower Hill Trail features "Talking Rocks" that describe the mining activities at Reed Gold Mine and various rocks found in the southeastern US. Numerous locations feature historic mining machinery, and an area on Upper Hill has the chimney and restored foundations of the 1854 mill house. The restored underground tunnels date to the 1830s. The reconstructed stamp mill represents machinery of the 1890s. Admission to the mine and exhibits is free. Panning is $3 per pan. Open 9 a.m. to 5 p.m. Tues through Sat.

where to eat

D'Anna's Kitchen. 11850 US 601; (704) 888-0935; dannaskitchen.com. This small restaurant in the center of Midland offers country cooking at its best for breakfast, lunch, and Sunday brunch. Big biscuits, liver mush, and other southern staples are served at breakfast, but look for hamburger steak and fried chicken for dinner. $$

There is some distance between good places to eat in these parts. The town of **Locust,** despite the entomological tone of its name, has a couple of good offerings; it lies between Midland and the next stop on this trip.

The Local Room. 215 S. Central Ave.; (704) 781-5373; localroomlocust.com. Well-prepared steak and salmon are served alongside ribs and locally sourced chicken. $$.

Tailgators Sports Grill. 1788 W. Main St., Locust; (704) 781-2055; tailgatorssportsgrill .com. A gator is the mascot here, and there is gator to be found on the menu, too. Wings, wraps, burgers, and salads go well with the dozen or so televisions. Open Sun through Thurs 11 a.m. to 11 p.m., Fri and Sat 11 a.m. to 1 a.m. $$.

mount gilead

Mount Gilead Historic District is listed on the National Register of Historic Places, but an even older piece of history provides greater reason to stop in this town of just under 1,500 people. It continues a country road jaunt through central North Carolina that is part of the Pee Dee River basin.

getting there

A little more than an hour and 60 miles outside of Charlotte, continuing on SR 27 east past the city of Albemarle and onto SR 73 east navigates to the town of Mount Gilead, about 30 minutes from Midland.

where to go

Town Creek Indian Mound. 509 Town Creek Mound Rd.; (910) 439-6802; historicsites .nc.gov. Another state historic site is located an hour's drive across the crystalline Lake Tillery at the edge of the Uwharrie National Forest. For 70 years archeologists have been conducting research at this site that offers evidence of human existence from the 11th century. During this period American Indian cultures constructed earthen mounds for their spiritual and political leaders. Archeological evidence from the site at the confluence of Town Creek and the Pee Dee River revealed as early as the 1930s that this was a significant center for craft, trade, and highly important spiritual ceremonies. Today visitors can tour the site, the rebuilt mound, temples, burial house, and stockade. A visitor center has exhibits that explain the excavations that have occurred here and the rich culture that they reveal to scientists. Free. Open Tues through Sat 9 a.m. to 5 p.m.

where to shop

Mount Gilead Antiques Mall. 126 N. Main St.; (910) 606-9166. Fifteen antiques dealers offer collectibles and more in this renovated hosiery factory in the historic downtown. In addition to glassware, furniture, and jewelry, there is a small Christmas shop. Open daily.

Memory Lane. 109 S. Main St.; (910) 439-4038. Also located in the historic district of Haithcock Square, Memory Lane has interesting finds that include funky retro art, North Carolina pottery, and handmade jewelry. Open Wed through Sat 10 a.m. to 5:30 p.m., Sun 1 to 5:30 p.m.

uwharrie national forest

The Uwharries are some of the oldest mountains on the planet. Formed by erupting volcanoes spewing lava from beneath the earth's crust, these peaks once towered 20,000 feet—as tall as Mount Kilimanjaro. Eons of erosion have worn the rugged slopes to their current 1,000 feet—about one-third the height of the average Blue Ridge peak. Badin Lake, the Yadkin and Pee Dee Rivers, and Lake Tillery make up the forest's western border, which includes Morrow Mountain State Park, situated between the two lakes. Declared a national forest in 1961, it is among the nation's youngest; and at 50,000 acres, among the smallest. It's special for many other reasons, too.

Two trail systems offer heads at multiple locations and with widely varying degrees of difficulty. At the park office on SR 24/27 near the town of Troy is the easiest: two loops for a total of three miles mostly along Denson's Creek. Separate biking and equestrian trails also wind throughout the forest. While fishing is the most popular activity in the forest waters, one might also see the occasional rock hunter or even hopeful people panning for gold. There are no formal mining operations here, but such activities are permitted with manual equipment.

Kings Mountain Point, located at the Badin Lake Recreation Area, includes a paved hiking trail that encircles the point and a fishing pier. The Badin Lake Hiking Trail crosses near the western end of the parking lot. Restrooms, benches, water spigots, and picnic tables are available at the site. It is open from 6 a.m. to 10 p.m.; no camping is permitted. Jumping Off Rock (one brochure warns against such activity) offers a vista of the surrounding terrain and is accessible via the Uwharrie Trailhead on Flint Hill Road. Big Rocks, also called Nifty Rocks, are accessible by a half-mile trail in the Badin Lake Recreation Area. The recreation area also has three camping areas with more than 100 tent and RV sites. Reservations can be made at recreation.gov and are $12 per night. Morrow Mountain State Park has campsites and cabins available for rent. Learn more about Morrow Mountain at ncparks.gov or by calling (704) 982-4402.

where to eat

The Burger Shack. 200 S. Wadesboro Blvd.; (910) 439-4204. Typical of many southern diners, The Burger Shack has dozens of items on the menu; in addition to burgers find fried chicken, greens, and other southern cooking. Open 6 a.m. to 9 p.m. Mon through Sat. $.

seagrove

While there is more than enough to fill a kitchen cabinet here, much Seagrove pottery passes for museum-quality art with crystalline glaze work going for thousands of dollars. Other area potters, who number more than 100 (roughly one-third of Seagrove's population), have garnered international attention for their creative work. The historically based work of potter Mary Ferrell has been featured on the sets of films such as *The Patriot* and *Cold Mountain*. Art pottery produced at Johnston & Gentithes Studios is anything but historical. Their work, once exhibited at the Smithsonian, is whimsical, unpredictable, and reflective of literature and nature.

The history of Seagrove pottery dates to the Revolutionary War, when English and German immigrants made utilitarian pottery due to the high quality of local clay. These practical pieces lost popularity, and the craft dwindled as the sale of mass-produced housewares grew. Potters began producing more artistic pieces in the 1920s, but their popularity would not catch on until the 1980s, when a group of local potters founded the North Carolina Museum of Traditional Pottery and organized the Seagrove Pottery Festival, an annual event still held each year on the weekend before Thanksgiving.

getting there

Seagrove is on the opposite side of the national forest from Mount Gilead. Take SR 109 to SR 27. Travel east on SR 27 through the town of Troy. Either US 220 or 220 Alternate will lead to Seagrove's famed SR 705, the Pottery Highway.

where to go

North Carolina Museum of Traditional Pottery. 127 E. Main St.; (336) 873-7736; seagrovepotterymuseum.net. This is a good first stop on a trip to Seagrove. Pick up maps and learn about different pottery before heading out to the shops. Free. Open Mon through Sat 9:30 a.m. to 3:30 p.m.

North Carolina Pottery Center. 233 East Ave.; (336) 873-8430; ncpotterycenter.org. Seagrove pottery is showcased along with permanent displays of North Carolina pottery, American Indian pieces, historical items, and changing exhibits. Admission is $2.50 for adults, $1 for students in 9th through 12th grades. Open Tues through Sat 10 a.m. to 4 p.m.

Seagrove Pottery. 106 N. Broad St.; (336) 873-7280; seagrovepotterygallery.org. This gallery represents more than 50 potters and artists from the Seagrove region. It offers a wide variety of face jugs, utilitarian and decorative pottery, basketry, candles, and hand-painted garden accessories.

where to shop

The potteries of Seagrove are more than places to shop. They are veritable museums of art and history. Often they are the homes of the artists themselves. They are places of great folk traditions passed down from generation to generation. While listing all potteries isn't possible here, the following is a list of stops to consider. **The Randolph County Tourism Development Authority** (800-626-2672; heartofnorthcarolina.com) has a complete list of potteries and **Seagrove Area Potter Association** (discoverseagrove.com) maintains another helpful website.

Ben Owen Pottery. 15 Ben's Place; (336) 879-2262; benowenpottery.com. The Owens and six other families living within a five-mile radius are credited with starting this resilient industry. The studio, one of the oldest potteries, was founded by the ancestors of Ben Owens III, a sixth-generation potter who operates the studio today. Open Tues through Sat 11 a.m. to 5 p.m.

Johnston & Gentithes Studios. 741 Fork Creek Mill Rd.; (336) 873-9176; johnstonand gentithes.com. Funky and fanciful might describe the work of Fred Johnston and Carol Gentithes. Though rooted in the southern folk tradition, it has definitive influences from around the world and mythical places beyond this world. Open Mon through Sat 10 a.m. to 5 p.m.

Jugtown Pottery. 330 Jugtown Rd.; (910) 464-3266; jugtownware.com. Jacques and Juliana Busbee founded Jugtown Pottery in 1921 just south of Seagrove in a shop that's on the National Register of Historic Places and where potters still work today. The Busbees also worked with the Owens and other families who started the pottery tradition here. Open Tues through Sat 8:30 a.m. to 5 p.m.

King's Pottery. 4905 Reeder Rd.; (336) 381-3090;. Operated by the King family, this studio specializes in wheel-thrown and hand-built utilitarian pottery. The wood-fired and salt-glazed items include folk art, face jugs, and specialty pieces. *Antiques Road Show* viewers might recognize the work from one of its broadcasts. Open by appointment and some Saturdays. The owners suggest calling first if you "are coming some distance."

Phil Morgan Pottery. 966 SR 705; (336) 873-7304. Morgan has gained recognition for a particularly elegant form of crystalline glaze pottery. These pieces are anything but practical. They are classic pieces that are the center of collectors' displays and even the displays of heads of state who receive them as gifts from US presidents. Open Mon through Sat 9 a.m. to 5 p.m.

Westmoore Pottery. 4622 Busbee Rd.; (910) 464-3700; westmoorepottery.com. The classic, historical pieces found at Westmoore can be seen in feature films, but the replicas can also be a part of your home decor. Open Mon through Sat 9 a.m. to 5 p.m.

where to eat

Seagrove Family Restaurant. 8702 SR 220 South; (336) 873-7789. Country-fried steak with turnip greens and other southern-style selections along with burgers and fries make this a nice choice for lunch, but the locals come here for breakfast. Lemon and coconut cream pies come highly recommended. Open Mon through Sat. 5:30 a.m. to 2 p.m. $.

Westmoore Family Restaurant. 2172 SR 705 South; (910) 464-5222. Westmoore offers a full line of fried and broiled seafood, pit-cooked barbecue, and daily meat and veggie specials. Open Thurs through Sat 11 a.m. to 9 p.m., Sun 11 a.m. to 8 p.m. $–$$.

where to stay

The Duck Smith House Bed & Breakfast. 465 N. Broad St.; (336) 872-4121; ducksmith house.com. This restored historic farmhouse is located within walking distance of potteries. The full country breakfast includes freshly picked fruits, jams, and other goodies from 50-year-old fruit trees on the property. $$.

Seagrove Stoneware Inn. 136 W. Main St., (336) 707-9124; seagrovestoneware.com. Owned and operated by potters David Fernandez and Alexa Modderno, the house features artwork from across the country. Rooms are decorated with pottery from both local and nationally known potters. $$.

day trip 02

east

hole-in-one:
pinehurst, southern pines

The famous Pinehurst/Southern Pines golf resort area provides golfers with luxurious accommodations; elegant, upscale shopping opportunities; fine culinary experiences; and plenty of green grass. Within this relatively small space (within a 15-minute drive) can be found more than 43 championship courses. That's fewer than 100 residents per golf hole, making it one of the highest-density golf areas in the country. Take in these facts: For the fourth time, the US Open will be held at the famed Pinehurst Number Two in June 2024. The area has more than 165 miles of fairways. This area is geographically designated as the "Sandhills" for its sandy soil, and its golf courses have 2,900 bunkers and no shortage of sand to fill them. Pinehurst Resort is the world's largest resort with eight courses. Old Number Two is the only course in North Carolina to receive a Five-Star Rating by *Golf Digest,* and it has done so since the rating system began in 1992. The magazine ranked Pinehurst Number Two at number six in the country. *Money Magazine* ranked Pinehurst at number four in its top 25 places to retire. More than 80 horse farms are located in the region, making it an Olympic Equestrian training ground. Olympic cyclists have trained here, too.

And there is more in the towns of Southern Pines and Aberdeen, which encompass the storybook charm of small villages. The Weymouth Center for the Arts & Humanities in Southern Pines offers writers and composers stays of up to two weeks to pursue their work. North Carolina's Literary Hall of Fame is also here. Nearby, quaint Aberdeen, named for a seaport in Scotland, reflects the strong Scottish heritage of this region. For more information,

86

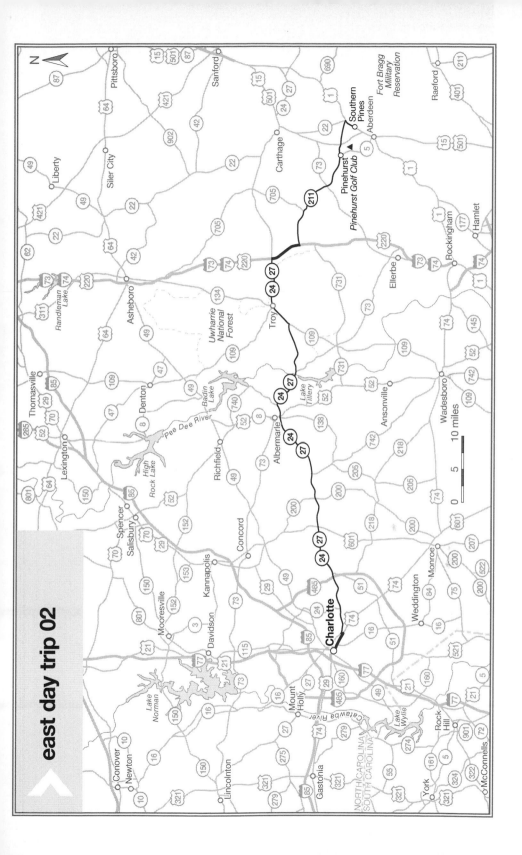

east day trip 02

contact the **Pinehurst, Southern Pines, Aberdeen Area Convention & Visitor Bureau** (155 W. New York Ave., Ste 300; 800-346-5362; homeofgolf.com).

pinehurst

Boston soda-fountain magnate James Walker Tufts, who wanted to build a southern winter retreat and a health resort to aid in recovery from the day's maladies, developed Pinehurst in 1895. Tufts purchased 5,000 acres in the Sandhills and built an inn and a New England–style village, designed by famed landscape architect Fredrick Law Olmsted. Originally he called it Tuftstown. He later changed the name to Pinehurst, after selecting the name from a runners-up list in a town-naming contest in the New England coastal area. Pinehurst officially opened December 31,1895, and has since hosted some of the most famous athletes, business leaders, philanthropists, government officials, golf champions, and heroes from America and beyond.

Pinehurst's evolution as a revered golf venue is rooted in the 1898 development of its first golf course. However, it was the hiring of Donald J. Ross as golf professional in 1900 that undeniably altered the focus of Pinehurst Resort. His famed Number Two course has laid claim to, and continues to serve as, the site of some of the most honored amateur and professional golf events in the world. In 1996 Pinehurst was declared a National Historic Landmark.

getting there

Pinehurst is about a flat two-hour drive from Charlotte, traveling on SR 27 to I-73/I-74 south. Take a left on SR 211 south.

where to go

Sandhills Horticultural Gardens. 3245 Airport Rd.; (910) 695-3882; sandhills.edu. Ten major gardens, covering 27 acres, are featured here, including the Ebersol Holly Collection, which is said to be the largest on the East Coast; a specialized conifer garden; the formal English Sir Walter Raleigh Garden; Hillside Garden; Azalea Garden; and the Desmond Native Wetland Trail Garden. Horticulture students at Sandhills Community College, whose graduates have gone on to find notable horticultural jobs at such places as the White House, maintain the gardens. Free. Open during daylight hours.

Given Library & Tufts Archives. 150 Cherokee Rd.; (910) 295-3642; www.vopnc.org /our-government/library-home. The story of Pinehurst unfolds in the displays of maps, letters, pictures, news clippings, and other documents that date from 1895, when Tufts first began to make this resort a reality. Free. Open Mon through Fri 9:30 a.m. to 5 p.m. and Sat 9:30 a.m. to 12:30 p.m.

where to golf

The **Pinehurst Number Two** course regularly rates high in *Golf Digest*'s biennial ranking of America's 100 greatest golf courses. Accordingly, in 2014 the US Open Championship returned to Pinehurst, which had hosted the event in 2005 and 1999. Seldom does the Open return to a golf course so quickly, but Pinehurst Number Two is an exceptional course and will host the men's and women's events again in future years.

Golf Digest regularly rates two dozen or more of the 43 golf courses in the Pinehurst, Southern Pines, Aberdeen Area with three stars or better. Those that weren't rated did not receive enough ballots because the course was either too new or it was a private or semi-private course. Most receive ratings of four stars or better.

Descriptions of the best courses follow. Be forewarned, however, that these courses can cost as much as $400 per person for 18 holes, and to play those holes properly, you'll want to hire a caddie for an additional $50 or so plus tip per round of golf. The region does feature less expensive golf courses. For more information, order the free *Area Golf Course Guide* from the Pinehurst, Southern Pines, Aberdeen Area Convention & Visitor Bureau, (155 W. New York Ave., Ste 300; 800-346-5362; homeofgolf.com).

Pinehurst Number Two. Pinehurst Resort & Country Club, 80 Carolina Vista; (877) 545-2124; pinehurst.com. Opened in 1901, and repeating host of the US Open, this course was called "the fairest test of championship golf I have ever designed" by architect Donald Ross. Players have to drive the ball well and hit long irons well. Most of all, players must have a razor-sharp short game because of small greens that fall off around the edge.

Pinehurst Number Four. Pinehurst Resort and Country Club, 80 Carolina Vista; (877) 545-2124; pinehurst.com. Officially opened in April 2000 and dubbed Tom Fazio's "tribute to Pinehurst," Number Four was built with crowned greens similar to those found on Number Two and is complemented by British-style pot bunkers and sand areas planted with native grasses.

Pinehurst Number Eight. Pinehurst Resort and Country Club, 80 Carolina Vista; (877) 545-2124; pinehurst.com. With an Audubon International Signature Sanctuary designation, Number Eight was the site of the 1997 and 1998 PGA Club Professional Championships. Solid, straightforward golf is free from theatrics like artificial earth moments and forced carries. The course was created by Tom Fazio to celebrate the 100th birthday of the resort in 1996.

where to shop

The Village at Pinehurst shops have storefront windows to mimic a turn-of-the-century New England shopping district that invites browsing, lingering, and strolling at a slow and steady pace. Be sure to stop at **The Theatre Building** (80 Carolina Vista; 877-545-2124), which has been graced by such luminaries as Helen Hayes, Will Rogers, and Gloria

Swanson. It now houses a group of stores, ranging from G. Monroe's, a clothing shop, to King's Gifts & Collectibles.

where to eat

Visitors to Pinehurst typically purchase packages that include meal plans. See restaurant descriptions under "Where to Stay."

where to stay

Magnolia Inn. 65 Magnolia St.; (877) 545-2124; pinehurst.com/accommodations/the -magnolia-inn. Old South hospitality can be found in this charming inn located in the center of the historic village of Pinehurst. Enjoy gourmet dinners ($$–$$$), particularly the crab cakes, served in the dining room, on the porch in the pub, or poolside. Golf packages are available. $$$.

Pinehurst Resort. 80 Carolina Vista; (877) 545-2124; pinehurst.com. Nestled among the pines, this AAA four-diamond resort has played host to travelers since 1895. Pinehurst has nine signature golf courses. There are opportunities to improve your golf game at the Pinehurst Golf Academy, play croquet at any of the resort's three full-size croquet courts, or play tennis. A 31,000-square-foot, $12 million spa features 28 private treatment rooms and eight salon stations. The spa also showcases a golf fitness studio. Also available from the resort are 30-minute guided carriage tours of the village of Pinehurst for $15 per person.

Pinehurst Resort offers three inns as well as condominium and villa rentals. All accommodations in Pinehurst are priced in the $$$ category. For reservations call (877) 545-2124.

Hotel Carolina. 80 Carolina Vista; (844) 330-1673. Built in 1901, the stately Victorian structure and the centerpiece of the resort houses 210 guest rooms and 12 suites. The hotel's **Carolina Dining Room** ($$$) serves breakfast, lunch, and dinner, and the **Ryder Cup Lounge** ($$) is for lighter meals and cocktails.

The Holly Inn. 155 Cherokee Rd.; (844) 330-1664. Originally opened December 31, 1895, this was the village's first inn. The Holly Inn has 85 rooms with period furnishings. The inn offers two distinctive dining options in Pinehurst Resort's modified American meal plan. **The 1895 Grille** ($$$) is the resort's premier dining experience, featuring regional cuisine in an elegant Southern grill, with a buffet breakfast and innovative New American–style cuisine for dinner. The cozy **Tavern** ($$–$$$), with its century-old hand-carved imported Scottish bar, working fireplace, and outdoor patio, is open daily for lunch and dinner.

Manor Inn. 5 Community Dr. ; (844) 330-1671; www.pinehurst.com/accommodations /the-manor. With 45 rooms, the inn has the intimate feel of a bed-and-breakfast and is a popular choice for golfing groups and families because of its value pricing and room configuration options.

southern pines

Southern Pines was first known as Vineland, but the US Postal Service refused to accept the name because the North Carolina town may have been confused with a New Jersey town by the same name. In search of a new name, the popular winter resort chose to identify itself with its geographic location along the edge of the longleaf pine belt, which has become a lasting symbol for the state. Downtown is divided by train tracks, mostly hidden by magnolia and pine trees. They divide Broad Street, where you'll find most of the tourist activity—on both sides of the tracks.

getting there

To get to Southern Pines from Pinehurst, take the quick 10-minute drive on SR 2, also known as Midland Road.

where to go

Historic Shaw House Properties. Morganton Road and SW Broad Street; (910) 692-2051; moorehistory.com. Operated by Moore County Historical Society are three historic homes—the Shaw, Garner, and Bryant Houses—built during a 50-year period beginning in 1770. Each is furnished with plain-style furniture depicting life in the Sandhills at the end of the 18th century. Also maintained by the historical society are the Britt Sanders and Joel McLendon Cabins (circa 1760–1790). Guests might be surprised at the rustic appearance of all the homes, but that is due in large part to the society's care in preserving them as accurately as possible. Free. Open Tues through Fri 1 to 4 p.m.

Creation Museum, Taxidermy Hall of Fame of North Carolina, and Antique Tool Museum; 156 N Broad St.; (910) 692-3471. This display is evidence that if one would like to find a hall of fame for a particular subject, it is probably possible. On exhibit is practically every kind of North Carolina wildlife (preserved, of course) and state and national taxidermy ribbon winners, all interspersed with messages about creationism. The museum is located in the Christian Book Store on Broad Street. The exhibit also includes a small collection of antique tools.

Weymouth Center for the Arts & Humanities. 555 E. Connecticut Ave.; (910) 692-6261; weymouthcenter.org. This 1920s Georgian mansion, situated on 24 acres with extensive gardens, offers arts and humanities activities. The former home of author James Boyd, it's listed on the National Register of Historic Places. The center is home to a writers' lecture series, writers-in-residence program, and chamber music presentations. **The North Carolina Literary Hall of Fame** here pays homage to the most distinguished Tarheel men and women of letters. Find displays, photographs, and lists of works from such notable writers as Thomas Wolfe, O. Henry (William S. Porter), Paul Green, and James Boyd. Open Mon through Fri 10 a.m. to 2 p.m. Admission is $5.

Weymouth Woods Sandhills Nature Preserve. 1024 N. Fort Bragg Rd.; (910) 692-2167; ncparks.gov. Named for Weymouth, England, the 898-acre nature preserve of long-leaf pine forest is home to the endangered red-cockaded woodpecker. A nature museum includes exhibits on the importance of the longleaf pine, prescribed burnings that have preserved it, as well as exhibits that present nature at night and underground. The preserve includes four and a half miles of year-round trails, and staff conducts regularly scheduled guided tours and programs. Open daily 9 a.m. to 6 p.m. Nov through Mar, 8 a.m. to 8 p.m. Apr through Oct.

where to shop

Campbell House. 482 E. Connecticut Ave.; (910) 692-2787; mooreart.org. The Arts Council of Moore County preserves this historic home as display space for the work of a featured local, state, or regional artist each month. Most artwork is offered for sale. Open Mon through Fri 9 a.m. to 5 p.m. and the third Sat and Sun of each month, 2 to 4 p.m.

where to eat

Ashten's. 140 E. New Hampshire Ave.; (910) 246-3510; ashtensrestaurantandbar.com. A winner of North Carolina's Best Dish for its asparagus strudel, Ashten's offers a comfortable fine dining atmosphere plus a pub that serves great Angus burgers. Open Tues through Sun for dinner only. $$–$$$.

Chef Warren's Bistro. 215 NE Broad St.; (910) 692-5240; chefwarrens.com. This cozy French bistro presents mouthwatering menus that feature nightly specials, tapas, and seasonal dishes. Many dishes are prepared with the harvest of the chef's own garden. Open for dinner only Tues through Sat. $$$.

The Ice Cream Parlor. 176 NW Broad St.; (910) 692-7273; icecreamparlorrestaurant. com. A popular spot with the lunch crowd, the Ice Cream Parlor specializes in old-fashioned handmade burgers served Southern-style with mustard, chili, slaw, and onions. It also serves homemade chicken salad, cakes, and, of course, ice cream hand-scooped out of the freezer. Open daily. $.

195 American Fusion. 195 Bell Ave.; (910) 692-7110; 195pinehurstdining.com. Specializing in all-natural fusion cuisine, this restaurant features Indian Butter Chicken and confit duck, and items as simple as chicken quesadillas. Open for lunch and dinner Wed through Fri, lunch only on Tues. Closed Sun and Mon. $$.

Sweet Basil. 134 NW Broad St.; (910) 693-1487. It's a good sign when you see lines outside the door of a restaurant. And that's often the case at Sweet Basil, popular for its soups, salads, and sandwiches, particularly the grilled eggplant sandwich with sweet roasted peppers and arugula on focaccia. Open Mon through Fri 11 a.m. to 3 p.m., Sat 11:30 a.m. to 3 p.m. $$.

where to stay

Jefferson Inn. 150 W. New Hampshire Ave.; (919) 893-4424; thecarolinaexperience.com. Established in 1902 and renovated in 2023, the Jefferson Inn is a noted landmark in the historic district of Southern Pines. The inn has 15 luxurious rooms and extravagant one-bedroom suites. Experience fine cuisine in the dining room of One Fifty West or slightly more casual dining at the Tavern and Courtyard. $$.

Knollwood Manor. 1495 W. Connecticut Ave.; (309) 253-4957. Five acres of longleaf pines, dogwoods, magnolias, holly trees, and flowering shrubs surround visitors at this English manor house, appointed with 18th-century antiques and the comforts of home. From the back terrace, it's 100 feet to the 15th fairway of championship golfing. Enjoy swimming, tennis, and golf. Full breakfast. Knollwood Manor has five guest rooms and suites with private baths. $$$.

south

>>>

day trip 01

south

>>> **highways, byways & country roads:**
rock hill, sc; mcconnells, sc; york, sc

Burning up the highway south on I-77, you leave the skyscrapers of Charlotte in your rear-view mirror. In minutes you cross the state line, passing Carowinds theme park as highway blends to byway blends to country road. The Rock Hill area is deeply embedded in history, and the tourism folks are betting most of their hotel tax dollars on that history getting visitors into their region. They lay claim to the Catawba Indian Cultural Center, Southern Revolutionary War Institute, Kings Mountain Battleground, one of the nation's largest Revolutionary War living history sites, and a big handful of other places where you can learn about American pre-history and history. There are also touches of science in an environmental center, a traditional natural history museum, a children's museum, and Snap, Crackle, Pop!—the home of the inventor of those colorful characters of Kellogg's fame. The Culture & Heritage Museums, a family of museums in York County, South Carolina, include Historic Brattonsville, McCelvey Center, Museum of York County, and Main Street Children's Museum.

rock hill, sc

Rock Hill is the fourth largest city in South Carolina, yet it has just slightly more than 75,000 residents. Once a strong textile center, Rock Hill is still rebounding from the recession of that industry, which it is attempting to replace with other manufacturing. Old Town, which encompasses the historic downtown area, Winthrop University, parks, and the city's original neighborhoods, has become an entertainment and shopping hub.

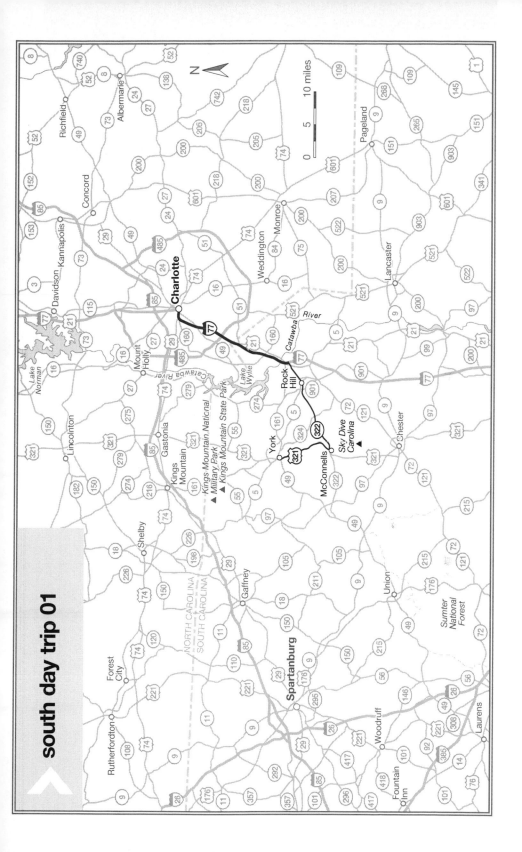

south day trip 01

getting there

Rock Hill is reached by traveling south of Charlotte on I-77 for about 30 minutes. Take exit 82A and follow US 21 into the city.

where to go

Catawba Cultural Center. 1536 Tom Steven Rd.; (803) 328-2427; https://catawbaculture. org/. Some written accounts exist that place the Catawba in this area around the middle of the 16th century. Archeologists argue that the Catawbas may have been the area's aboriginal humans existing here some 4,500 years ago. John Lawson, the explorer who first surveyed the Carolinas, wrote extensively about the "people of the river" in his accounts early in the 1700s, and from that time the Catawbas' relationship with settlers and the state and federal governments was tumultuous at best. A reservation was carved out of several hundred acres in the 1840s, but that reservation was terminated in 1960. It would take more than 30 years before the federal government recognized the Catawba Indian Nation. Now members of the Nation are establishing this center of exhibits that include a dugout canoe, two replicas of a barkhouse, a replica of an old Catawba Indian Garden, and walking trails. The most resilient aspect of the Catawbas has been their production of pottery, which they still do today. It is available for purchase here. Admission is free, but fees are charged for a growing list of classes and programs. Open Mon through Fri 9 a.m. to 5 p.m.

Ebenezer Park. 4490 Boatshore Rd.; (803) 366-6620; yorkcountygov.com. Joggers, bikers, and boaters turn out in droves at this picturesque 26-acre waterfront park. Picnicking, swimming, and fishing are also popular pastimes here. The park has campsites for RVs and tents. An entrance fee of $6 is charged for out-of-county visitors. A fee of $15 is charged for campsites. The park is typically open during daylight hours.

Glencairn Garden. 725 Crest St.; (803) 329-5620; http://glencairn.yorkmg.org/. David and Hazel Bigger could not have imagined when they built their bungalow-style house and designed this southern garden in 1928 that 80 years later it would be a major attraction in the center of this city. When Dr. Bigger died in 1958, his widow donated their home and garden that started with a gift of a few azaleas from a friend and bloomed into a tranquil respite. It is 11 acres of dogwoods, camellia, wisteria, and other traditionally southern plants. Admission is free. Typically open during daylight hours.

Main Street Children's Museum. 133 E. Main St.; (803) 327-6400; chmuseums.org. Inspired by the artwork of Snap, Crackle, and Pop creator Vernon Grant, this children's museum is part of the Cultural & Heritage Museums of York County. A tree house, a train, a sailing ship, and other interactive components make up this fun hands-on learning experience for preschool-age children. Admission is $6 for ages 1 and over. Open 10 a.m. to 5 p.m. Tues through Sat, noon to 5 p.m. Sun.

Museum of York County. 4621 Mount Gallant Rd.; (803) 329-2121; chmuseums.org. Impressive, realistic dioramas are at the heart of this natural history museum that takes visitors from the South Carolina Piedmont to the African Serengeti. A large collection of some of the world's largest animals are on display—all preserved, of course. A Naturalist Center allows guests to learn about natural history hands-on with animal skins, skulls, and rocks and minerals curated especially for that purpose. Other exhibits include the Carolina Piedmont Hall's Landscapes and Lifeways: The Carolina Piedmont 600 Years Ago and Today. Settlemyre Planetarium takes visitors out of this world. Curiously, the museum also pays tribute to Vernon Grant, the creator of Kellogg's Rice Krispies characters Snap, Crackle, and Pop, in an exhibit about his life growing up in York County. Admission is $8 for adults, $7 for seniors, and $5 for youth ages 4 to 17. Open Tues through Sat 10 a.m. to 5 p.m., Sun 1 to 5 p.m.

The White Home. 258 E. White St.; (803) 329-1020; historicrockhill.com. Not to be confused with the home of the same color on Pennsylvania Avenue in D.C., The White Home, circa 1840, evolved over 40 years from humble beginnings as a small one-room house to what guests see today. It is named for the White family that lived in the house until the historical society bought it in 2005. It's a window into the lives of this family who were leaders in the community and into the city's development. The White Home operates as a private event venue but holds frequent events for the public.

where to shop

Gettys Art Center. 201 E. Main St.; (803) 328-2787; yorkcountyarts.org. This art center, managed by the Arts Council of York County, includes the Rock Hill Pottery Studio and Gallery; Grace with Fire pottery studio; the South Carolina Arts Alliance headquarters; Social Design House; artist studios; and Gallery Up, a fine arts retail store, gallery, and custom frame shop. The artist-run gallery sells jewelry, sculpture, paintings, photos, woodwork, and scarves, all by local artists. Open Mon through Fri 10 a.m. to 5 p.m.

A Lasting Touch. 2210 India Hook Rd.; (803) 324-5503; alastingtouch.com. Rock Hill has a handful of antiques stores, but this is one of the largest and most diverse. It sells artwork, books, china, collectibles, figurines, glassware, jewelry, and new home decor items. Open Tues through Fri 10 a.m. to 6 p.m., Sat 10 a.m. to 4 p.m.

The Mercantile. 153 E. White St.; (803) 366-6372; cdmerchantile.com. This trendy collective of shops, an art gallery, and a farmers' market is also a gathering place and event venue for the city. Look for the colorful murals on the renovated buildings.

where to eat

The Flipside Restaurant. 129 Caldwell St.; (803) 324-3547; theflipsiderestaurant.com. Located downtown, Flipside walks the line between upscale and laid back with lunch being on the more laidback side. Look for soups, salad, or a fried green BLT for lunch, but settle in for short ribs or shrimp and grits for dinner. $$$.

Legal Remedy Brewing. 129 Oakland Ave.; (803) 324-2337; legalremedybrewing.com. The original brewery is located here in this restored car dealership in what Is known as Old Towne. In addition to about a dozen locally crafted beers, cured and smoked meats are the specialty of the house. Try the smoked turkey for a slight deviation from the typical pork. Open Thurs 4 to 8 p.m., Fri and Sat noon to 8 p.m. and Sun noon to 6 p.m. $$.

The Pump House. 575 Herrons Ferry Rd.; (803) 329-8888; rockhillpumphouse.com. This striking structure was the actual pump house that supplied water to the Celanese Factory on the Catawba River. Now it's a restaurant pumping out interesting southern cuisine with locally sourced ingredients. Start with lump crab cake or a salad and finish with filet mignon or drunken lamb chops. For lunch try the Pump House Steak Burger. Open daily 11 a.m. to 10 p.m. $$$.

where to stay

Harmony House B&B. 3485 Harmony Rd., Catawba; (803) 403-1912; harmonyhousebb .wordpress.com. Staying at Harmony House on Harmony Road will certainly put guests at harmony with the world around them, if only for a while. Surrounded by beautiful gardens and lit fountains, this Victorian-style bed-and-breakfast isn't likely to disappoint. Its location is convenient to I-77, but on a large countryside property. $$.

mcconnells, sc

There's not much more to McConnells than Historic Brattonsville. In fact, the 700-acre site is really dedicated to the Scotch-Irish Bratton family, and thus to the many families who settled the South Carolina Upstate from the middle of the 18th century.

getting there

SR 322 to the west of Rock Hill is also known as McConnells Highway, and it heads straight into McConnells (about 15 minutes).

where to go

Historic Brattonsville. 1444 Brattonsville Rd.; (803) 684-2327; chmuseums.org. The sprawling Historic Brattonsville is part of the family of museums in York County, but is located a short ride into the country in the town of McConnells. At the heart of this Revolutionary War living history site is the plantation of the Bratton family, which provides a glimpse of how the people of the Carolinas lived from the middle of the 18th century to the period just before the Civil War. The restoration is an ambitious undertaking that includes the meticulous renovation or replication of more than 30 structures, whose many stories are told by costumed guides. Hightower Hall, featured in the Mel Gibson film *The Patriot*, is the Italianate villa mansion where the Brattons lived. Part of the heritage farm exhibit includes animals not often seen, such as Gulf Coast sheep, Devon cattle, and Ossabaw Island hogs, cared for here just as they were hundreds of years ago. Other restorations and replicas are also part of the tour. The Walt Schrader Trails are an eight-and-a-half-mile network of back country paths. Admission is $8 for adults, $7 for seniors, and $5 for youth ages 4 to 17. Open Mon though Sat 10 a.m. to 5 p.m., Sun 1 to 5 p.m.

Sky Dive Carolina. 1903 King Air Dr., Chester; (803) 581-5867; skydivecarolina.com. Sky Dive Carolina is located just south of McConnells on US 321. After only 30 minutes of instruction, the adventurous can take a tandem free fall at 120 miles per hour, strapped to the front of an instructor. Sky Dive Carolina also offers more advanced courses in skydiving.

york, sc

The town of Yorkville was the town closest to the middle of the county, so in 1785 it became the county seat of York. In 1915 citizens voted to shorten the name to York, just to make things a little more confusing for visitors. Today it holds a population of around 7,000, who mostly appear to value small-town life. During the nation's bicentennial, about 180 buildings in downtown were listed on the National Register of Historic Places, preserving forever the remarkable architectural features and character of the small-town South.

getting there

A 15-minute drive on US 321 north leads directly into York. This day trip could easily be done in reverse, heading to York from Charlotte on SR 49.

where to go

McCelvey Center. 212 E. Jefferson St.; (803) 684-3948; chmuseums.org. In addition to fulfilling its mission as the home of the Southern Revolutionary War Institute, the McCelvey Center houses the 500-seat Lowry Family Theater, which hosts an annual performing arts series. As a historical center it is a must-see for the history buff, providing opportunities for genealogical and historical research through extensive collections of documents, photographs, York County court records, microfilm reels, rare books, maps, church and cemetery indexes, and family genealogical books. The building, historic itself, opened in 1852 as the Yorkville Female Academy, one of the state's leading schools for women. It later became part of the public school system, which turned it over to the McCelvey Center in 1987. Admission is free except for performances. Open Mon through Fri 10 a.m. to 4 p.m.

western york county scenic highway

*From York, drivers can choose to take scenic **SR 161** north to the North Carolina state line, passing farm and field as well as the historic **McGill's Store,** now **Lauren's Café** (1598 SR 161 South; 803-222-3785) that's been open since 1883. This route points you back to Charlotte, but a southerly route down US 321 will extend the day trip along SR 322 starting at McConnells and further west to **Bullocks Creek,** along the way passing **Bullock Creek Cemetery,** which dates to the Revolution, and the site of a patriot refuge, **Lacey's Fort.** Turning north, SR 49, SR 211, and SR 97 run north along the Broad River through the towns of **Sharon, Hickory Grove,** and **Smyrna,** population 59. Here hungry travelers can stop for lunch at the **Sharon Grill** (3718 York St.; 803-927-7821.)*

kings mountain battleground

*There are two parks (a South Carolina state park and a national military park) and one North Carolina city named for **Kings Mountain,** and the Charlotte day-tripper could actually visit any one of the three during any number of these day trips. So why all the Kings Mountains? Many historians believe that the **Battle of Kings Mountain** on October 7, 1780, was the turning point in the Revolution. It was the first patriot victory since the British took Charleston five months earlier. A ragtag but determined bunch of militia known as the Overmountain Men fought for only an hour before beating back more than 1,000 redcoats. A film on the battle is shown at the National Park Visitor Center, located on SR 216 near Blacksburg. A one-and-a-half-mile loop trail features monuments and highlights important parts of the battle. The adjacent **Kings Mountain State Park** (803-222-3209; southcarolinaparks .com) is located on SR 161 near Blacksburg, and features a living historic farm and camping facilities. Also located here just off I-85 is the Catawba Two Kings Casino (538 Kings Mountain Blvd.; 704-750-7777; twokingscasino.com.)*

where to shop

Windy Hill Orchard & Cider Mill. 1860 Black Hwy.; (803) 684-0690; windyhillorchard .com. This has become a York County traveler's tradition, and it must be because of the cider donuts. You'll also find traditional favorites such as pies, cider, peach, pumpkin, and strawberry butter. In the fall enjoy apple slushes. Tours, hayrides, and other fun events are scheduled seasonally throughout the year. Open Aug through Dec.

day trip 02

south

>>>

a capitol idea for a day trip:
columbia, sc; lake murray, sc

Columbia is the capital of South Carolina and the state's largest city. While more than 760,000 people live in the metropolitan area, only about 130,000 people call the city proper home, making it a friendly southern city rich in cultural and recreational activities. Easy to navigate and affordable, the Columbia-Lake Murray area consistently ranks high on lists of the country's best places to retire. While the city has been vitally important throughout history to the development of the state and the entire South, it can't lay claim to any specific industry. The energy powerhouse SCANA was once the only Fortune 500 Company based here but even it dropped off the list. Still, a diverse selection of companies has decided to do business in Columbia, leaving philanthropic benefits to museum and cultural attractions in their tracks. The city beams with pride over its University of South Carolina Gamecocks and as home to Darius Rucker and the 1990s band Hootie and the Blowfish. The Saluda and Broad Rivers meet here to form the Congaree River; as a result, the area is rich in recreational opportunities.

Historically, South Carolina's capitol city has taken its share of beatings. In the Civil War General William Sherman burned the city almost to the ground, destroying military holdings, homes, and reportedly bales of cotton in retaliation for the city's taking the lead in the state's secession from the Union. Visitors can follow the path that Sherman and his men followed and see the structures that did survive. One would think that after 145 years, the city would put the Civil War in the history books, but southern pride reared its head in the 1990s when many resisted pressure by the NAACP and others to remove the Confederate flag that flew along with Old Glory over the statehouse. The resisters succumbed, agreeing to place it near

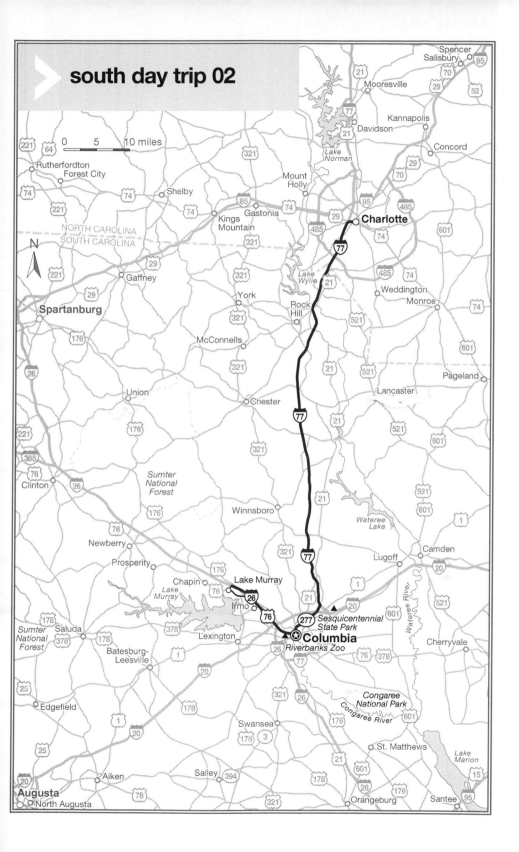

south day trip 02

one of the monuments on the Sherman trail. Strangely, that move became part of a revitalization effort in the downtown area. The Congaree Vista district along Gervais Street, once known as a warehouse district, became a thriving area of museums, art galleries, shops, and restaurants. Before long, a new arena, convention center, and hotels opened.

Columbia's restored park system is only the tip of the natural offerings that abound in this day trip. Lake Murray is an integral part of the region, and the state's zoo is located here, too. Surrounding the 720 miles of Lake Murray's shoreline are golf courses, restaurants, access areas, and the east side towns of Lexington, Irmo, and Leesville. Each of them offers limited but worthwhile stops for the day-tripper.

columbia, sc

Columbia, centrally located in the Palmetto State, became the capitol in 1786 when the legislature voted to move it from Charleston. The Santee River near here and the Cooper River near Charleston were connected by canal in 1800. That was only important for a half century, when most of its use was replaced by the railroad system. What did remain important was the city government's commitment to a downtown. City streets were built wide initially with the mistaken belief it would somehow control the mosquito population, but later it proved advantageous when city leaders began to revitalize downtown. Cotton had become the area's lifeblood; thus the state was quick to secede from the Union to protect its institution of slavery, thrusting it into the middle of the Civil War. Emerging from virtual destruction by Sherman's army in 1865, the area returned to it cotton roots, becoming a textile manufacturing center for much of the 20th century. But again Columbia found itself embroiled in a national controversy over segregation. Through the mid-1900s the city was cast into the national limelight over equal pay for Black teachers, voting rights, and segregation. Jim Crow laws were beginning to be overturned in 1963 when the University of South Carolina admitted its first Black student and *Newsweek* praised the city for liberating "itself from the plague of doctrinal apartheid."

By the end of the 20th century, the city had recommitted itself to making Columbia a great place to live and visit. In addition to turning the warehouse district into a thriving center for the arts, Columbia restored parks to what is better than their original glory. They relocated the Nickelodeon theater and attracted a Mast General store. Taking advantage of the city's museum culture, a new children's museum and science center opened downtown, and a new fountain and sculpture gave new lift to the Boyd Plaza in front of the Columbia Museum of Art.

getting there

From Charlotte, I-77 crosses I-20, ending at Columbia's I-26 in less than two hours from Charlotte. These three highways come together to create a handy loop around Columbia.

where to go

701 Center for Contemporary Art. 701 Whaley St.; (803) 779-4571; 701cca.org. This center includes an artist-in-residence program and presents contemporary art exhibits by area artists. The center also conducts concerts, workshops, and other programs. Free. Admission charged for various events. Open Wed through Sun 1 to 5 p.m.

Columbia Fire Museum. 1800 Laurel St.; (803) 545-3700; https://colafire.net. Located in the downtown historic museum in the city's fire department headquarters, the Columbia Fire Museum displays artifacts of firefighting equipment from the mid-1800s. A photo history of fire fighting in Columbia and a history of Black firefighters in the department are also on exhibit. Free. Open Mon through Fri 8:30 a.m. to 5 p.m.

Columbia Museum of Art. 1515 Main St.; (803) 799-2810; columbiamuseum.org. This is a traditional art museum with flair. Located in front of the former department store building is a 25-foot-tall piece, entitled *Apollo's Cascade*. The enthusiast will find European and American fine and decorative art, including one of the largest collections of Baroque and Renaissance art in the Southeast. Recent innovative exhibitions included a photographic history of rock 'n' roll and contemporary exhibitions from artists such as Chihuly. Temporary programs and exhibitions also provide an artistic window into the community and its history with exhibits that feature local works about the area. The museum also has a focus on collection and curation of Asian art and antiquities. Also of particular interest are Sandro Botticelli's *Nativity*, Claude Monet's *The Seine at Giverny*, Canaletto's *View of the Molo*, and art glass by Louis Comfort Tiffany. Admission is $10 for adults, $5 for students, and $8 for seniors. Open Tues through Sun 10 a.m. to 5 p.m. and until 8 p.m. on Thurs.

EdVenture Children's Museum. 211 Gervais St.; (803) 779-3100 edventure.org. EdVenture is a combination science center and children's museum that has more than enough room for visitors to expand their minds. While it is geared to children middle school age and younger, their accompanying adults are likely to learn a thing or two here as well. Eddie, the world's largest child (taller than the Lincoln Memorial) allows young visitors to climb on and through his body. Kids can explore a farm, a grocery store, and other places of work. Butterflies flutter seasonally in an outdoor exhibit, while other outside exhibits explore solar power, recycling, and conservation. Admission is $13. Open Mon through Sat 9 a.m. to 5 p.m., Sun noon to 5 p.m.

Elmwood Cemetery & Gardens. 501 Elmwood Ave.; (803) 252-2133. History buffs, particularly those interested in the Civil War, will want to make their way to this 1854 cemetery. A complete Confederate cemetery can be found on the site. Historical walking tour maps available in the office, open Mon through Fri 9 a.m. to 5 p.m.

Fort Jackson Museum. Building 4442 Fort Jackson Blvd.; (803) 751-7419. Camp Jackson was established here in 1917 as an artillery replacement depot through the First World War. Just before World War II it was reactivated as Fort Jackson and now is the US Army's largest initial training center. Half of all new soldiers come through here. While there are few formal public attractions on the 52,000-acre site, the museum displays military weapons, uniforms, and other equipment to illustrate how American soldiers train, live, and work. The displays are supplemented by exhibits of special areas of interest. Free. Open Mon through Fri 9 a.m. to 4 p.m.

General Sherman's March on Columbia Self-Guided Walking Tour. (803) 252-7742; shermansmarch.com. On February 17, 1865, following an 18-day march from Georgia, Union General William Tecumseh Sherman and his soldiers looted and burned the city in what has been described as drunken retribution for the city's role in starting secession. Visitors to Columbia can follow that treacherous path to see the preserved ruins and other landmarks that mark that day. Mostly what remains are historical markers, but still to be seen are remains of Saluda River Bridge, the statehouse now marked with stars where cannonballs struck it, the Horseshoe Buildings at the university, the 1949 McCord House, Hampton-Preston House, Mills House, the 1853 First Presbyterian Church, the First Baptist Church where the secession convention met in 1860, and a handful of other sites. Some buildings are open to visitors. A tour can be downloaded from the website.

Governor's Mansion. 800 Richland St.; (803) 737-1710. Spared by Union soldiers, the South Carolina governor's mansion became the official residence for state governors in 1868. It was built in 1855 as a residence for officers of Arsenal Military Academy. Today its features include some of the most spectacular magnolia and crepe myrtle trees in the state, under which guests are welcome to picnic. Tours are offered Tues and Wed mornings, but appointments are required. Gardens are open 9:30 a.m. to 4:30 p.m.

congaree national park

*The Congaree River ambles out of the southeastern corner of Columbia to **Congaree National Park** and a pristine assemblage of flora and fauna. Declaration as a national park protects these 22,200 acres of the nation's largest contiguous tract of old-growth bottomland hardwood forest. Interspersed among the hardwoods are towering pines that compose one of the tallest forests on the East Coast, and plants and animals that provide fodder for research among students and scientists alike. To the traveler it is miles of hiking trails, places to canoe, and unexpected wilderness. The Harry Hampton Visitor Center (100 National Park Rd.; 803-776-4396; www.nps.gov/cong), open daily 8:30 a.m. to 5 p.m., includes an exhibit on the park's inhabitants and is a starting point for a boardwalk loop through the swamp. Rangers also offer regularly scheduled walks and canoe tours. Access to the park is off I-77, exit 5. You can access it directly from Charlotte or via I-26 out of Columbia.*

Hampton-Preston Mansion & Gardens. 1615 Blanding St.; (803) 252-7742; historic columbia.org. Built by a wealthy local merchant in 1818, the federal-style home of Wade Hampton integrated some Greek Revival influences. His daughter, Caroline, along with her husband, John Preston, expanded the home to twice its original size in the 1850s. Sherman spared the home for use by nuns as a temporary convent after their building was destroyed. Through its history the estate served as College for Women, Chicora College, Westerveldt Academy, and Columbia Bible College. In 1947 the gardens were bulldozed, and the four-acre tract was subdivided for various commercial uses. Tours of the house begin at the top of the hour. Purchase tickets in the museum shop on the grounds of the Robert Mills House, 1616 Blanding St. Admission is $12 for adults, $11 for seniors, and $8 for children ages 6 to 17. A discount is offered for multiple historic home tours. Open Wed through Sat 10 a.m. to 4 p.m., Sun 1 to 5 p.m.

Mann-Simons Cottage. 1403 Richland St.; (803) 252-7742; historiccolumbia.org. The historical society has narrowed construction of what they believe was a one-room house to the late 1820s. It is equally unclear how Celia Mann, a slave in Charleston, acquired the home. It is believed she arrived in Columbia on foot and earned a living as a midwife as early as 1844. She left the home to her youngest daughter, Agnes Jackson, who married Bill Simons and lived there until she died in 1907. This home is one of several structures on the site that served as various residences and businesses. Purchase tickets in the museum shop on the grounds of the Robert Mills House, 1616 Blanding St. Admission is $12 for adults, $11 for seniors, and $8 for children ages 6 to 17. A discount is offered for multiple historic home tours. Open Tues through Sat 10 a.m. to 4 p.m., Sun 1 to 5 p.m.

McKissick Museum. 816 Bull St.; (803) 777-7251; sc.edu. Located on the University of South Carolina campus on what is known as the Horseshoe, McKissick Museum was founded as the university's museum. It has become a sort of unofficial museum of the region with exhibits that range from rocks, gems, and minerals to rare books and an unusual collection of 18th-century British silver. The museum is located in a beautiful 1839 building that was the university's first library and is a nice combination of natural science, art, and history. Free. Open Mon through Fri 8:30 a.m. to 5 p.m., Sat 11 a.m. to 3 p.m.

Melton Memorial Observatory. 1429 Greene St.; (803) 777-8105; sc.edu. Stars, moons, planets, and other celestial objects come into view thanks to the powerful telescopes and expert direction at the Melton Observatory on the university campus. Tours of the facility are conducted along with night sky viewing on clear Monday nights throughout the year. Free. Hours are Mon 9 to 11 p.m.

Memorial Park. Corner of Gadsden and Hampton Streets; (803) 545-3100; experienceco lumbiasc.com. This park, occupying about a city block, memorializes South Carolinians who served in wars throughout American history. Monuments honor the USS *Columbia* warship and those who served with her during World War II, the China-Burma-India Theater veterans of World War II, South Carolina casualties of the Pearl Harbor attack, South Carolina Holocaust survivors, and the state's Vietnam War veterans. The park was dedicated in November 1986 along with the unveiling of the South Carolina Vietnam Monument. In June 2000 the Korean War Memorial was dedicated at Memorial Park.

Nickelodeon Theatre. 937 Main St.; (803) 254-3433; nickelodeon.org. With only 75 seats in this storefront theater near the university, it is hard to get a bad seat. Credited with helping to revitalize downtown, the Nickelodeon shows independent and low-budget films and is the only nonprofit theater in the state. It also hosts regular film festivals. Regular ticket prices are $9. Two screenings are typically held each evening with occasional matinees.

Riverbanks Zoo & Garden. 500 Wildlife Pkwy. (just off I-126 at Greystone Boulevard in Columbia); (803) 779-8717; riverbanks.org. While the zoo and garden have different addresses that technically put them in different cities, they are adjacent and can be visited together. About 1 million people visit this massive attraction each year, making it the state's largest attraction, the largest zoo and aquarium in the Southeast, and one of the nation's most spectacular combinations of flora and fauna. The zoo's bar-free exhibits benefit from the garden's horticulturalists that create lush naturalistic surroundings for the zoo's residents. Here friendly lorikeets, birds from Australia, will land on your shoulder (or head), and you can feed giraffes, see penguins from the bottom of the world, or come face to face with Galapagos turtles. Across the river in the Botanical Garden (1300 Botanical Pkwy., off SR 378 in West Columbia), native and exotic plants likewise provide a look at environments that are worlds away. Located on the peaceful Saluda River, the garden includes a spectacular walled garden, trails, and more. Riverbanks is listed on the National Register of Historic Places with structural remains dating back to the early 1800s. The ruins of Saluda Mill, one of South Carolina's oldest textile mills set ablaze by Sherman and his troops, can be found along Riverbanks' Garden River Trail. An interpretive center includes artifacts, descriptions, and other historical exhibits. Admission is $21.99 for adults, $18.99 for children ages 3 to 12. Open daily 9 a.m. to 5 p.m. with additional hours to 6 p.m. weekends Apr through Sept.

Robert Mills House & Gardens. 1616 Blanding St.; (803) 252-1770; historiccolumbia.org. Designed by the same architect responsible for the design of the Washington Monument, this home is one of only five National Historic Landmarks in Columbia. Robert Mills was the first architect born and trained within the US and designed the home at the request of Englishman Ainsley Hall, who died before it was completed. His wife, Sarah, soon sold it to the Presbyterian Synod of South Carolina and Georgia, which established a seminary there. It also served as Westerveldt Academy and later the Columbia Bible College. Purchase tickets in the museum shop on the grounds of the Robert Mills House, 1616 Blanding St. Admission is $12 for adults, $11 for seniors, and $8 for children ages 6 to 17. A discount is offered for multiple historic home tours. Open Tues through Sat 10 a.m. to 4 p.m., Sun 1 to 5 p.m.

Sesquicentennial State Park. 9564 Two Notch Rd.; (803) 788-2706; southcarolinaparks .com. The focal point of this park is a 30-acre lake with meandering trails and beautiful spots to picnic under shady trees. Locals and travelers come here to fish or camp, and they can rent canoes, kayaks, and pedal boats for a nominal fee. In 1969 the state moved what is believed to be the oldest house in the county: a two-story log house, dating back to the mid-18th century to this park. Daytime admission is $6 for adults and $3.50 for children. Generally open during daylight hours.

South Carolina Military Museum. 1 National Guard Rd.; (803) 299-4440; scmiliatarymu seum.com. A collection of equipment from Colonel Melvin Purvic, who shot John Dillinger at the Biograph Theatre, is on display along with many military exhibits from the Colonial period to current conflicts. Exhibits include the Hall of Heroes, a memorial to those South Carolin-ians who received the Congressional Medal of Honor; an exhibit on "Carbine" Williams, who developed the smaller, lighter, more accurate carbine rifle used in World War II; and more. Free. Open Mon through Sat 10 a.m. to 4 p.m.

South Carolina State House. 1100 Gervais St.; (803) 734-2430; www.studentconnection .scstatehouse.gov. Appropriately, palmettos line the entrance of the copper-capped state-house, home to the state's collection of art, historical portraits, sculpture, and monuments. The building was under construction when Sherman invaded in 1865 and burned what was then the statehouse, where most of the drawings for the new legislative building were kept. After those delays and the passing of the jobs to several architects due to death and politi-cal jockeying, the building was completed in 1903 and renovated from 1995 to 1998. While most of those renovations were to bring the building up to contemporary code, the House and Senate chambers both received serious face-lifts as did other public areas to include new marble floors and a refurbished dome. Open Mon through Fri 9 a.m. to 5 p.m.

South Carolina State Museum. 301 Gervais St.; (803) 898-4921; scmuseum.org. This massive four-story facility is the official state museum and stages major exhibitions of art, sci-ence, and history. The museum is located in what was the world's first totally electric 1894 textile mill. Giant sharks hang overhead, and a large collection of fossils provides the basis for a dinosaur exhibit and active research of prehistoric life. Well-done dioramas take visi-tors from the foothills of The Upstate to the state's coastal habitats. Progressive technology exhibits focus on advances and uses of laser technology, space science, and aviation. South Carolina's history is covered through a series of artifacts that include some of the oldest ever found in the state and tell the area's story that begins 14,000 years ago. The Revolution, the state's role in the Civil War, and its Black history are covered with exhibits of tools, weapons, modes of transportation, and other artifacts. The museum also houses the South Carolina Confederate Relic Room and Military Museum. Even with all that, the museum has saved space for national touring exhibitions. Admission is $8.95 for adults, $7.95 for seniors, and $6.95 for children ages 3 to 12. Open Tues through Sat 10 a.m. to 5 p.m., Sun 1 to 5 p.m.

Woodrow Wilson Family Home. 1705 Hampton St.; (803) 252-7742; historiccolumbia .org. Historic Columbia renovated the childhood home of the nation's 28th president and turned it into the Museum of the Reconstruction Era. The Italianate villa home was built in 1872 as the city began to rebuild from the Civil War. Admission is $12 for adults, $11 for seniors, and $8 for children ages 6 to 17. A discount is offered for multiple historic home tours. Open Tues through Sat 10 a.m. to 4 p.m., Sun 1 to 5 p.m.

where to shop

Adluh Flour Mills. 804 Gervais St.; (803) 779-2460; adluhstore.com. A blinking neon sign attracts customers to this mill that has become famous for its flour and cornmeal over the past 100 years. It is so famous, in fact, the state department of agriculture declared it the official state flour. Though it is sold at grocers and restaurants throughout the Southeast, you can stop by the plant to make a purchase. Open Mon through Thurs 7:30 a.m. to 5 p.m., Fri 7:30 a.m. to noon.

Blue Sky Gallery. 1332 Main St.; (803) 318-4326. The memorable art created by the artist known as Blue Sky, who was born and attended college here, is available for purchase at this gallery. Sky's murals and sculptures can also be viewed throughout the city. Among them are *Busted Plug Plaza*, a giant fire hydrant, and *NEVERBUST,* a giant piece of chain. The gallery is open by appointment and "occasionally on Saturday afternoons."

Devine Street. https://devinestreetcolumbiasc.com/. This trendy neighborhood street east of downtown Columbia has two dozen shops and boutiques and almost as many restaurants. Some merchants sell home decor while others focus on women's fashions. At Silver Spoon Bake Shop you can satisfy the taste of any sweet tooth.

where to eat

Cafe Strudel. 300 State St., West Columbia; (803) 794-6634; cafestrudel.com. Attention to details such as cooking with sunflower oil make Cafe Strudel special. Breakfast dishes like the Hangover Hashbrowns make it memorable. During lunch and dinner, Cafe Strudel offers Philly cheesesteaks, off-the-charts burgers, and similar fare. Local art is also for sale. Open Mon through Wed 8:30 a.m. to 3:30 p.m., Thurs through Sat 8:30 a.m. to 10:30 p.m., and Sun 10 a.m. to 2:30 p.m. $.

Carolina Ale House. 277 Columbiana Dr.; (803) 407-6996; carolinaalehouse.com. Though branches of this sports bar are slowly popping up across the Carolinas, the rooftop dining and bar at this location make it a special kind of sports bar good for families by day and evening, and partiers by night. Burgers, wings, and other hearty food synonymous with sports bars are on the menu. Open daily 11 a.m. to 2 a.m. $$.

The Gourmet Shop. 724 Saluda Ave.; (803) 799-3705; thegourmetshop.net. If you don't try anything else, check out the chicken salad at the Gourmet Shop. The cafe offers shady outdoor seating and delectable food that comes out of a renowned bakery. After lunch, shop for gourmet cheeses, wines, and even gourmet kitchen gadgets. Open daily 9 a.m. to 4 p.m. $$.

Motor Supply Bistro. 920 Gervais St.; (803) 256-6687; motorsupplycobistro.com. This high-end, farm-to-table restaurant, located in the Vista District, changes menus daily, as evidenced by handwritten menus. Its contemporary selections blend American, French, Italian, and Asian cuisine. Open for lunch Tues through Sat 11 a.m. to 2 p.m. Open for dinner Tues through Thurs 5 to 9 p.m., Fri and Sat 5 to 10 p.m., and for Sunday brunch 11 a.m. to 2 p.m. $$$.

where to stay

Chesnut Cottage Bed & Breakfast. 1718 Hampton St.; (803) 256-1718; chesnutcottage .com. Confederate President Jefferson Davis once addressed the citizens of Columbia from the porch of Chesnut Cottage. Today there is more rocking going on here than stumping. It was the home of author Mary Boykin Chesnut, but now it has guest rooms with period antiques as well as a library with Civil War artifacts. $$$.

Graduate Columbia. 1619 Pendleton St.; (803) 779-7779; graduatehotels.com. Once simply called the Inn at USC, this stately and elegant boutique hotel, located on the campus of the University of South Carolina and close to downtown attractions, is now a part of the Graduate Hotels chain. Located in college towns their properties are often themed after the home team. Marble floors and luxurious furnishings designed for the Gamecock mascot make this one of the most desirable places to stay in Columbia. $$$.

lake murray, sc

Resorts, golf courses, marinas, and other recreational facilities dot the 650 miles of shoreline around Lake Murray. At the time it was built in the 1930s to accommodate production of hydroelectricity, it was the largest man-made reservoir in the world. Still covering 50,000 acres, it is central South Carolina's premier recreational center. **Lake Murray Visitor**

Center is located on SR 6, 2184 N. Lake Dr. in Columbia. For more information visit lake murraycountry.com or call (803) 781-5940. Keep in mind this is a *big* lake; it would take the better part of a day to travel over all of it. Target your destinations carefully.

getting there

Lake Murray is less than 30 minutes from Columbia via I-26 west.

where to go

Dreher Island State Park. 3677 State Park Rd., Prosperity; (803) 364-4152; southcarolinaparks.com. Two bridges and a causeway connect the three islands of this 342-acre recreation area located on a finger jutting out on the northern side of Lake Murray. Hiking and fishing are the main pastimes here with a short nature trail along the shore and more strenuous trails up to two miles. Both RV and tent camping sites are available. Several cabins with kitchens and screened porches are also available for rent. Daytime admission is $3 for adults and $1.50 for children. Typically open during daylight hours.

Lanier Sailing Academy. 3072 US 378, Leesville; (803) 317-9070; laniersail.com. Lanier offers sailboat rentals to qualified sailors and teaches those that want to learn to be qualified sailors. In addition, the academy runs skippered trips for those who just want a taste of the life on the lake. There are 2- to 8-hour trips available for up to 8 people. Cost is between $120 and $350 per sail.

Lexington County Museum. 231 Fox St. at US 378, Lexington; (803) 359-8369; lexingtoncountymuseum.org. Take a tour offered by costumed guides at this large complex of two antebellum homes and three cabins, located just south of Lake Murray in Lexington County. The seven-acre site actually includes a total of 36 structures that give a glimpse of life in the late 1700s through the Civil War. Most notable is the 10-room, two-story John Fox House, circa 1832. Originally a plantation home, the John Fox House is furnished and decorated with period pieces. Admission is $5 for adults and $2 for children. Open Tues through Sat 10 a.m. to 4 p.m., Sun 1 to 4 p.m.

Lorick Plantation House. 2184 N. Lake Dr., Irmo; (803) 781-5940; www.lakemurraycountry.com/businesses/lake-murray-country-visitor-center-2. This historic plantation house, circa 1840, also known as Green Acres, houses the Lake Murray Country Visitor Center and offers exhibits and an aquarium with various species of fish from Lake Murray. Heart pine floors in the dining room show evidence of fire damage by Sherman's troops. Free. Open Mon through Fri 9 a.m. to 5 p.m., Sat 10 a.m. to 4 p.m., Sun 1 to 5 p.m.

chitlin' struttin'

To find **Salley,** South Carolina, the weekend following Thanksgiving, just follow your nose. On that weekend the town of Salley cranks up the fryers and cranks out the chitlins for the **Chitlin' Strut.** Bands play, the area's most beautiful girls strut their stuff in a beauty pageant, idols sing, and callers call hogs. But really it's all about the chitlins.

For those who don't know, chitlins (or chitterlings) are a southern delicacy made from certain elongated innards of pigs. The folks in Salley make no bones about the fact that it sounds disgusting, but they also claim if you give chitlins a try, you won't regret it. They have been the center of attention in these parts since 1966, when gutsy Mayor Jack Able spearheaded the effort to raise money for the town's Christmas decorations. Today as many as 50,000 people attend, consuming more than 10,000 pounds of chitlins. Should anyone be interested in anything other than chitlins, they will find typical festival food vendors alongside craft vendors. There are rides and games and all manner of fun activity.

For more information check out chitlinstrut.com or call the town of Salley at (803) 258-3485. The festival is held at the Civic Center and Fairgrounds. To get there, head south on I-77 and take exit 1 for US 321 south to SR 3 south.

Lunch Island (aka Bomb Island or Doolittle Island). Owned by the South Carolina Electric and Gas Company, this may well be the site of the largest purple martin roosts in the world. In late afternoons during July and August, what is estimated to be nearly a million purple martins arrive in a cloudlike form over Lake Murray as they settle to feed and roost. The daily phenomenon occurs until they head off to South America for winter hibernation. While the satiny birds can be seen from various areas, there are multiple companies in the area that offer cruises out to the island for a closer look. Contact **Spirit of Lake Murray** (3340 Highway 378, Leesville; spiritoflakemurray.com) to catch a ride.

where to eat

Alodia's Cucina Italiana. 2736 North Lake Drive, Irmo; (803) 781-9814; alodias.com. With locations in both Irmo and Lexington, this nice italian restaurant could be visited on a day trip to the lake or Columbia. They say the recipes served here come from the family of founder Adam Huneau and the restaurant was named after his great-grandmother. Start with calamari or bruschetta, feast one of a dozen entrées and finish with cannoli or crème brûlée. Open for dinner only. $$$

The Flight Deck. 109 Old Chapin Rd., Lexington; (803) 957-5990; flightdeckrestaurant .net. A World War II theme includes aircraft memorabilia and artwork. The family-friendly restaurant also includes an arcade. Sandwiches, burgers, steaks, and blue plate specials make up the diverse menu. Open Mon through Thurs 11 a.m. to 9 p.m., Fri and Sat 11 a.m. to 10 p.m. $.

Liberty Tap Room on the Lake. 1602 Marina Rd., Irmo.; (803) 667-9715; libertytaproom .com. The small chain location overlooks one of the marinas on Lake Murray. A broad list of beer and ciders on tap combine with a food menu that is nearly as broad. Pizza, sandwiches, burgers, steak, and fish all are served here. Open Mon through Thurs 11 a.m. to 9 p.m., Fri and Sat 11 a.m. to 10 p.m., Sun 11 a.m. to 9 p.m. $$

Rusty Anchor. 1925 Johnson Marina Rd, Chapin; (803) 749-1555; rustyanchorrestaurant .com. Located at the Lighthouse Marina, the Rusty Anchor appropriately serves various kinds of seafood. Steaks and salads are also on the menu. Finish up with Godiva chocolate cake or key lime pie. Open seasonally Wed through Fri 5 to 9 p.m., Sat and Sun 11 a.m. to 9 p.m. $$–$$$.

southwest

>>>

day trip 01

southwest

Marketers say there are more Revolutionary War battle sites in the Spartanburg area than anywhere else in the country. The city and county of the same name were indeed named for the Spartan Regiment of the South Carolina Militia that formed in this area. But of more modern significance were the arrival of the railroads and Spartanburg's part in the Industrial Revolution as it began to develop textile mills along the banks of its plentiful rivers. Spartanburg became known as the Hub City, partly because of its central location in the foothills of the Blue Ridge between Charlotte, Atlanta, Columbia, and Ashville, but initially and primarily because of the number and layout of rail lines in the city.

The area dates from 1753, when settlers negotiated a treaty with the native Cherokee. In 1785 it emerged as a frontier trading post with Scotch-Irish, German, and American Indian traders. Not much of this history remains, but standing sentinel over downtown Spartanburg's Morgan Square is a statue of General Daniel Morgan, who led the American forces to victory at the Battle of Cowpens during the Revolutionary War, frequently recognized as a tactical masterpiece.

The area economy is a literal melting pot, with international industry anchored by a BMW plant that employs 4,000 and the largest peach-producing area in the state that picks 4,000 boxcar loads of peaches each year.

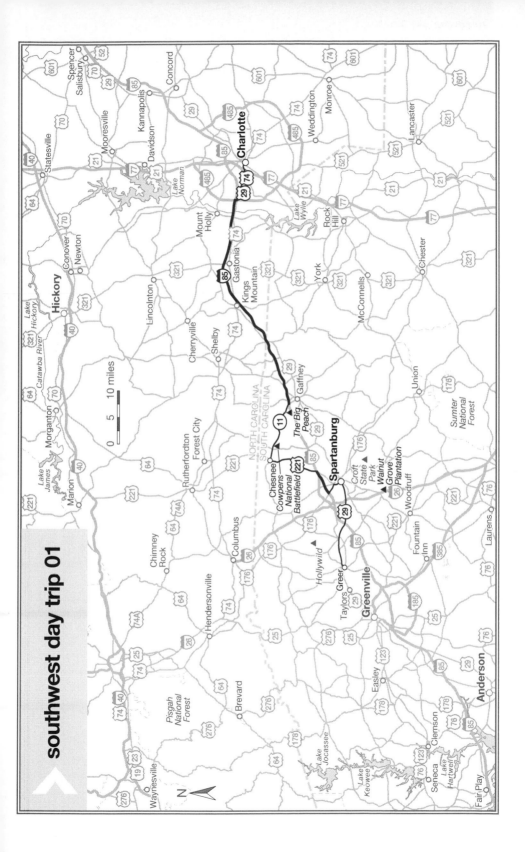

southwest day trip 01

chesnee, sc

Don't confuse the location of Cowpens Battleground, the site of what some historians say was the turning point in the Revolutionary War, with the town of Cowpens. The national park is located just outside the town of Chesnee, a small farming community of about 1,000 people. Other than that significant contribution to American history, Chesnee is little more than an intersection on US 221. But its historical significance, an emerging art scene, and a healthy selection of farms make it more than a worthwhile day trip.

getting there

Chesnee is just over an hour's drive from Charlotte, traveling west on I-85. Take exit 92 at Gaffney and make your way to Chesnee via SR 11, the Cherokee Foothills Scenic Highway.

where to go

Cowpens National Battlefield. 4001 Chesnee Hwy.; (864) 431-2828; nps.gov. It was on this site, on January 17, 1781, that a force of militia from Virginia, Georgia, and the Carolinas, commanded by General Daniel Morgan, won a decisive Revolutionary War battle over the British. Afterward British General Cornwallis abandoned South Carolina and marched north to his surrender at Yorktown. Considered a tactical masterpiece, this battle is a staple of many formal military educations. That strategy is interpreted well by park rangers and signage at the park. Events on this site each year include an anniversary re-enactment. Free. Open daily 9 a.m. to 5 p.m.

> ## the butt of many jokes
>
> *A million-gallon water tank standing four stories tall between exits 90 and 92 on I-85 has taken its share of grief over the years for its resemblance to what is usually a covered part of the human body. Some refer to it as* ***"Moon Over Gaffney."*** *Regardless, this peach has done its job. The Gaffney Board of Public works commissioned an artist to paint the tank, built in 1981, to resemble a peach, attempting to make clear that South Carolina produces more peaches than its neighbor to the south—Georgia. So maybe the unfortunate design is a good thing if you believe what Oscar Wilde said: "The only thing worse than being talked about is not being talked about."*

where to shop

Strawberry Hill Cooley Farms. 3097 SR 11; (864) 461-7225; strawberryhillusa.com. Operating here for more than 60 years, Strawberry Hill is one of the largest pick-your-own farming operations in the state. It is a sweet 1,000 acres of strawberries, peaches, cantaloupes, blackberries, and other fruits. Guests also find a cafe where they can get scratch-made biscuits, burgers, and ice cream. Cafe is open year-round Mon through Sat 6 a.m. to 2:30 p.m. Pick your own is seasonal, check the website for latest information.

spartanburg, sc

Today Spartanburg is part college town and part emerging city of music. It has eight institutions of higher learning, including Wofford College, Converse College, and a campus of the University of South Carolina. It's also the home of southern rock's The Marshall Tucker Band, still touring after three decades and more than two dozen albums. A music trail highlights the city's unexpected musical background, adding to the appeal of this midsize southern town. In Morgan Square new restaurants are emerging to complement the cultural opportunities that have materialized over the past couple of decades. Traditional culinary landmarks such as the Beacon Drive-in, which once served President Bill Clinton, still stand tall on the eatery scene.

getting there

US 221 in Chesnee takes you to I-85 Business so you don't have to backtrack. It's only a 30-minute shot into Spartanburg. Take exit 5A off of I-85 Business to get on I-585/US 176. Take the Church Street/US 221 exit and turn right off the ramp onto N. Church Street, which will lead you into the city.

where to go

Chapman Cultural Center. 200 E. Saint John St.; (864) 542-2787; chapmanculturalcenter .org. Art exhibits, performances by local and national artists, and other arts programming are offered at this complex of three buildings, opened in 2007. Included are two theaters: a beautiful traditional theater with seating for 500, and an intimate black box theater that is also used for instructional space. The Spartanburg Science Center (864-583-2777; spartan-burgsciencecenter.org), located here, includes four exhibit spaces, one each for the human body, physics, life science, and earth science. The corresponding Spartanburg Regional History Museum is also on the property. Admission to the science center is $5. In addition to evening performance times, the center is open Tues through Sat, 10 a.m. to 5 p.m.

Croft State Park. 450 Croft State Park Rd.; (864) 585-1283; southcarolinaparks.com. The 150-acre Lake Craig is the centerpiece of this park, known for its equestrian facilities. Horse shows are held frequently here, but the park also offers biking trails, camping, fishing, and other outdoor activities. Admission is $3 for adults $1 for children. Typically open during daylight hours.

Hollywild Animal Park. 2325 Hampton Rd.; Wellford; (864) 472-2038; hollywild.com. Hollywild is a small zoo featuring exotic animals, shows, feeding stations, and demonstrations. Its name comes from the fact that so many of its residents have appeared in movies and commercials, some living out retirement here. A safari ride takes visitors through about 70 acres where animals roam free. Admission is $9 for adults, $7 for seniors and children. Children under 2 are admitted free. Open Sat and Sun 10 a.m. to 5 p.m.

Hub-Bub. 149 S. Daniel Morgan Ave.; (864) 582-0056; scartshub.com/venues/hub-bub/. This has been called one of the leading artist-in-residence programs in the nation. The program is based in the former Nash Rambler car dealership that has been converted into a gallery and performance hall where staged throughout the year are concerts, films, progressive art exhibits, poetry readings, experimental theater, workshops, and more artistic endeavors. A display gallery features work of resident artists and is open Mon through Fri 9 a.m. to 5 p.m.

Hub City Railroad Museum. 298 Magnolia St.; (864) 594-5050; hubcityrrmuseum.org. Railroad enthusiasts learn more by visiting the train depot of the Southern Railway. The museum includes artifacts of the city's textile heritage and its continuing agricultural industry. Also included are artifacts from the Hayne Shops of Southern Railway, the area's only freight and passenger car repair shop. Free. Open Wed and Sat 8 a.m. to 2 p.m.

Walnut Grove Plantation. 1200 Otts Shoals Rd., Roebuck; (864) 576-6546; spartanburg history.org. Located in the unincorporated community of Roebuck—just south of Spartanburg near the intersection of I-26 and US 221—is this well-preserved 18th-century plantation. Built by Charles Moore for his wife, Mary, and eight children (two more were born at Walnut Grove), the home amazingly stayed in the family until 1961. Several patriot military units were formed on the property, including the Spartan Regiment, from which the county and city eventually took their names. The family donated the plantation to the Spartanburg County Historical Society, which restored the home and still operates it as a museum today. Admission is $10 for ages 6 and older. Open Tues through Sat 11 a.m. to 5 p.m., Sun 2 to 5 p.m. Apr through Oct, and Sat 11 a.m. to 5 p.m. Nov and Mar. Guided tours begin hourly.

where to shop

Hub City Bookshop. 186 W. Main St.; (864) 577-9349; hubcity.org. This independent bookstore looks out on Morgan Square downtown and specializes in new releases and regional authors, including its own Hub City Press titles. Little River Coffee Bar and Cake-head Bakery are also located in the building, which was once the Masonic Temple. Open Mon through Sat 10 a.m. to 7 p.m.,

where to eat

Beacon Drive-In. 255 John B White Sr. Blvd.; (864) 585-9387; beacondrivein.com. J.C. Strobel was at the Beacon counter calling out orders in his big, booming, rhythmic voice for decades until his death in 2014. Place your order quick and "move on down the line," J.C. would say during his walk and talk. He had lot to do with The Beacon, which opened in 1946, becoming a beloved landmark. It literally offers tons of items, but is best known for its sweet tea (made with 3,000 pounds of sugar per week,) generous portions of fries (made from three tons of potatoes per week,) and big, sloppy burgers known as burger a-plenty. Open Mon through Thurs 7:30 a.m. to 9 p.m. and Fri and Sat 7:30 to 10 p.m. $.

Converse Deli. 551 E. Main St., Ste. 105; (864) 585-5580; conversdelieast.com. A little easier on the cholesterol and calorie counts are the lunch offerings at the Converse Deli. This popular lunchtime restaurant is part of a farm-to-table program that even has a small garden in front of the restaurant. The selections, however, resemble those of a traditional deli. Open Mon through Sat 10 a.m. to 9 p.m., Sun 11 a.m. to 3 p.m. $.

Gerhard's Cafe. 1200 E. Main St.; (864) 591-1920; gerhardscafe.net. Gerhards is an Austrian and German restaurant with an extensive menu that includes American dishes as well. You'll find hearty, rich food and some exotic selections like wild boar chops and pheasant. Open Mon through Thurs 5:30 to 10 p.m., Fri and Sat 5:30 to 10:30 p.m. $$.

Wades. 1000 N. Pine St.; (864) 582-3800; eatatwades.com. This little meat and potatoes restaurant regularly wins accolades from the media and others. It has been operating in Spartanburg since 1947, and although the menu and buildings have changed through the years, the locals keep coming back for the quality and consistent food and service. Open Mon through Fri 11 a.m. to 8 p.m., Sun 11 a.m. to 3 p.m. $.

where to stay

Clevedale Inn. 1050 Willis Rd., (864) 345-2394; clevdaleinn.com. While this inn's main focus is on weddings and events, the Clevedale also has four rooms for overnight stays, including a renovated 1947 Southern Railway Caboose. Whichever accommodation you select you are not likely to be disappointed, with the luxurious attention to detail. $$

The Inn on Main. 319 E. Main St.; (864) 585-5001; innonmainofspartanburg.com. This nostalgic 1904 inn has a grand façade with big columns, big porches, and a red brick exterior. Inside, rooms are elegant and bright and represent some of the city's Revolutionary-era history. It has operated as a bed-and-breakfast since 2002, and it's readily recommended. $–$$.

greer, sc

Thanks to the good folks at BMW, Greer is the second-fastest-growing city in South Carolina. The BMW plant opened in Greer in the mid-1990s, expanded in 2002, and the population grew to 26,000 by 2008. By 2020, about 33,000 people called Greer home. Dozens of suppliers have also moved into the area, bolstering the economy even more. Day-trippers can visit the BMW production facility, but the city also offers some historical perspective. Greer Station, 12 blocks, and 40 buildings downtown, are included on the National Register of Historical Places. Thanks in part to these new developments, the area is experiencing the beginning of a cultural revolution, a beneficiary of an increased tax base and philanthropic offerings of new companies looking to make an impression.

getting there

From Spartanburg, it's a straight shot west on US 29 to Greer. The trip takes less than 30 minutes.

where to go

BMW Factory. 1400 SR 101 South; (864) 802-6000; bmwusfactory.com. The BMW *Zentrum* (the German word for center) is the visitor center and museum that reflects and displays BMW's heritage of engineering and innovation. Four galleries take guests from the 1930 Dixi to the X6 Sports Activity Coupe. Visitors experience the heritage of BMW that includes production of aircraft engines, motorcycles, and automobiles designed specifically for racing. The plant offers guided tours Mon through Fri 9:30 a.m. to 5:30 p.m. $15 per person; reservations are required.

Greer Heritage Museum. 106 S. Main St.; (864) 877-3377; greerheritage.com. When city hall moved down the street, the heritage museum moved into what was built as a post office in 1935. While it maintains typical artifacts and documents from the city's history, it also offers a series of temporary exhibits that originate from various community archives and collections, on subjects as random as technology and as expected as photos from the past. Free. Open Tues and Thurs 9 a.m.to 3 p.m. and Sat 9 a.m. to 5 p.m.

Suber's Mill. 2002 Suber Mill Rd.; (864) 430-3675; scmills.com. This corn mill, built around 1908, still grinds corn using water power. It's one of few such mills still operating in the state. Open Sat 9 a.m. to noon.

where to eat

The Southern Growl. 155 N. Buncombe Rd., (864) 655-7444; thesoutherngrowl.com. As many as 60 taps, 20 made by Southern Growl, pour beer at this pub. The menu is specifically designed to pair well with beer and staff is anxious to help diners with finding the perfect salad or sandwich to go with that beer.

where to stay

James House Inn. 401 W. Poinsett St.; (864) 982-5300; thejameshouseinn.com. Built in 1921 and on the National Register of Historic Places, the James House maintains much of its historic charm. Antiques are combined with amenities such as Tempurpedic mattresses to assure guests a memorable, relaxing stay. $$

day trip 02

southwest

heartland to death valley:
greenville, sc; clemson, sc;
lake hartwell, sc

This day trip doesn't go to the California Mojave Desert, only to Clemson University where the Tigers football team plays. It begins in the vibrant and surprisingly progressive city of Greenville and winds up at one of the state's largest man-made reservoirs, offering this part of the state's best recreational activities.

greenville, sc

A bridge seemed to change everything for Greenville. Much of this city's history is inglorious at best. Little distinguishes its early history from that of surrounding cities and foothill communities of The Upstate. A trading post since 1768, Greenville was founded originally as Pleasantburg; no one really knows for sure why its name changed in 1831 or even for whom it is named. Greenville didn't have a vital role in the Revolutionary War and it didn't change the Civil War, although it was home to Donaldson Air Force base during World War II. In the middle of the 20th century it struggled with a littered downtown, a polluted Reedy River, and a less-than-positive image. This all began to change in the 1970s when the city began a revitalization effort that is unmatched in this region. Trees and decorative light fixtures were added to narrowed streets, creating friendly parks and plazas. But that was only the beginning. In the 1980s the city began a project that created a 20-acre park downtown, highlighted by a suspension pedestrian bridge over the falls on Reedy River. A

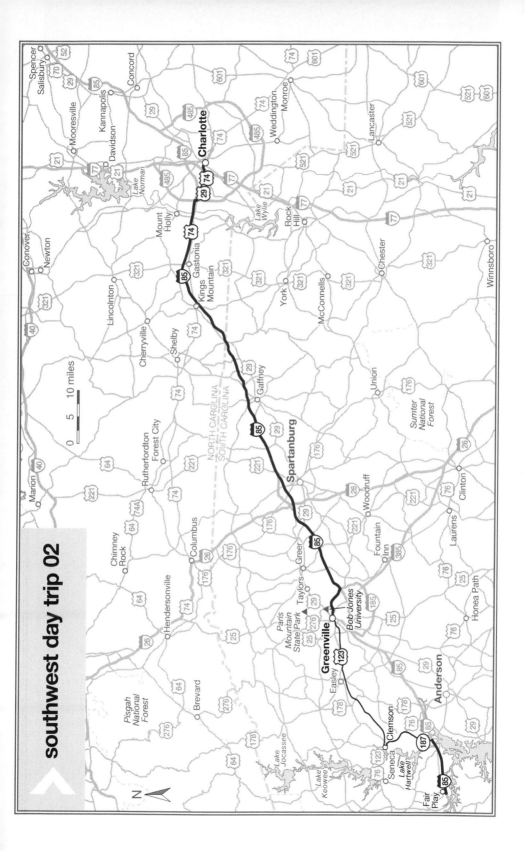

southwest day trip 02

much talked-about design curiosity, opened in 2004, the 345-foot Liberty Bridge sweeps around the falls and through the tops of trees planted some 40 years ago.

The city has managed to maintain the natural charm that existed all this time, but since its revitalization, its historic treasures are valued even more. The National Trust for Historic Preservation awarded Greenville with the Great American Main Street Award in 2003 and 2009. Probably most important, the city has become known as a bastion of the arts and culinary delights. A busking program called Acoustic Cafe is a city effort to offer daily performances at several key locations. Main Street Gallery offers the same opportunity to visual artists to showcase their talents. In addition, the city commissioned original works of sculpture to honor Greenville's past as well as more contemporary whimsical works. Greenville has also become a hotspot for specialized tours focused on food, beer, wine, history, and more. Get more information about the city and those tours at greenvillecvb.com.

getting there

Greenville is located off I-85 south less than two hours from Charlotte. This Greenville should not be confused with the Greenville in the eastern part of North Carolina that's more than four hours from Charlotte.

where to go

American Legion War Museum. 430 N. Main St.; (864) 271-2000. Although most of Greenville's military history is more connected to the 20th century, the war museum displays artifacts from the Revolutionary War, Civil War, Spanish/American War, World War I, World War II, Korean War, Vietnam, Persian Gulf, and Iraq. It also traces the history of what was originally the Greenville Army Air Base in 1942 but was taken over by the US Air Force during World War II, up until 1963 when it then became Donaldson Air Force Base. Free. Open Sat 10 a.m. to 4 p.m. and Sun 1 to 4 p.m.

Bob Jones University. 1700 Wade Hampton Blvd.; (864) 242-5100; bju.edu. South Carolina's largest private liberal arts university has created a host of cultural opportunities for the city. With 4,000 students, it is the largest fundamental Christian college in the world with a 200-acre campus. A museum and gallery with a significant collection of religious art that dates to 14th-century Europe is open to the public. Period furniture, sculpture, and tapestries are displayed among traditional baroque paintings and Egyptian, Roman, and Hebrew antiquities.

Centre Stage. 501 River St.; (864) 233-6733; centrestage.org. Centre Stage is Greenville's professional theater, bringing to the city current Broadway and original comedies, dramas, and musicals. The theater space is also used by local arts groups.

Greenville Zoo. 150 Cleveland Park Dr.; (864) 467-4300; greenvillezoo.com. Operated by the city is this small zoo located within Cleveland Park. The animals and displays are an interesting mix from around the world. Included are big animals such as elephants and other African species as well as favorites such as monkeys. A reptile house contains various slithery species. A picnic shelter and playground are also located here. Admission is $12 for adults, $11 for children ages 3 to 15. Open daily 10 a.m. to 5 p.m. in fall and winter except Thanksgiving, Christmas, and New Year's Day, and 9 a.m. to 5 p.m. in spring and summer.

Heritage Greens. College Street; heritagegreensc.org. A part of Greenville's cultural heritage since the 1970s, Heritage Green is a parklike setting downtown that includes five major attractions:

> **Greenville Theatre.** 444 College St.; (864) 233-6238; greenvillelittletheatre.org. The Greenville Little Theatre company has been in continuous operation since 1926 and produces professional-quality musicals, mysteries, comedies, and dramas.

> **The Children's Museum of the Upstate.** 300 College St.; (864) 233-7755; tcmupstate.org. This is one of the largest children's museums in the country with exhibit space that spans 80,000 square feet. It includes 18 galleries with typical children's museum and interactive exhibits of work places, stores, a hospital, supermarket, television studio, farm, and other environments. A traveling exhibit hall provides space for national touring exhibits based on children's educational programs and literature. Admission is $15 per person ages 2 and up. Open Tues through Sat 9 a.m. to 5 p.m., Sun 11 a.m. to 5 p.m.

> **Greenville County Museum of Art.** 420 College St.; (864) 271-7570; gcma.org. The popular contemporary work of Andrew Wyeth is among the most significant at the Greenville County Museum of Art. The museum also collects a wide range of American art from Josef Albers, Jasper Johns, Andy Warhol, and Romare Bearden. Free. Open Wed through Sat 10 a.m. to 5 p.m., Sun 1 to 5 p.m.

> **Sigal Music Museum.** 516 Buncombe St.; (864) 520-8807; sigalmusicmuseum.org. Located in the former Coca-Cola Bottling Company, the Sigal museum collects and exhibits a range of historical musical instruments. There are more than 1,000 items on display at any given time from the museum's collection and special exhibitions. It's also a performance venue. Admission is $7 for adults, $6 for seniors and $4 for children. Open Tues through Sat 10 a.m. to 5 p.m. and Sun 1 to 5 p.m.

> **Upcountry History Museum.** 540 Buncombe St.; (864) 467-3100; upcountryhistory .org. Audiovisual and interactive displays take visitors through 300 years of history of Upcountry South Carolina. Admission is $10 for adults, $9 for students and seniors, $8 for children ages 4 to 12. Open Tues through Sat 10 a.m. to 5 p.m., Sun 1 to 5 p.m.

Kilgore-Lewis House. 560 N. Academy St.; (864) 232-3020; kilgore-lewis.org. Built between 1835 and 1838, this historic home is the headquarters of the Greenville Council of Garden Clubs. It includes about five acres of garden displays and plays host to frequent weddings and other events. Visit the gardens anytime. The public can tour the home Wed through Fri 10 a.m. to 2 p.m.

Museum & Library of Confederate History. 15 Boyce Ave.; (864) 421-9039; confederatemuseum.org. Located in the city's historic district in an unassuming house is a large collection of Confederate-period artifacts and a research library that explores military and home life of the period. Cannons, guns, uniforms, and other wartime items are on display, but the museum also presents civilian housewares, clothing, and furnishings to illustrate life just before, during, and after the Civil War. It is operated by the Sons of the Confederate Veterans. Free. Open Mon and Wed 10 a.m. to 3 p.m., Fri 1 to 9 p.m., Sat. 10 a.m. to 5 p.m., and Sun 1 to 5 p.m.

Paris Mountain State Park. 2401 State Park Rd.; (864) 244-5565; southcarolinaparks .com. Originally built by the Civilian Conservation Corps during the Great Depression, the renovated bathhouse, now called the Park Center, serves as the hub of activity at Paris Mountain. Once a rural retreat, it is now frequented by bicyclists, hikers, and picnickers. Swimming and fishing are allowed in 15-acre Lake Placid. Admission is $6 for adults, $3.75 for seniors, $3.50 for children. Generally open during daylight hours.

The Peace Center for the Performing Arts. SW corner of Broad Street and Main Street; (864) 467-3030; peacecenter.org. This performing arts center opened in 1990 in the heart of downtown and became the heart of the city's cultural community. It was built from three nearly dilapidated factory buildings and includes the Peace Center Hall, the Gunter Theatre, the Dow Brand Amphitheatre, and the Wyche Pavilion. The center hosts performances by the Greenville Symphony, Greenville Chorale, Carolina Ballet Theatre, South Carolina Children's Theatre, and Greenville International Ballet. The center also presents intimate concerts by national acts and independent films in a state-of-the-art, high-definition theater.

Shoeless Joe Jackson Museum & Baseball Library. 356 Field St.; (864) 346-4867; shoelessjoejackson.org. In 2006 the home of Shoeless Joe Jackson was dismantled to be moved to its current location near Fluor Field, home of the Greenville Drive baseball team, a Class A affiliate of the Boston Red Sox. Jackson, who is third on baseball's all-time batting average list, grew up here and returned to Greenville following his major league career. He is remembered, unfortunately, for being part of the shunned 1919 Chicago White Sox team accused (and later acquitted) of throwing the World Series, an episode that would lead to his and seven other players' banishment from the game. In addition to personal effects, the museum includes records, artifacts, photographs, film, and other items associated with Jackson. A book collection related to baseball and its role in American culture is housed in Joe's former trophy room. Free. Open Thurs through Mon 11 a.m. to 7 p.m.

where to shop

Art Crossing at Riverplace. 101 Swamp Rabbit Tr.; (864) 242-2100; artcrossinggreenville .com. Art Crossing at Riverplace includes about 20 studios converted from parking garages. For sale are works in paint, ceramics, photographs, jewels, and mosaics. Open Tues through Sat 11 a.m. to 5 p.m.

Christopher Park Gallery. 610-C S. Main St.; (864) 232-6744; chickenmanart.com. The goal of this gallery is to present non-traditional and even quirky art for sale in a non-pretentious atmosphere. It has a mix of wall art, pottery, and other functional and decorative pieces that are displayed casually as they may be displayed in your home. Hours vary according to season and even the weather.

Village of West Greenville. Located along Pendelton St. west of downtown; villagewgvl .com. More than 60 local artists, retailers, and restaurants are located in this former textile village. Here you find clothing boutiques, art galleries, housewares, and more.

where to eat

Brick Street Cafe. 315 Augusta St.; (864) 421-0111; brickstreetcafe.online. Located in the historic district of the West End, Brick Street serves home cooking with a little something added in. You can get fried green tomatoes alongside halibut or shrimp and grits. It's also a pretty place to eat, with fresh flowers and colorful decor. Save room for sweet potato pie! Open Mon through Sat 11 a.m. to 2:30 p.m. and Thurs through Sat 5:30 to 9:30 p.m. $$.

Soby's. 207 S. Main St.; (864) 232-7007; sobys.com. Located in a 100-year-old cotton exchange, a loft overlooks the busy kitchen at Soby's. Creating a warm atmosphere, its architectural character is preserved with exposed brick and beams surrounding diners who sit on chairs and eat off tables from wood salvaged from the building. The food can be described as New South cuisine with familiar ingredients with a twist. Open Mon through Thurs 5:30 to 10 p.m., Fri and Sat 5:30 to 11 p.m., Sun brunch 10:30 a.m. to 1:30 p.m., and 5:30 to 9 p.m. $$$.

The Trappe Door. 23 W. Washington St.; (864) 451-7490; trappedoor.com. Locating a restaurant with Belgian food and beer in Greenville seems to have been a stroke of genius. It takes its name from the beer-brewing Trappist monks, who, like the restaurant, established the operation in a basement. It has become one of the most popular dining spots in Greenville. Selections range from short ribs to schnitzel. Open daily at 5 p.m. $$.

where to stay

Modal, Coffee & Hostel. 813 Augusts St.; (864) 884-2834; staymodal.com. Hostels aren't easy to come by in South Carolina, but targeting those with an interest in the arts seems to work here. Modal has a combination of bunk-style rooms for traveling artists as well as private accommodations that are more B&B-style for daytrippers. $$.

Pettigru Place. 302 Pettigru St.; (864) 242-4529; pettigruplace.com. An English garden on the picturesque tree-lined street leads guests into this Georgian Federalist home built in 1920. The interior is stately yet informal and comfortable, with guest rooms that reflect various themes. Victorian decor fills one room, while another has an African rainforest theme. $$$.

worth more time

Campbell's Covered Bridge. 101 Campbell's Covered Bridge Rd., Landrum. Built in 1909, this is the only remaining covered bridge in South Carolina. From US 25 north of Travelers Rest, take SR 414 through Tigerville. Turn right on Pleasant Hill Road, right on Campbell's Covered Bridge Road, and travel approximately a quarter-mile to the bridge.

clemson, sc

The home of the Tigers and Clemson University forms the southern border of the city of Clemson in Pickens County. Lake Hartwell forms its western border. The university and its 15,000 students create most of the cultural opportunities in the area, which includes a great botanical garden and a renowned geology museum.

getting there

From Greenville take US 123 south to arrive in the heart of Clemson in about 30 minutes.

where to go

Bob Campbell Geology Museum. 140 Discovery Ln.; (864) 656-4600; clemson.edu. This geology museum at Clemson University is as dynamic as a geology center can be. Its collection of 10,000 rocks, minerals, fossils, and other objects tells a story from beneath the earth's surface with a goal of delivering connections to today. A skeleton of a saber-tooth tiger, meteorites, and other unusual holdings are on display. Free. Open daily 10 a.m. to 5 p.m.

Fort Hill/John C. Calhoun House Museum. 103 Tillman Hall; (864) 656-4789; clemson .edu. Fort Hill is the home of the John C. Calhoun Mansion and Library, a National Historic Landmark that was once the home of John C. Calhoun, at the center of the university campus. Calhoun was considered a leading statesmen in antebellum South Carolina. A proponent of slavery, he would go on to serve as vice president of the United States. The home includes a presentation of antebellum furnishings and family artifacts that tell the story of how the home was passed down to the Clemson family through marriage.

South Carolina Botanical Garden. 102 Garden Trail; (864) 656-7697; clemson.edu. With 270 acres, this spectacular garden features thousands of varieties of ornamental plants, an arboretum that spans 70 acres, and other horticultural gems. Visitors can hike miles of nature trails along streams and through forests; a butterfly garden and wildflower meadow offer additional opportunities to explore nature. More formal displays offer an extensive collection of camellias, holly, and hydrangea. The 1716 Hanover House was reconstructed on Clemson's campus in 1941 and moved here in 1994. Free. Open daily dawn to dusk.

where to shop

'55 Exchange. Hendrix Student Center, 720 McMillan Rd., Clemson University; (864) 656-2155. Clemson's class of 1955 established this student-run shop as a gift on its 50th anniversary. It had been known as the Agricultural Sales Center and still carries on the tradition of selling the acclaimed Clemson University ice cream, blue cheese, and other agricultural products. Open Mon through Fri 11:30 a.m. to 6 p.m. (until 8 p.m. in summer), Sat and Sun 1 to 6 p.m.

where to eat

Esso Club. 129 Old Greenville Hwy.; (864) 654-5120; theessoclub.com. Old Esso Gas Station signs hang at this Clemson University tradition that was established in 1933. Salads, barbecue wings, and other menu items stay loyal to a university theme. Hours vary according to university events. $.

Pixie & Bills Restaurant. 1058 Tiger Blvd.; (864) 654-1210; https://pixieandbills.com/. Located in the heart of Tiger Country is this fine dining restaurant with a focus on steak and seafood. Open Mon through Fri 11:30 a.m. to 1:30 p.m. and Mon through Sat 5:30 to 9:30 p.m. $$$

Tiger Town Tavern. 368 College Ave.; (864) 654-5901; tigertowntavern.com. What started as a pool hall became a full-service restaurant in the mid-90s. It now serves typical college bar food, including sandwiches named after ACC college teams. Hours vary according to college events. $.

where to stay

The Conference Center & Inn at Clemson University. 230 Madren Center Dr., Clemson University; (864) 654-9020; clemson.edu. This luxurious four-story hotel is located on campus, providing a great starting point for day trips. It affords views of gardens, the campus, and nearby Lake Hartwell. $.

lake hartwell, sc

The 56,000-acre Lake Hartwell reservoir provides a massive amount of recreational opportunities for the day-tripper. Its shoreline spans nearly 1,000 miles from north of Clemson south to the Northeast Georgia Mountains, bisecting I-85 near Anderson and providing dozens of boat launches, parks, and access areas. Anglers, both professional and amateur, come from miles around seeking one of the lake's whopping striped bass. Fresh produce stands, pick-your-own orchards and farms, flea markets, and antiques malls dot the landscape.

getting there

Take SR 28 east out of Clemson and SR 187 15 minutes to I-85 south. Within a few minutes of getting on the interstate there are a number of exits to Lake Hartwell.

where to go

Lake Hartwell State Recreation Area. 19138-A SC Hwy. 11 South; (864) 972-3352; southcarolinaparks.com. The park's information center displays a wide variety of vintage fishing equipment, getting visitors ready to wet a line as they seek bass, largemouth, crappie, bream, and catfish. In addition to lake access, this park has a camp store and opportunities for hiking and camping. One-room camper cabins are available for rent. These are on the primitive side, but feature bunk beds, a porch, and electricity but no running water or bathroom. Other campground facilities are located throughout the area. Admission to the park is $3 for adults, $1.50 for seniors; $1 for children ages 15 and under. It's typically open during daylight hours.

where to shop

Curiosity Shoppes & Gem Mine. 15298 SC Hwy. 11, Fair Play; (864) 972-0463. Located in nearby Fair Play within the area visitor center, this shop is a fun potpourri of guidebooks, nautical items, T-shirts, jewelry, and pottery. The stop is an attraction in itself—mine for gems, have a picnic, or even play a round of Frisbee golf on the grounds. Hours vary according to season.

west

>>>

day trip 0 i

west

>>> **across the river:**
belmont, gastonia, dallas,
kings mountain

Charlotte day-trippers need only look a couple dozen miles beyond their doorsteps to escape the hustle and bustle of metropolitan life. Across the Catawba River is an abundance of natural adventures waiting in the county of Gaston, extending from a world-class botanical garden in the east to a rather unusual geographic formation on its western edge some 100 miles from the Blue Ridge.

In the South Carolina day trip to York, the importance of the Catawba began to emerge. These American Indians settled the Gaston area, too. In fact, they inhabited this area first and stayed here until 1772, when they began to move to the reservation near Fort Mill as Scotch-Irish, Pennsylvania Dutch, and English began to settle the area. More on the Catawbas is found at the Schiele Museum of Natural History and its replica of a Catawba Indian village.

In the middle of the 19th century, Gaston County joined the Industrial Revolution and began to discover its industrial legacy in cotton mills, established throughout the county but particularly in the towns of Lowell, McAdenville, and Belmont, where Daniel J. Stowe, one of the 20th-century leaders in the mill business, established a botanical garden. Stowe, an avid collector of a wide range of items, also helped enhance the Gaston County Museum of History in Dallas with a collection of carriages.

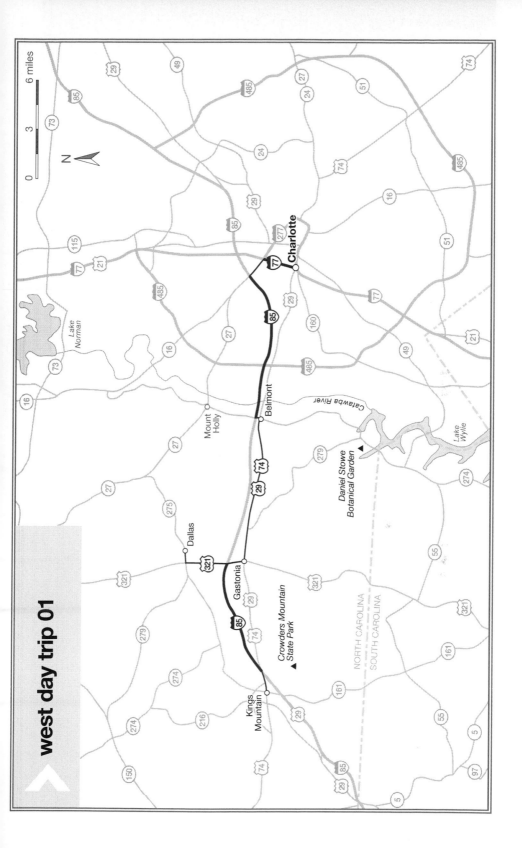

west day trip 01

belmont

Located at exit 26 on I-85, Belmont was settled in the 1750s with the establishment of the Fort at the Point near the junction of the South Fork and Catawba Rivers. It would be nearly 100 years before Jasper Stowe opened one of the area's first textile plants to help establish the city, giving anchor to its economic stability for more than 100 years. In 1872 a Roman Catholic priest, Father Jeremiah O'Connell, purchased a small tract of land on which the Benedictine monks established a religious community and school. That property is now Belmont Abbey College, and the monks are among the area's largest landholders.

getting there

Travel west about 15 minutes on I-85 and take exit 27. Follow SR 273 into Belmont.

where to go

Belmont Abbey Basilica. 100 Belmont-Mount Holly Rd.; (704) 461-6675; belmontabbey .org. Founded in 1876 by Bishop Leo Haid, Belmont Abbey is a monastery of about 20 men who operate Belmont Abbey College, a Roman Catholic undergraduate liberal arts school. The Abbey Players and other college arts groups perform in a theater named for the bishop. Central to the 700-acre campus is Abbey Basilica of Mary Help of Christians (its original and formal name). The striking German Gothic–Revival building was the largest Catholic church in the state at the time of its construction, and the Benedictine monks of Belmont did much of the actual work themselves. One of those monks crafted the ceiling in the style of a sailing vessel. Notably, the windows are painted and heat-fused instead of stained, allowing for greater, magnificent detail. The spectacular clock tower was added in 1909. The interior of the church, then classified as a cathedral, was completely renovated in 1964–1965. The Vatican elevated the cathedral to the rank of a minor basilica in 1998, and it is on the National Register of Historic Places. A brochure on the basilica provides information for a self-guided tour and is available inside the entrance to the Abbey Basilica or by request by calling (704) 461-6891. Masses and prayer services are held daily throughout the day from 7 a.m. to 7 p.m.

Belmont Historical Society & Heritage Learning Center. 40 Catawba St.; (704) 825-4848; thebelmonthistoricalsociety.org. Housed in the R.L. Stowe home, built originally as a log structure in 1899, the historical society collects, preserves, and restores artifacts from the area. A stop here shows why the name Stowe is so prominent in this town built around the business the philanthropic family led. Exhibits include American Indian arrowheads and tools, an old-time spinning wheel, and other artifacts from the textile industry as well as the Belmont Sports Hall of Fame. Free. Open Fri through Sun 1 to 5 p.m.

Daniel Stowe Botanical Garden. 6500 S. New Hope Rd.; (704) 825-4490; dsbg.org. Textile magnate Daniel J. Stowe established this garden of 400 acres on the banks of Lake Wylie in 1991. Its main facility, 12 acres of manicured gardens, and a large visitor center, opened in 1999. Among those gardens is a southern cottage garden, a subtropical garden, and beautifully designed perennial gardens that draw thousands of birds, bees, and butterflies. The Orchid Conservatory, which features orchids among other tropical plants, opened in 2008. The young garden, noted for its sparkling fountains, has received accolades nationally from the horticultural world and the media, including HGTV. It's constantly expanding with trails that lead to the lakefront and promises for botanical attractions to open over the next several decades. Admission is $12 for adults, $11 for seniors, and $6 for children 4 to 12. Open daily 9 a.m. to 5 p.m.

Stowe Park. 24 S. Main St.; (704) 825-8191; www.cityofbelmont.org/stowe-park. Located in the middle of downtown, the oak trees are taller today, but this shady park still looks much as it did when it opened in the 1950s. Named for Robert Lee Stowe Jr., brother of Daniel Stowe, it is still a gathering spot for locals, whose children take advantage of the playground or get ice cream at the snack bar. A bandstand at the bottom of a grassy amphitheater provides space for bands during frequent seasonal events.

where to shop

Catawba River Antique Mall. 406 Catawba St.; (704) 825-2383. The big fiberglass Shoney's Big Boy in red and white checkered overalls that used to greet diners now greets shoppers at this massive mall. More than 300 booths fill more than 67,000 square feet of vintiques shopping bliss.

Piccalo Antique Mall. 134 N. Main St.; (704) 825-5656; piccoloantiquemall.com. This massive treasure trove of antiques features more than 70 dealers in collectibles, furniture, garden accessories, and funky finds of all types. It is the largest of a handful of secondhand shops to open in the downtown area in recent years. Open Mon through Sat 10 a.m. to 6 p.m., Sun 1 to 6 p.m.

where to eat

Nellie's Southern Kitchen. 36 N. Main St.; (704) 396-7169; nelliesouthernkitchen.com. It might be a little hard to understand why photos of pop singers The Jonas Brothers hang at the back of this restaurant until you understand the brothers' father established this restaurant to honor his grandmother who lived in the area until she died in 2011. Chicken and dumplings, meatloaf, and more are modeled after her recipes. $$.

Old Stone Steakhouse. 23 S. Main St.; (704) 825-9995; oldstonesteakhouse.com. The downtown location of Old Stone provides for great outdoor seating as well as a warm and handsome wood-paneled interior dining room. The steaks are good, but you can also get well-prepared crab cakes and crab legs. Open for lunch and dinner Mon through Sat. $$$.

Sammy's Deli & Pub. 25 S. Main St.; (704) 825-4266; sammyspub.com. This is the place in Belmont to get a drink from a selection of top-shelf liquors and specialty cocktails offered seasonally. Sammy serves up typical pub food like burgers and sandwiches, but you can also get a surprisingly tasty barbecue salad. Open Sun through Thurs 11 a.m. to 10 p.m., Fri and Sat 11 a.m. to 11 p.m. $–$$.

String Bean Fresh Market & Deli. 106 N. Main St.; (704) 825-3636; stringbeanmarket .com. Chef and owner Chad Hutchinson named his restaurant String Bean for the affection- ate memories he had of stringing green beans with his family as a child in North Georgia. "People just don't have time to sit and string beans anymore," he says. But his cooking gives them that time. String Bean offers surprisingly innovative soups, salads, sandwiches, and sides such as duck fat fries, a fried green tomato BLT, and a southern Reuben on Texas toast with coleslaw and barbecue sauce. $–$$.

gastonia

Gastonia, the county seat, is an area manufacturing center. It is the corporate headquarters of the world's largest spun yarn manufacturer and several other key manufacturing busi- nesses. I-85 continues to bisect Gastonia with a number of exits convenient to local attrac- tions, shopping, and restaurants. One of the area's premier attractions, Crowders Mountain, has a Kings Mountain address, but it can be accessed from either I-85 or US 74 in Gastonia.

getting there

Take SR 7 to US 29/74 from Belmont into Gastonia. The drive takes only about 15 minutes.

where to go

Schiele Museum of Natural History & Planetarium. 1500 E. Garrison Blvd.; (704) 866-6900; schielemuseum.org. During his 38 years as an executive with the Boy Scouts, Bud Schiele amassed an incredible collection of preserved birds, mammals, rocks, miner- als, photos, and documents. But this wasn't a typical merit badge collection; it included bear, buffalo, and other big animals. He donated them to the community, and that col- lection became what is now the vast Schiele Museum. Today it boasts a large collection of specimens of large and small North American animals in dioramas and a collection of North Carolina specimens. A collection of Native American tools, weapons, and ornaments tells the story of the American Indian. The James H. Lynn Planetarium presents seasonal shows about the nighttime sky, combining traditional projections on the dome with images captured by the Hubble telescope. Outside, guests find a nature trail and Catawba Indian

fish camping

When my older brother first brought his fiancé down from Pennsylvania years ago, the family planned to go to the fish camp on Friday night. She didn't know what she was in for! Are we going fishing? Are we going camping? Is it a combination of the two? Will there be clean restrooms there?

*Even if a person knows that a **fish camp** is a place where you eat fish, they still might not know what they are in for. Fish camps, typically located near local bodies of water like Lake Wylie on the North and South Carolina border, are restaurants that serve calabash-style, or deep-fried, fish, shrimp, and other seafood. It's usually served with hush puppies and slaw in a casual atmosphere.*

Gastonia is known for fish camps, so here are a few local favorites. Even though they have addresses other than Gastonia, all are easy to find from local attractions and all are in the $$ range.

TwinTops Fish Camp. *4574 S. New Hope Rd., Gastonia; (704) 825-2490*

Catfish Cove. *1401 Armstrong Ford Rd., Belmont; (704) 825-3332*

Long Creek Fish Fry. *1031 Lower Dallas Hwy., Dallas; (704) 922-3998*

Riverside Fish House. *1341 Dallas-Stanley Hwy., Dallas, (704) 922-8360*

village that interprets four centuries of Catawba culture through replicas of a prehistoric bark-covered house, council house, and log cabins. A Stone Age heritage site provides a glimpse of the area's aboriginal man, and an 18th-century backcountry farm reveals the lives of early settlers, complete with hogs, sheep, chickens, and cattle. Regular demonstrations are held at each of the sites. Admission is $7 for adults, $6 for children ages 4 to 18 and for seniors. Open Mon through Sat 10 a.m. to 4 p.m. and Sun 1 to 5 p.m.

where to eat

Pita Wheel. 110 S. York St.; (704) 747-3224; pitawheel.com. Originally located in an old gas station in nearby Dallas, Pita Wheel is now a popular gathering spot in an old gas station in downtown Gastonia. Various forms of pitas with chicken, beef, and veggies are on the menu alongside other bar favs such as burgers and craft beer. $.

R.O.'s Barbecue. 1318 Gaston Ave.; (704) 866-8143; rosbbq.com. R.O.'s (pronounced ar-ohs) serves barbecue with a different twist. Throughout North Carolina a battle rages between eastern- and western-style barbecue. An R.O.'s sandwich is neither western nor eastern; it's piled high with sliced, roasted pork and topped with a zesty slaw that is now packaged and distributed regionally as a dip. Try it with a Cherry-Lemon Sundrop, a locally produced soft drink. $.

Tony's Ice Cream. 604 E. Franklin Blvd.; (704) 867-7085; tonysicecream.com. The blonde brick might make you hesitate. The yellow tile inside is old, but Tony's has something going for it. In business since 1947, it offers burgers, sandwiches (including fried bologna and liver mush), and awesome hot dogs. But think about it before you order; the milkshake that comes in 28 flavors might just be a meal on its own. $.

dallas

Dallas is a small historic town situated between New Hope Road and US 321, accessible via either of those roads from I-85 depending on which way you are traveling. It was once the county seat, but that changed to Gastonia in 1909.

getting there

Take US 321 north out of Gastonia; it's about 10 minutes to Dallas.

where to go

Gaston County Museum of History. 131 W. Main St.; (704) 922-7681; gastoncounty museum.org. Located in the former Hoffman Hotel, this simple, elegant 1852 Greek Revival building served travelers coming to do business at the courthouse across the street. Furnished period rooms include the "hands-on" parlor, a gift shop, and changing exhibits that explore art, history, and historic preservation. The Daniel Stowe Carriage House displays North Carolina's largest public collection of horse-drawn vehicles, including sleighs, drays, and buggies. Free. Open Tues through Fri 10 a.m. to 5 p.m., Sat 10 a.m. to 3 p.m.

Historic Dallas. 131 W. Main St.; (704) 922-7681. Starting at the history museum or any nearby point, stroll through the oak tree-lined streets of the town square, listed on the National Register of Historic Places. Notable features include the old jail and courthouse, several distinct homes and businesses, and the Carolina and Northwestern Railway Depot. Pick up a map at the museum or download one from its website in advance.

where to eat

Tommy's Drive-In. 2708 Gastonia Dallas Hwy.; (704) 922-3849. Located on US 321, Tommy's is an old-fashioned drive-in with burgers, shakes, and onion rings. The menu also extends to fried chicken and barbecue, too. Open Mon through Thurs 10 a.m. to 9 p.m., Fri and Sat 9 a.m. to 10 p.m. $.

kings mountain

Not to be confused with the battle that occurred in Blacksburg, South Carolina, several miles to the southwest, Kings Mountain has gained some notoriety in its own respect as a small, warm community. It was so named in 1874 because it was the community closest to the battle location of the same name. It, too, is easily accessible from I-85. Highway signs make it easy to find. There is also an **NC Welcome Center** on I-85 at mile marker 2 in Kings Mountain (704-937-7861) that has information on area attractions and accommodations. It is accessible to northbound traffic.

getting there

To get to Kings Mountain from Dallas, you will want to backtrack. Take US 321 south to I-85 and travel west about 10 minutes to Kings Mountain.

where to go

Catawba Two Kings Casino. 538 Kings Mountain Blvd.; (704) 750-7777; twokingscasino .com. This casino was opened in 2021 by the Catawba Indian Reservation with a name that honors 18th century Catawba Chief King Hagler and the city where it's located. At press time it had limited facilities for gambling, dining and entertainment with plans for extravagant additions in the coming years.

Crowders Mountain State Park. 522 Park Office Ln.; (704) 853-5375; ncparks.gov. Crowders Mountain, rising 800 feet above the surrounding terrain and 1,625 feet above sea level, is popular among rock climbers because of its 150-foot sheer vertical cliffs. It and the adjacent Pinnacle's Peak, at 1,705 feet, are remnants of an ancient mountain range from which the Appalachian range was formed. Hiking trails vary from easy to strenuous and feature mountain laurel, wildflowers, and an extensive number of birds. Fishing is permitted at the lake near the park office, where visitors can rent a canoe for a modest fee. The office also houses a small nature center on the mountain's history and ecology. The park is typically open during daylight hours.

Kings Mountain Historical Museum. 100 E. Mountain St.; (704) 739-1019; kingsmoun tainmuseum.org. The museum presents seasonal rotating exhibits from its collection of 1860s vintage clothing, World War I and II memorabilia, textiles, and archival collections of documents and photos. The historical society also owns two nearby local homes: the Barber House, circa 1810–1840, and the Cornwell House, circa 1876, both located behind the main exhibit hall and available only for special events or by appointment. The grounds, however, are open to the public during normal operating hours. Open Tues through Sat 10 a.m. to 4 p.m.

> ## american legion world series

*After 85 years, the **American Legion Baseball league** has found a permanent home for its World Series in the city of Shelby, a few minutes west of Kings Mountain on US 74. Nearly 100,000 athletes between the ages of 15 and 19 from all 50 states and Canada participate in the league built to foster sportsmanship, healthy living, and active citizenship. Today it is recognized as one of the highest levels of amateur baseball competition. After a couple of trial runs, in 2011, the league established Shelby's Keeter Stadium (230 E. Dixon Blvd.) as the home of its championship to be held each August.*

*The honor has helped facilitate the growth of fun things to do throughout the area, including the establishment of the **Earl Scruggs Center** (103 S. Lafayette St.; 704-487-6233; earlscruggscenter.org), a museum to honor the famed banjo player in the former Cleveland County Courthouse, and the **Don Gibson Theater** (318 S. Washington St.; 704-487-8114; dongibsontheater.com), named for two country music talents who have ties to the area. Recent years have also seen a growth in Shelby's arts community and the establishment of a small wine-producing district.*

where to eat & stay

The Inn of the Patriots. 301 Cleveland Ave., Grover; (704) 937-2940; theinnofthepatriots .com. An interesting bed-and-breakfast located in the town of Grover that is accessible to all points of interest. Built in 1879 by Dr. Alfred Frederick Hambright, it is the brainchild of Marti Mongiello, a former White House chef. Guests stay at the inn to eat among elegant decor and furnishings that reflect an 18th-century theme. $$.

day trip 02

west

The hilly area from Hendersonville to Flat Rock was once a hunting ground for the Cherokee, and in the early 1800s became a refuge from the sweltering southern heat for the wealthy in Charleston and other cities. Writer Carl Sandburg chose this area as his home, and Thomas Wolfe referenced a statue in Oakwood Cemetery, located near downtown Hendersonville, in his novel *Look Homeward, Angel*. The area is famous now for its apples and apple festival, but there is more deep down at the core of this great day trip. For more information stop in at **Henderson County Travel & Tourism** (201 S. Main St., Hendersonville; 800-828-4244, 828-693-9708; visithendersonville.org, historicflatrockinc.com).

flat rock

The Village of Flat Rock has always been a tourist destination, but the families from South Carolina's Lowcountry didn't necessarily come here just for a little R&R. Beginning in the early part of the 19th century, they came to escape epidemic outbreaks of yellow fever and malaria. Many of Charleston's wealthy built large summer estates, which still exist today. These structures and the entire village, in fact, are on the National Register of Historic Places.

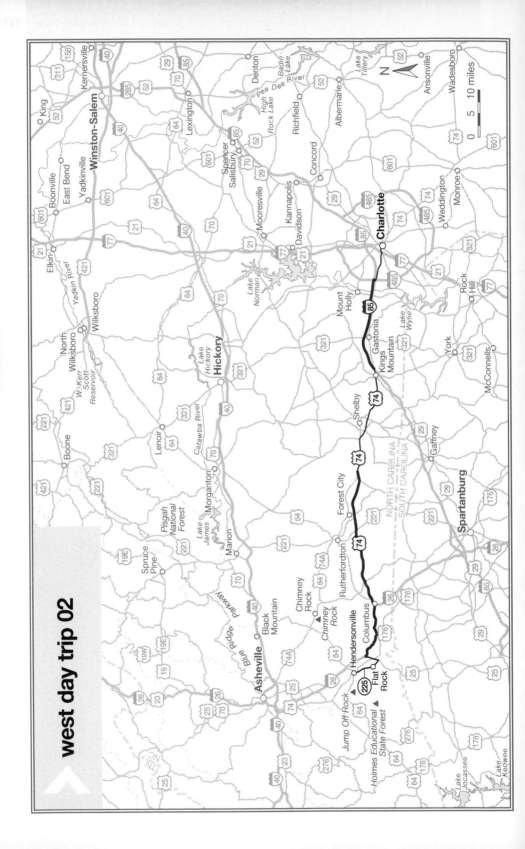

west day trip 02

getting there

This day trip begins about an hour and 45 minutes from Charlotte. Head west on I-85 and take US 74 West from Kings Mountain. US 74 merges with I-26 North near Tryon. From I-26 take exit 64, SR 25 South to Zirconia and then travel north on SR 225 to Flat Rock.

where to go

Carl Sandburg Home National Historic Site. 81 Carl Sandburg Ln.; (828) 693-4178; nps .gov/carl. Carl Sandburg won two Pulitzer Prizes but only received an eighth-grade education. A prolific poet, historian, author, and lecturer, Sandburg spent the final 22 years of his life, which ended in 1967, at this 1838 estate, Connemara. Known as the "Poet of the People," Sandburg was Abraham Lincoln's biographer, but he wrote most about the struggle of the American working class. Today the site preserves the dairy goat farm his wife, Lilian, operated and displays more than 65,000 artifacts from Sandburg's life and work. The site offers walking trails on 264 acres where visitors can explore nature or sit on the same rock on which Sandburg sat and asked the question "Who am I, where have I been, and where am I going?" Admission to the site is free. Thirty-minute guided tours cost $5 for visitors ages 16 and over and are offered Thurs through Sun at 11 a.m., 1, and 2 p.m. The site is open daily during daylight hours except Christmas Day, the home and visitor center is open Thurs through Sun 10 a.m. to 3 p.m.

Flat Rock Playhouse. 2661 Greenville Hwy.; (828) 693-0731; flatrockplayhouse.org. The State Theatre of North Carolina is acclaimed in the industry and features the Vagabond Players. The playhouse, founded in 1952, is located in a barnlike structure and fits appropriately on the campus, which also includes the 1885 Lowndes House, where the administrative offices are located, and other structures that house the theater's education programs, storage and production units, and rehearsal halls. The theater runs a six-month season, presenting selections for every age and taste. Usually on the schedule are Broadway hits, classics, comedies, and even whodunits. It also offers holiday productions after the regular season concludes in October. Matinees and evening performances are presented Wed through Sun mid-Apr through mid-Oct.

St. John in the Wilderness Episcopal Church. 1895 Greenville Hwy.; (828) 693-9783; stjohnflatrock.org. The Flat Rock area wasn't reserved for only the wealthy of Charleston. It also became the home of Charles Baring, a wealthy banker from England, who built Mountain Lodge for his wife, Susan. As Baring continued to accumulate land in the area (as much as 3,000 acres at one point), he began to desire a house of worship, in the middle of this Baptist stronghold, that was loyal to the Church of England. So in 1833 he built this private chapel, and in 1836 deeded it to the Bishop of North Carolina. The church's graveyard includes plots for signers of the Declaration of Independence, members of the

Confederate government, and others significant to area history. Open Tues through Sun 9 a.m. to 4 p.m.

where to shop

The Gallery at Flat Rock. 2702 Greenville Hwy.; (828) 698-7000; galleryflatrock.com. Contemporary art is at the heart of this fine gallery. Owner Suzanne Camarata represents more than 60 local, regional, and national artists. In addition to fine art, you will also find jewelry, cards, books, and other gifts.

The Wrinkled Egg. 2710 SR 225; (828) 696-3998; thewrinkledegg.com. The Wrinkled Egg is at the heart of this small shopping district known as "Little Rainbow Row," a nod to the Charlestonians and their big Rainbow Row. It's located in the (circa 1890) building known until the 1980s as Peace's Grocery. It has developed a specialty in serving the summer campers who make their way here, but you will also find eclectic folk art and other local items.

where to eat

Flat Rock Village Bakery. 2710 Greenville Hwy.; (828) 693-1313; villagebakerync.com. The bakery offers organic wood-fired breads and pizzas, salads, and sandwiches. If you stop in for lunch, save room for pastries, brownies, cookies, and a cup of joe from a local blend. Open Mon through Sat 7 a.m. to 5 p.m., Sun 8 a.m. to 5 p.m. $.

Hubba Hubba Smokehouse. 2724 Greenville Hwy.; (828) 694-3551; hubbahubbasmoke house. squarespace.com. Barbecue is cooked low and slow in the backyard and served on the deck or in the courtyard. There's limited indoor seating and you might get a visit from a free-range chicken or friendly cat (in the outdoor seating area, that is.) It's a cash-only operation. Open Sun, Mon, and Thurs 11 a.m. to 3 p.m., Fri and Sat 11 a.m. to 7 p.m. Closed in winter. $.

Season's Restaurant. 86 Lily Pad Ln.; (828) 696-9094; hliresort.com/seasons. Located in Highland Lake Inn, the restaurant serves a healthy selection from its organic garden. Its dining options are among the more sophisticated in Flat Rock, with a menu that includes local trout, top cuts of steak, lamb, and more. Open Mon through Sat 11:30 a.m. to 2:30 p.m. and 5 to 9 p.m. as well as for Sunday brunch 10:30 a.m. to 2 p.m. $$$.

where to stay

Highland Lake Inn & Resort. 86 Lily Pad Ln.; (800) 635-5101; hlinn.com. This elegant retreat with several buildings and room types is nestled in the woods on a 26-acre site. A lake on site is just big enough for the complimentary canoes and paddleboats. Fancy hens, a peacock, and other animals rambling on the property add to the countryside atmosphere, complemented by a selection of games like badminton, croquet, and horseshoes. $$$.

Mansouri Mansion. 2905 Greenville Hwy.; (828) 693-6016; mansourimansion.com. Completed in the early 1850s on 28 rolling acres and originally known as the Farmers Hotel, this inn served as the first stagecoach stop along the Old Indian Trail. During the Civil War, Confederate soldiers were garrisoned here, and it is rumored that they hid gold and jewelry from Union troops and renegades in a secret room that is still accessible from one of the second-story rooms. Today the inn is on the National Register of Historic Places with unique expansive gardens and slate walkways. $$.

Mill House Lodge. 1150 W. Blue Ridge Rd.; (800) 736-6073; millhouselodge.com. Until the middle of the 20th century, this mill operated to produce ground corn and wheat. Today its seven lodges surround a seven-acre lake in the heart of Flat Rock. All units offer either a kitchenette or a full kitchen, which may come in handy for making breakfast before a day of sightseeing. $$.

hendersonville

It seems the sweet smell of apples hangs around for weeks following North Carolina's official Apple Festival on Labor Day weekend (see appendix on page 211 for more details). Production of red and golden delicious apples, galas, Rome beauties, and other varieties makes Henderson County the largest apple producer in North Carolina, which ranks seventh among all states in apple production. That farm life has merged with a rich history and a spectacular climate to create a unique tourist spot. The city's architecture is reflective of the late 19th and early 20th centuries. Downtown's designation on the National Register of Historic Places in 1988 led to a renaissance of sorts through much of the 1990s. Storefronts that were unoccupied for years, in some cases, were reopened as stores, galleries, restaurants, or other businesses. For additional information contact **Downtown Hendersonville Inc.** (828-697-2022; downtownhendersonville.org).

getting there

Hendersonville is about 10 minutes from Flat Rock on SR 225/Greenville Highway.

where to go

Elijah Mountain Gem Mine. 2120 Brevard Rd.; (828) 692-6560; elijahmountain.com. Emeralds and rubies, along with other stones, are often found at this tourist mining operation. Flumes are covered to make mining comfortable for patrons. Prices per bucket range from $14.99 to $300. Open daily 10 a.m. to 6 p.m.

Hands On! Children's Museum. 318 N. Main St.; (828) 697-8333; handsonwnc.org. This children's museum is reflective of the region with exhibits based on mountain life. It includes a grocery store, a costume theater, and even an apple seed to pie exhibit. Admission is $10 for all. Open Mon through Sat 9 a.m. to 5 p.m.

Henderson County Heritage Museum. 1 Historic Courthouse Sq.; (828) 694-1619; hendersoncountymuseum.com. Learn about the area's history at this center located in the old courthouse that now houses county offices. The story begins with the Cherokee who once hunted here and the pioneers who made the area their home in the wilderness. It houses documents, archives, artifacts, and other items. Free. Open Wed through Sat 10 a.m. to 5 p.m.

Hendersonville Depot. 650 Maple Street; (828) 890-8246; avmrc.com. When the first steam engine took on the Saluda Mountain Grade to Hendersonville in 1879, it might have said, "I think I can; I think I can." But it couldn't. The engine needed a help engine to push it up the steepest mainline standard-gauge railroad in the US. That didn't stop Southern Railway from running service to this town and eventually building this—a second, bigger depot. In 1911 regular routes of the Carolina Special began to run between Charleston and Cincinnati. Today the exterior paint has been restored to its original yellow color and a Southern Railway caboose is on display. The depot's baggage room houses the Apple Valley Model Railroad Club and its HO scale model railroad, a replica of Hendersonville, Asheville, Brevard, and Saluda. Free. Open Wed 1 to 3 p.m. and Sat 10 a.m. to 2 p.m.

Holmes Educational State Forest. 1299 Crab Creek Rd.; (828) 692-0100; ncesf.org. This small park offers a series of trails that are easy to navigate. "Talking trees" inform visitors about the variety of species living in the forest. Also on the site is an exhibit on fire control, including a watch tower and helicopter. Open 9 a.m. to 5 p.m. Tues through Sat and 11 a.m. to 6 p.m. Sat and Sun mid-Mar through late Nov, and Tues through Fri 9 a.m. to 5 p.m. the rest of the year.

Historic Johnson Farm. 3346 Haywood Rd.; (828) 891-6585; hendersoncountypublicschoolsnc.org. Now part of the Henderson County School System, Johnson Farm was built between 1876 and 1880. Additions were made up until 1923 as it became a popular tourist retreat. The main house was constructed of handmade bricks fired on site from French Broad River mud. It was the home of a wealthy tobacco farmer, Oliver Moss, and includes an elegant house, smokehouse, granary, blacksmith shop, barn, boarding house, and cottage. Sallie Johnson purchased the home early in the 20th century, and her sons donated it to the schools in 1987. It is listed on the National Register of Historic Places. The farm follows the school schedule, but the public is welcome. Admission is $10 for adults, $8 for students. Open Tues through Fri 8 a.m. to 2:30 p.m. Sept through May, Mon through Thurs 8 a.m. to 2:30 p.m. June through Aug. Guided tours are offered at 10:30 a.m. and 1:30 p.m.

Jump Off Rock. 4501 Laurel Park Hwy.; (828) 693-4840; laurelpark.org You can see Jump Off Rock from miles around, and the view from atop it is even more impressive. It juts out from the surrounding terrain like a monolithic diving board at an elevation of 3,100 feet, providing stunning views of the rolling hills of the Blue Ridge and Pisgah mountain ranges. Three trails offer easy, moderate, and difficult hiking challenges. Perhaps most interesting is the legend that more than 300 years ago a Cherokee maiden threw herself off the rock upon receiving news that her young chief had been killed in battle. According to the legend, you can see the ghost of the maiden on moonlit nights. Free. Open during daylight hours.

Mineral & Lapidary Museum of Henderson County. 400 N. Main St.; (828) 698-1977; mineralmuseum.org. Established in 1997, the Mineral and Lapidary Museum is the result of 15 years of work by the local gem and mineral society. It includes exhibits that range from gems, geodes, and fluorescent minerals to American Indian artifacts and even a replica of a skeletal T-Rex head. Free. Open Mon through Fri 1 to 5 p.m., Sat 11 a.m. to 5 p.m.

Aquarium & Shark Lab by Team ECCO. 511 N. Main St.; (828) 692-8386; teamecco. org. This attraction, a popular school field trip destination and research center, has blossomed from an 800-square-foot lab with a 90-gallon tank to serving more than 10,000 with its 2,000-gallon shark tank with more than 300 species. Open Wed through Fri 1 to 4 p.m. and Sat noon to 4 p.m. Admission is $6.75 for adults and $4.75 for children.

Western North Carolina Air Museum. 1340 E. Gilbert St.; (828) 698-2482; western northcarolinaairmuseum.com. More than a dozen restored and replica antique and vintage airplanes that date mostly to the 1930s and 1940s are displayed in two hangers at the Hendersonville Airport. Free. Open Wed, Sat, and Sun noon to 6 p.m., Sat 10 a.m. to 5 p.m. Apr through Oct; Wed, Sat, and Sun noon to 5 p.m. Nov through Mar.

where to shop

Curb Market. 221 N. Church St.; (828) 692-8012. All vendors at this farmers' market are required to be residents of Henderson County. Thus, shoppers get only homegrown and locally handmade products from people who have been doing business here for generations. Shoppers will find crafts, baked goods, jellies, plants, flowers, toys, and seasonal produce. The market has been in continuous operation since 1924. Open Tues, Thurs, and Sat 8 a.m. to 2 p.m. Apr through Dec; and Sat 8 a.m. to 1 p.m. Jan through Mar.

Granddads Apples. 2951 Chimney Rock Rd.; (828) 685-1685; granddadsapples.com. This farm, run by the same family for four generations, sells apples and pumpkins and a selection of other produce. The bakery sells tasty apple cider doughnuts and other goodies. There's also a corn maze and other seasonal activities.

Narnia Studios. 408 N. Main St.; (828) 697-6393; narniastudios.com. With a theme from the popular C.S. Lewis stories, this shop features flowers, fragrances, and fairies of all types. Open Mon through Sat 9:30 a.m. to 6:30 p.m.

Needful Things II. 10 Francis Rd.; (828) 686-8745. With 55,000 square feet and 200-some vendors you could easily spend three hours or so here. There is nice variety spread over two stories.

where to eat

Flat Rock Wood Room. 1501 Greenville Hwy.; (828) 435-1391; flatrockwoodroom.com. Woodfired Neapolitan pizzas and panino sandwiches of a broad variety are the specialty at this nice Hendersonville restaurant. It also serves barbecue and burgers. Open Wed, Thurs, and Sun 11:30 a.m. to 8 p.m., Fri and Sat 11:30 a.m. to 9 p.m. $$.

Hannah Flanagan's Pub & Eatery. 300 N. Main St.; (828) 696-1665; theoriginalhannah flanagans.com. This is a busy hangout for locals. A long list of beer matches up well with classic Irish dishes like corned beef and cabbage, fish and chips, and Reubens. You'll also find a selection of burgers, and the fried mushrooms on the appetizer menu are a must. Open daily 11 a.m. to 11 p.m. $$.

Mike's on Main. 303 N. Main St.; (828) 698-1616. This 1950s diner and soda shop even has occasional sock hops on Sat nights. The patty melt might really take you back. Open Mon through Thurs 8 a.m. to 7 p.m., Fri 8 a.m. to 9 p.m., Sat 8 a.m. to 7 p.m., Sun 8 a.m. to 5 p.m. $.

where to stay

1898 Waverly Inn. 783 N. Main St.; (828) 693-9193; waverlyinn.com. The rocking-chair front porch beckons at this inn on Main Street. The warm and friendly environment is accompanied by a host of amenities like a big DVD collection, board games, and sitting rooms. In addition to breakfast, the inn also offers fresh baked treats in the afternoon and wine and cheese at evening socials. $$$.

The Charleston Inn. 755 N. Main St.; (828) 693-6737; thecharleston.net. Among the larger bed-and-breakfasts in the area, formerly called the Claddagh, it is listed on the National Register of Historic Places. Its construction dates to the 1880s. The inn was originally named the Charleston Boarding House—a reference to a fishing village in Ireland. Several of the rooms have fireplaces and claw-foot tubs, but the wraparound porch can be enjoyed by all. $$.

Echo Mountain Inn. 2849 Laurel Park Hwy.; (828) 693-9626; echomountaininn.com. This inn overlooks Hendersonville and the surrounding area from one of the town's peaks. Constructed of local stone, the two-story inn has a handsome exterior and comfortable interior with lots of personality. Four-poster beds in two rooms add a touch of elegance, while other rooms have simpler homey touches. $$.

The Henderson. 201 3rd Ave. West; (828) 696-2001; thehendersonnc.com. Located downtown, this hotel is one of the few that remain from construction at the turn of the last century. Although it is a downtown storefront, the rooms are pretty and bright with immaculate attention to detail as in other area bed-and-breakfasts. The innkeepers also operate a gourmet restaurant here. $$.

The Melange Inn. 1230 5th Ave. West; (828) 697-5253. A popular and elegant wedding location, the Melange feels secluded but is within walking distance of popular attractions. Rooms are decorated with Victorian antiques but it lacks no modern amenity. $$$.

day trip 03

west

the land of waterfalls:
brevard

brevard

Known today as Transylvania County, this area was once part of the state of Georgia and was fought over by North and South Carolina. Brevard became part of the Old North State in 1811. It wasn't until 1861 that Transylvania was formed and so named because of the fact that there are more than 250 waterfalls in the county. Literally translated, Transylvania means "across the woods (or land)." At the heart of this day trip is Pisgah National Forest, which holds one of North Carolina's most popular waterfalls, Sliding Rock, giving proof that waterfall hunting is truly an interactive activity. It is also home to a puzzling population of unusual white squirrels.

getting there

Brevard is just two hours from Charlotte, traveling west on I-85 to US 74 at Kings Mountain. US 74 converges with I-26 at Tryon. Follow it west to US 64 west. From there it is less than 20 miles to the center of Brevard.

where to go

Brevard Music Center. 349 Andante Ln.; (828) 862-2100; brevardmusic.org. Since 1936 the Brevard Music Center has offered study opportunities to some of the country's most promising young musicians. It presents a seven-week festival featuring those students and

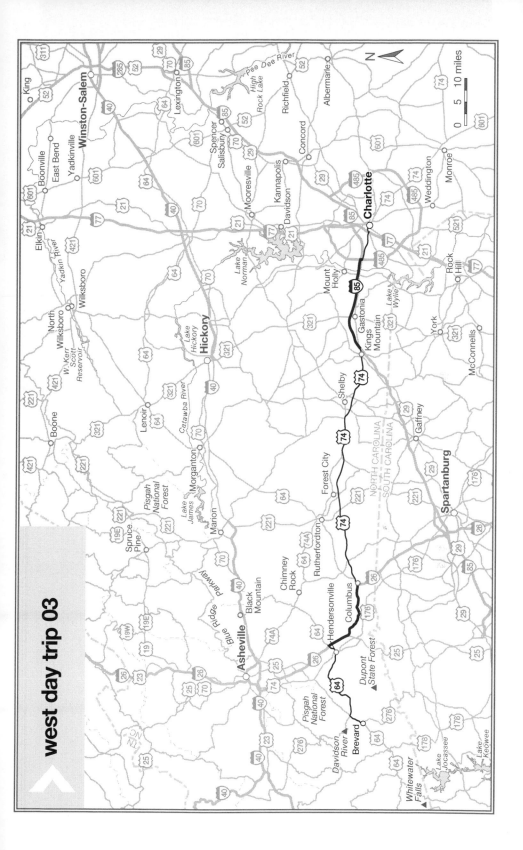

west day trip 03

professionals each summer. The center also works in conjunction with the Paul Porter Center at Brevard College.

The Cradle of Forestry in America & Forest Discovery Center. 11250 Pisgah Hwy. (US 276); (828) 877-3130. Congress set aside this 6,500-acre site to commemorate the beginnings of a more conservation-minded forestry industry more than a century ago, when George Vanderbilt began buying land in this area. A visitor center features a short film about Vanderbilt and other pioneers in forestry conservation. An exhibit gives examples of how forestry conservation has advanced in the past century. The center offers young children the Forest Fun exhibit with puppets, puzzles, and costumes. Admission is $6 for ages 16 and older, $3 for children. Open daily 10 a.m. to 5 p.m.

Downtown Sculpture Tour. (828) 884-2787. This tour is both a nod to the cultural community in Brevard and a teachable moment about the wildlife in the area. It includes 20 works of woodland creatures in steel, bronze, copper, marble, and stone.

Pisgah Center for Wildlife Education. 1401 Fish Hatchery Rd.; (828) 877-4423. Featuring life in mountain waters and on land, this center includes a trail with interactive exhibits, including realistic models of animals typically found in the forest. A trout raceway where brook, rainbow, and brown trout are bred for stocking mountain waters helps visitors understand the breeding process. **The Bobby N. Setzer State Fish Hatchery,** adjacent to the center, is the state's largest trout hatchery. The facility consists of 16 indoor rearing tanks and 50 outdoor raceways, where the fish are grown until they are catchable size. A nature center features exhibits on native wildlife and includes several habitats with fish, frogs, salamanders, and snakes. Free. Open Mon through Sat 8 a.m. to 4:45 p.m. Closed on Easter weekend and other state holidays except for Good Friday, Memorial Day, Independence Day, and Labor Day.

Pisgah Forest Riding Stables. 476 Pisgah Dr.; (828) 883-8258; pisgahstables.com. These stables offer one- to three-hour rides through the forest trails that feature waterfalls or mountain vistas. Riders must be at least 7 years old. Cost is $35 to $100 per person. Open Mon through Sat Apr through Oct from 9 a.m. to 5 p.m.

Pisgah National Forest. (828) 877-3265; fs.usda.gov. This expansive national forest offers a half million acres of some of the country's best outdoor activities. Opportunities for hiking, camping, picnicking, fishing, and horseback riding abound. The forest actually covers 12 North Carolina counties, but its best offerings are accessible by entering on US 276 at the intersection of US 64/280 in Brevard. Start exploring at the ranger station on the right, one and a half miles inside the forest entrance. Here you can pick up information about the forest and the surrounding area. A small nature center gives visitors an idea of the plant and wildlife species they will likely experience. Davidson River cuts through the forest and typically runs along the forest road. Several stores and outfitters at the entrance of the forest rent inner tubes that allow for a lazy afternoon drifting down the river. To make things easier, a designated driver can drop off riders upstream and pick them up at a predetermined location. Roadside camping is permitted for free on a first-come, first-served basis, but private facilities are also available for a fee. Among the attractions are the Pink Beds area, a valley that features spectacular mountain laurel, rhododendron, and azaleas that bloom in spring and summer. Public access areas are generally open during daylight hours.

Sliding Rock. US 276 about seven miles from the ranger station; (828) 877-3350. Mother Nature has provided this exhilarating slide with 11,000 gallons of chilly 60-degree water rushing over the rock every minute. Sliding down the rock is a quick but memorable 60-foot trip that ends with a plunge into a deep pool. Lifeguards are on duty. Admission is $5 for sliders and non-sliders. Open 10 a.m. to 5:30 p.m. Memorial Day to Labor Day.

Waterfall Trail. With 250 waterfalls near Brevard, a day trip just won't do it. Local marketers say this area has the largest concentration of falls in the country, and setting out on the road to find them takes the day-tripper to some captivating sites. Space won't permit the listing of all the waterfalls, but here's a short list of the most interesting and prominent falls in the Brevard area. Most don't have addresses, but we've provided directions. You can also use an interactive component at https://explorebrevard.com/the-great-outdoors/waterfalls.

Hooker Falls. This waterfall is located in Dupont State Forest on the Little River at the former grist mill near Cascade Lake. Travel south from Brevard on US 276, take a left on Cascade Lake Road, and travel two and a half miles before taking a right on Staton Road.

Triple Falls. You can walk to Triple Falls from the Hooker Falls parking lot in Dupont State Park, too. Cross over Staton Road and hike upstream to find these three falls.

High Falls. At 150 feet this is the tallest of the Dupont State Park waterfalls. Continue upstream to High Falls Trail. Take a left, walk 2,000 feet, and take a right to stay on the well-marked trail. High Falls is accessible by either of the two trails near here.

Bridal Veil Falls. One of the area's favorite falls, Bridal Veil was featured in the movie *The Last of the Mohicans.* You can actually walk under the waterfall. Find Bridal Veil in Dupont State Park off Conservation Road.

Looking Glass Falls. Located just off US 276 (Forest Road) about five miles into Pisgah National Forest, the 65-foot-high waterfall is easily accessible via stairs leading to the base.

Moore Cove Falls. About one mile from Looking Glass, find a small footbridge from a parking lot that leads to the waterfall about a half mile away.

Slick Rock Falls. Travel about three and a half miles from the ranger station at the forest entrance, and take the first left on Forest Road 475B. The trailhead is located about one mile from the Forest Road on the right. The 35-foot-high waterfall is just a short walk up the trail.

Cove Creek Falls. The hike to Cove Creek is a little more challenging at one mile, but this waterfall is worth the trip. Take US 276 3.5 miles from the ranger station and turn left on Forest Road 475. Take this road to Cove Creek Group Campground just beyond the state fish hatchery and park there.

Falls at Graveyard Fields. There's not a real graveyard here. The waterfall derives its name from the tree stumps in the surrounding area. Get here by traveling 14 miles on US 276; take a right to access the Blue Ridge Parkway. Turn left and travel south on the parkway. Park at Graveyard Fields Overlook at milepost 419 and take the short but moderately difficult hike from there.

Toxaway Falls. Take SR 215 to US 64 west. Travel 14 miles. At 125 feet, this waterfall is one of the larger falls in the area. US 64 actually crosses over the top of it.

Whitewater Falls. At 411 feet, this narrow waterfall is the tallest east of the Mississippi. It is located 18 miles west of Brevard on US 64 and is easily accessible down a short paved path.

Connestee Falls. This double, crisscrossing waterfall is one of the most interesting. Take US 276 south of Brevard five and a half miles. A number of trails lead to Connestee Falls from the parking area.

where to shop

Art Galleries. A half dozen art galleries are located along E. and W. Main Streets in downtown Brevard. Travelers will also find a 13-mile stretch of shops, studios, potters, and artists of all types on US 276 south of Brevard to the state line. For more information contact the Transylvania County Arts Council, 349 S. Caldwell St.; (828) 884-2787.

D.D. Bullwinkles. 60 E. Main St..; (828) 862-4700; ddbullwinkels.com. This general store features a soda fountain and grill. It seems you can find everything here, from blue jeans to jellies and jams to pottery and jewelry. Open Mon through Thurs 10 a.m. to 5:30 p.m., Sun 11:30 a.m. to 5:30 p.m.

O. P. Taylors. 16 S. Broad St., (828) 883-2309; optaylors.com. Owner John Taylor promotes this as the coolest toy store on the planet. At more than 6,000 square feet, this toy store is part of a dying breed that offers just about any toy you could imagine. Taylor has established a store that does everything in a big, wacky fashion. Promotions include singing or tap dancing for a discount at the register. Open Mon through Sat 10 a.m. to 6 p.m. and Sun noon to 5 p.m.

White Squirrel Shoppe. 6 W. Main St.; (828) 877-3530; whitesquirrelshoppe.com. Pick up a souvenir white squirrel key chain or any number of other white squirrels in this fun gift shop. Open Mon through Thurs 9:30 a.m. to 5:30 p.m., Fri and Sat 9:30 a.m. to 6 p.m., Sun 1 to 5 p.m.

where to eat

Jordan Street Café. 48 W. Jordan St.; (828) 883-2558; thejordanstreetcafe.com. Burgers, wraps, salads, and more are offered at this downtown restaurant. The tasty and creative desserts are all offerings of owner Susan Nemath. Open Thurs through Sun for dinner only. $$.

Mayberry's Soups and Sandwiches. 30 W. Main St.; (828) 862-8646; mayberrys.com. The folks at Mayberry's aren't having deli meats shipped in; they roast all their meats themselves. And no cans for the soup; all are homeade. Open for breakfast Fri through Sun, for lunch daily, and dinner Mon through Sat. $$.

The Square Root. 33 Times Arcade Alley; (828) 884-6171; squarerootrestaurant.com. The old Brevard newspaper building is now home to this charming restaurant just inside a downtown alley. Selections on the menu include comfort food like meatloaf and comfort food with a twist like curry meatballs. Open Mon through Thurs 11 a.m. to 9 p.m., Sunday brunch 11 a.m. to 3 p.m., and dinner 5 to 9 p.m. $$.

where to stay

Boulder Ridge Bed and Breakfast. 74 Lazy Branch Rd., Pisgah Forest; (828) 577-1848; boulderridgebedandbreakfast.com. Since this inn is located in the forest, it feels secluded, yet it is only a few minutes from downtown Brevard. The mountaintop home also affords spectacular views and nice accommodations. $$.

The Bromfield Inn. 60 Woodside Dr.; (828) 577-0916; thebromfieldinn.com. Right out of the roaring '20s comes this grey, stone house that's just a short walk from downtown Brevard. Six bedrooms are offered for nightly stays that also come with use of quiet courtyards and luxurious amenities. Start your day with a three-course gourmet breakfast. $$$.

The Inn at Brevard. 315 E. Main St.; (828) 884-2105; theinnatbrevard.com. Located on 100 spectacular acres, this inn is one of the nicest in Brevard. It is a European-style mansion with big white columns in front, but the Yagers, who own the property, still provide plenty of southern charm. A collection of renaissance art is on display in the home's public areas and rooms. $$$.

day trip 04

west

Chimney Rock, purchased in 2009 as a state park, is one of the state's most recognizable and visible natural attractions, but Gen-Xers might also recognize another scene on this day trip. This adventure traces the steps of Jennifer Grey and Patrick Swazye in the 1987 film *Dirty Dancing,* filmed largely at Lake Lure, which also offers some of the state's most spectacular views. The expansive area is known as Hickory Nut Gorge, a swath of land created by the Rocky Broad River slicing through the hills. The gorge in the foothills between the Blue Ridge and Great Smoky Mountains is home to dozens of rare plants and a handful of rare animal species, making it one of the most significant centers of biodiversity in the state.

lake lure

The 720-acre Lake Lure was created with the completion of a dam on the Rocky Broad River in 1926, submerging the small community that was there. In 1931 the power company that built the dam sold it to Carolina Mountain Corporation. It would be more than 35 years before the community would buy the lake and take control of its recreational opportunities. Today the stunning lake has 27 miles of shoreline with resort homes, accommodations, restaurants, and attractions.

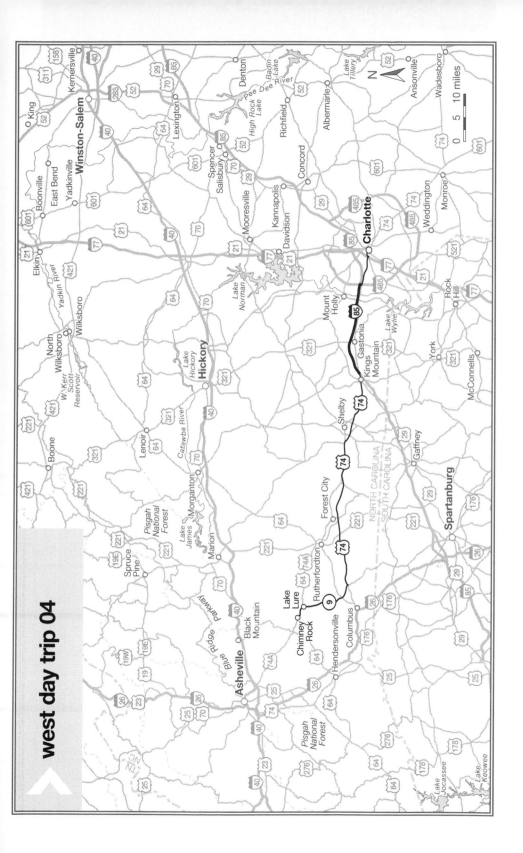

west day trip 04

getting there

Located in the foothills of the Blue Ridge Mountains, Lake Lure is less than 100 miles and two hours from Charlotte via I-85 West and US 74 West at Kings Mountain. From US 74, take exit 167 to SR 9. Arrive in Lake Lure in 15 minutes.

where to go

The Beach at Lake Lure. The large sandy beach is accessible from Memorial Highway on the southern edge of the lake, surrounded by beautiful vistas of the surrounding mountains. An adjacent water park has a water slide, water cannons, and other games. Lifeguards are on duty. Admission is $10 for adults, $9 for seniors, and $8 for children ages 4 to 12. Open daily 10 a.m. to 6 p.m. Memorial Day through Labor Day.

Cedar Creek Stables. 542 Cedar Creek Rd.; (828) 625-2811; cedarcreekstables.com. The stable offers one- and two-hour trail rides as well as pony rides for children under 8. The stable also operates a small gem mine and petting park. Rides start at $35 per person. Open daily 8 a.m. to 5 p.m.

Lake Lure Flowering Bridge. 3070 Memorial Hwy.; lakelurefloweringbridge.org. Giving even full botanical gardens a run for their money, this beautiful and creative display is maintained by the Friends of Lake Lure Flowering Bridge. It includes more than 2,000 species of plants maintained all by volunteers to create a stunning display. The 30 gardens are always open and always free.

Lake Lure Tours. Departing from Lake Lure Marina, 2930 Memorial Hwy.; (877) 386-4255; lakeluretours.com. Covered boats take day-trippers on a two-hour tour of the lake. A guide explains the lake's history, spins tales, helps examine nature, and ventures to some of the more interesting spots, including the area where Jennifer Grey practiced the lift dance move in the water with Patrick Swayze in *Dirty Dancing*. Admission is $20 for adults, $17 for seniors, and $10 for children. Tours are offered daily beginning at 10 a.m. Last tour time changes seasonally. The marina also offers lunch and dinner cruises.

the ghosts of lake lure

Flooding a town to build a resort is just asking for trouble. Sometimes when the air is still and the water's calm in the middle of the lake, you can still hear church bells ring. The legends (and tour guides at Lake Lure Tours) say that when the power company flooded the area and forced the 12 farming families off their land, a spirit remained in the town's church. Because it's at a depth of 130 feet, it has been miraculously preserved—its wood siding never rotted (they say). Even today, nearly a century later (they also say), if you listen carefully you can still hear those bells.

where to eat

The Highlands Kitchen + Bar. 454 Memorial Hwy.; (828) 436-4023; thehighlandskitchen bar.com. The lunch menu at Highlands that includes chicken and waffles, tacos and burgers give way to filet mignon and rack of lamb at dinner. Its good and comfortable anytime. $$-$$$.

LakeHouse Restaurant. 1020 Memorial Hwy.; (828) 625-4075; lakehouselakelure.com. Formery Larkin's, the LakeHouse offers casual dining overlooking the lake. Start with spinach artichoke dip and finish with a thick steak. At lunch get a burger or barbecue. Open daily 11:30 a.m. to 9:30 p.m. $–$$.

Veranda Restaurant. 2771 Memorial Hwy.; (828) 625-2525; lakelure.com. Beautiful antiques adorn the dining room in The 1927 Lake Lure Inn & Spa overlooking the lake. Food includes local trout and steaks. Dinner is served Wed through Sat 5 to 8 p.m. The inn is also famous for its lavish brunch, served every Sun 10:30 a.m. to 2:30 p.m. You might want to hit the Bloody Mary bar, too. $$$.

where to stay

The 1927 Lake Lure Inn & Spa. 2771 Memorial Hwy.; (828) 625-2525; lakelure.com. This grand 1927 hotel, built when the lake was filled, is the center of activity for the town. It has been restored to its original grandeur. Amenities include the Irongate Spa and an antiques tour. $$.

Lodge on Lake Lure. 361 Charlotte Dr.; (828) 625-2789; lodgeonlakelure.com. This country inn is located on a beautiful hillside garden lot with spectacular views. It offers 16 rooms on the lake where guests can fish, swim, or canoe. In addition to breakfast, the inn offers afternoon tea. $$$.

chimney rock

Chimney Rock opened to the public in 1885, but it wasn't until Lucius B. Morse began purchasing the rock and surrounding property in 1902 that it would set out to be the large popular attraction it is today. In those days tourists came by horseback from nearby railroad stations, but Morse, who also had the vision for developing Lake Lure, realized its potential. He and his brothers began to build trails, bridges, and steps to help visitors navigate the terrain. With a population of fewer than 200 people, the town of Chimney Rock is now a popular tourist destination, but its down-home mountain charm is preserved.

getting there

Chimney Rock is about five minutes north on SR 9, which merges with US 64 and US 74A at this point.

where to go

Chimney Rock Gemstone Mine. 397 Main St.; (828) 625-5524; chimneyrockgemmine .com. Here guests pan for gold and gemstones; the mine guarantees a find for everyone. Bucket prices range from $9 to $5,000. Open daily 10 a.m. to 6 p.m.

Chimney Rock Park. US 64/74A; (828) 625-9611; chimneyrockpark.com. Visible from Lake Lure, Chimney Rock is the newest of the state parks and includes more than 4,000 acres. The chimney is a 315-foot rock at an elevation of nearly 2,500 feet. From the top, which you can reach via elevator or steps, you can see more than 75 miles away—almost back to Charlotte. Other attractions at the park include 404-foot Hickory Nut Falls, the Opera Box with outcroppings underfoot and overhead, Devil's Head, and Exclamation Point. Hiking the park trails offers an opportunity to peer inside Moonshiner's Cave. Admission is $17 for adults and $8 for children ages 6 to 15; reduced rates in winter. Open daily 8:30 a.m. to 5:30 p.m. Apr through Oct, daily 10 a.m. to 4:30 p.m. the rest of the year. Closed Tues and Wed Jan through Apr.

Rocky Broad River Walk. Main Street. Among the shops and attractions of Chimney Rock Village is the scenic Rocky Broad River. Have a picnic at the tables between the roadway and river, then mosey down to the river and get your feet wet.

where to shop

Chimney Rock Village, with an old-time country atmosphere, is located on both sides of Main Street and includes shops where you can get a bite of fudge or buy housewares and souvenirs. Park and shop here—most storefronts have only a parking place or two. Here are a few examples of what you will find:

Bubba O'Leary's General Store. 385 Main St.; (828) 625-2479; bubbaolearys.com. This old-timey store offers everything under the sun, from candy and coffee to hiking boots. Open daily 10 a.m. to 6 p.m.

Chimney Sweeps. 400 Main St.; (828) 625-9000. Pick up souvenirs, including moccasins, dolls, and other American Indian items. Open daily 10 a.m. to 6:30 p.m.

Gales Chimney Rock Shop. 418 Main St.; (828) 625-4126. Gales is probably the oldest of existing shops, having been here since 1947. This eclectic store offers unique souvenirs and a look back on the area's history.

Mountain Traders. 410 Main St.; (828) 625-9801. Handcrafted jewelry, wind chimes, and other home decor are offered here. Open daily 10 a.m. to 6 p.m.

Native Rest Candles. 382 Main St.; nativesrestcandles.com. Environmentally responsible soy candles are offered for sale here.

Willow Creek. 375 Main St.; (828) 625-1111. This shop sells mountain crafts and packaged foods you can sample before buying. Open 10 a.m. to 5 p.m. with some extended hours on weekends.

where to eat

Chimney Rock Brewing Company. 461 Main St.; (828) 436-5461; chimneyrockbrewing .net. The brewery and tap room has four spectacular decks that extend to the Rocky Broad River. The food menu extends to England with European flavors like bangers and mash, fish and chips and Shepherd's pie. $$.

The Old Rock Cafe. 431 Main St.; (828) 625-2329; oldrockcafe.com. Located at the entrance of Chimney Rock Park, this full-service restaurant has a deck on the river. It serves sandwiches, salads, and burgers. Handcrafted beers are also available. Hours coincide with Chimney Rock Park. $.

where to stay

Broad River Inn. 339 Main St.; (828) 625-8870; broadriverinn.com. Beautifully landscaped, this elegant inn offers an amazing location and accommodations that include jacuzzi tubs, private balconies, and more amenities in the middle of all the action at Chimney Rock. $$$.

Carter Lodge. 273 Main St.; (828) 625-8844; carterlodge.com. Located at the base of Chimney Rock, the Carter Lodge comes with its own fishing stream. The rooms are simple, but clean and comfortable. The exterior might remind you of a ranch house. Balconies overlook the Rocky Broad River. $.

The Esmeralda. 910 Main St.; (828) 625-2999; theesmeralda.com. This is a beautiful mountain lodge with a stone fireplace and hand-hewn logs in the lobby. The big leather couches beg you to set here awhile. The rooms are four-star quality, but the atmosphere is that of a familiar bed-and-breakfast. Though its style is largely rustic, it comes with contemporary touches. The Esmeralda closed in winter 2023 for renovations. $$–$$$.

Hickory Nut Falls Family Campground. 639 Main St.; (828) 625-4014; hickorynutfalls familycampground.com. Close to town, this campground offers tent and trailer camping. Several tent sites have covered decks. $.

northwest

>>>

day trip 01

northwest

not secondhand furniture:
hickory, lenoir

Like a well-crafted mortise-and-tenon joint, the Hickory area has fashioned a substantial tourist spot around a furniture industry that has supported this area for more than a century. Names like Bernhardt, Thomasville, Kincaid, and Broyhill dominate the region. But after the new dining room suite is ordered for delivery, you can enjoy an afternoon of arts and science on Hickory's Salt Block or window shopping in the town of Lenoir. This certainly isn't a tourist trap, but it's not the countryside either. It's a pleasant blend of the best of both worlds.

The **Hickory Metro Convention & Visitor Bureau** is a great resource for things to see and do, and it can help guide you through what first appears to be a maze of furniture dealers. Contact the fine folks at the bureau by calling (800) 509-2444, or visit them online at visithickorymetro.com.

hickory

This day trip begins in a city whose name originated from a tavern. Hickory Tavern was built of logs under a big hickory tree in the 1850s. Apparently it was a pretty popular place. The name stuck, and the city of Hickory Tavern was established in 1863, becoming simply Hickory in 1873. The city's proximity to wood resources and stable transportation led to the establishment of Hickory Manufacturing Company in 1902 and a host of others that would follow suit.

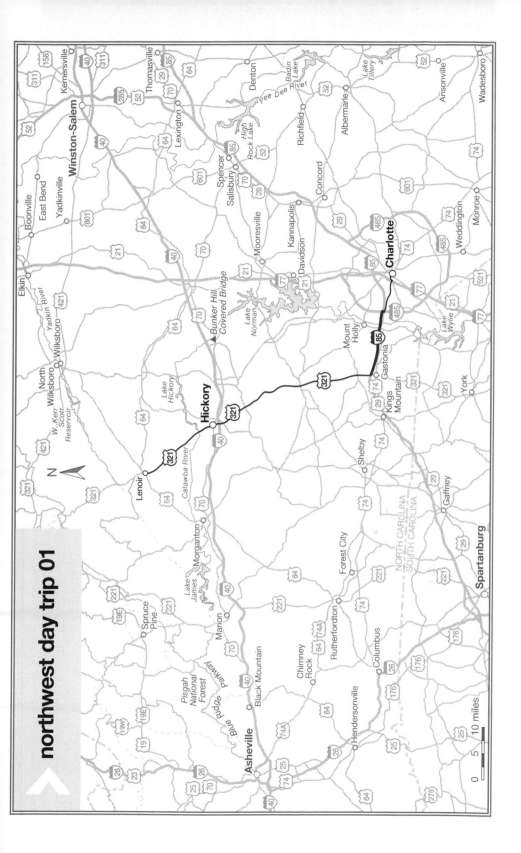

northwest day trip 01

The massive Hickory Furniture Mart with more than 100 furniture and home decor retailers is the heart of the retail industry. The Salt Block is simply the city's offering of "Science, Art and Literature Together," but it has added much to the traveler's experience.

getting there

You will find little difference in the route you choose from Charlotte to Hickory. Heading west on I-85 to US 321 north is the shortest and might prove the quickest at just more than an hour. Departing from north of the city, you might choose the slightly longer I-77 North to I-40 West route, putting you in the heart of Hickory in just over an hour. Hickory is a bit of a maze when it comes to roads. Numerically named roads with directional qualifiers might give you pause. Your GPS will likely work, but you might want to confirm directions with a detailed printed map.

where to go

Catawba Science Center. 243 3rd Ave. Northeast; (828) 322-8169; catawbascience.org. Most science centers focus on things to push, pull, turn, and trip to help kids learn about scientific phenomena. Families can do that at the Catawba Science Center, but adults can also learn about organic gardening, or take in a lunch and learn or other lecture. By day, families come to check out the aquarium of sharks, stingrays, frogs, and fish. They learn about the night sky in the astronomy exhibit or in the Millholland Planetarium. They learn, hands-on, about nature and technology. Admission is $12 for adults, $10 for seniors and for youths ages 3 to 18. Admission includes the planetarium. Open Tues through Sat 10 a.m. to 4 p.m., Sun 1 to 4 p.m.

Catawba Valley Furniture Museum. 2220 US 70 Southeast; (800) 462-6278; hickoryfurniture.com. Located on the ground level of the Hickory Furniture Mart, this museum traces the roots of the area's furniture industry and presents a family tree of furniture-making clans. Vintage tools, a reproduction of an early woodworking shop, and some of the first furniture produced here are on display. Free. Open Mon through Sat 9 a.m. to 6 p.m.

Harper House. 310 N. Center St.; (828) 465-0383; catawbahistory.org. The Hickory History Center and Catawba County Historical Society, which preserve and operate a number of area historical facilities, are based in this circa 1887 Victorian home. Built by local banker Daniel Webster Shuler, the house passed to several owners until 1923, when the Harper family purchased it. The most notable features of the home are the ornate brasswork, the stained-glass window in the foyer, and the silhouettes of the Harpers' friends on the walls of the attic, where they entertained during Prohibition.

Moved to the same site in 2004, the Craftsman-style Lyerly House, circa 1912, was built by E. Josephine Bonniwell Lyerly and her husband, Eubert Lyerly. A mayor of Hickory, Lyerly was owner and president of Elliott Knitting Mills, president of Clay Printing Company,

and publisher of the *Hickory Daily Record* at its 1915 inception. Also architecturally significant, it houses an exhibit on area history. Tours of the Harper House are $10; admission to
Bonniwell-Lyerly House is free. Open Thurs through Sat 9 a.m. to 4 p.m.

Hickory Museum of Art. 243 3rd Ave. Northeast; (828) 327-8576; hickoryart.org. Founded
in 1944, the Hickory Museum of Art is the second-oldest art museum in the state. Now
located in what was Claremont High School, its permanent collection includes a wide range
of American art in a number of media. It also hosts temporary exhibits from other museums
and private collections. Free. Open Wed through Sat 10 a.m. to 4 p.m., Sun 1 to 4 p.m.

Maple Grove Historical Museum. 542 2nd St. Northeast; (828) 322-4731; hickoryland
marks.org. The Hickory Landmarks Society is responsible for this and other architectural
restorations in the community. Listed on the National Register of Historic Places, Maple
Grove is a restored Italianate-style house completed in 1883, and one of the city's oldest
remaining homes. This was the home of Adolphus Lafayette Shuford, one of Hickory Tavern's founding fathers. The two-story frame house has a distinctive two-tier front porch and
simple but intricate interior and exterior detail. It's furnished with authentic Victorian furnishings. Free. Open Mon through Fri 9 a.m. to 5 p.m.

Propst House. 534 3rd Ave. Northwest; (828) 322-4731; hickorylandmarks.org. This Second Empire–style cottage with French detail was competed in 1883 and is listed on the
National Register of Historic Places. *House Beautiful* said it was a "Victorian gem," built by
J. Summie Propst, a local carpenter. The historical society moved the house to its current
location at Shuford Park from Main Avenue. Using his skills as a woodcarver, Propst included
carved details throughout the home. It is topped with a cupola tower glazed on all four sides.
Free. Docents offer guided tours Wed and Sun 1:30 to 4:30 p.m., Mar 15 through Dec 15.

where to shop

Catawba Furniture Mall. 377 US 70 Southwest; (866) 702-7361; catawbafurniture.com.
Eight acres of furniture spread over two levels. Carolina brands such as Broyhill and Bob
Timberlake combine with national brands like Better Homes and Gardens and Paula Deen
Home under one roof. Open Mon through Sat 10 a.m. to 6 p.m.

Hickory Antiques Mall. 348 US 70 Southwest; (828) 322-4004. If eclectic describes your
home decor, stop by the Hickory Antiques Mall to add a touch of character. Eighty vendors
offer furniture, collectible dolls, Depression glass, coins, china, and silver. Open Mon through
Sat 10 a.m. to 6 p.m., Sun 1:30 to 6 p.m.

Hickory Furniture Mart. 2220 US 70 Southeast; (800) 462-6278; hickoryfurniture.com.
More than 100 factory outlet stores populate this monstrous complex of four levels. Everything to decorate the home and even a design center are here. Shoppers find home furnishings, accessories, lighting, art, rugs, fabrics, and on and on. There's even a cafe and coffee

bar complete with Wi-Fi. The best time to visit for good deals is following the High Point wholesale market in the fall. Open Mon through Sat 9 a.m. to 6 p.m.

Valley Hills Mall. 1960 US 70 Southeast; (828) 328-6327; valleyhillsmall.com. If you aren't in the market for furniture but need a little retail therapy, this is the best place around for it. Valley Hills is the only enclosed shopping center for miles. It includes major brands, including anchors Belk and Dillard's.

where to eat

Bubblys. 2101 Catawba Valley Blvd. Southeast; (828) 855-2020. This Asian Fusion restaurant has been well received in Hickory since it opened in 2020. Wings, bowls, and burgers (both Asian and American style) all come together well on the menu. It gets its name from the popular bobo drinks served there. Open Wed through Mon 11 a.m. to 8 p.m. $$.

Cafe Rule & Wine Bar. 242 11th Ave. Northeast; (828) 324-2005; caferule.com. You'll need to make reservations for your Cafe Rule experience. Meals served here are done so with the close attention of a trained team of servers and chefs who take a moment to explain their methods and dishes. The experience begins with appetizers on the patio and then proceeds to the intimate dining room. Open Mon through Sat for dinner and Sun for brunch. $$$.

Hickory Social House. 2039 N. Center St.; (828) 328-3432; hickorysocial.com. Located outside Hickory on SR 127 in the former Bistro 127, this bistro is now home to Bootleggers Whiskey Bar, with top shelf offerings of whiskey, bourbon, rye, and moonshine. Elsewhere on the menu are gourmet pizzas, burgers, pastas, and entrees made from local meats and produce. Live entertainment is presented most evenings. Open for brunch and dinner Tues through Sat. $$.

Olde Hickory Tap Room. 222 Union Sq.; (828) 322-2965; oldehickorytaproom.com. Olde Hickory is one the state's oldest and more notable breweries, located just a few blocks from the restaurant. The big cheese cheeseburger, fish and chips, and other similar offerings make fair accompaniments to the brews. Open Thurs through Sun at 11 a.m. $$.

where to stay

2nd Street Inn. 13 2nd St. Southeast; 2ndstreetinn.com. Fourteen unique suites have been located in this renovated historic 160-year-old warehouse downtown. The rooms are big, airy, and modern with all new floors and details such as exposed brick and stylish art. $$.

worth more time

Bunker Hill Covered Bridge and **Murrays Mill Historic District** (US 70; 828-241-4299; catawbahistory.org) are located at the intersection of SR 10 and US 70 near the town of Claremont. Also operated by the historical society in the boucolic countryside along the banks of Balls Creek outside Hickory's moderately busy streets is this example of a late 19th-century town. Water from a placid pond slips over a mill dam, and the 28-foot waterwheel and a porch swing await at the general store. Preserved intact are the 1913 mill, the 1880s wheat house, and the 1913 John Murray House. Bunker Hill Covered Bridge, built in 1895, is one of two covered bridges remaining in North Carolina. Admission is $3 per person. Open Fri and Sat 9 a.m. to 4 p.m., Sun 1:30 to 4:30 p.m.

lenoir

For a century Broyhill and several other furniture manufacturers were the largest employers in Lenoir, but that began to change in the 1990s when jobs moved to production facilities overseas. Today, area employment is growing in the medical, education, and technology sectors; still this 2008 All-American City nestled in the foothills works hard to maintain its hometown charm. The city was named for Revolutionary War figure and statesman General William Lenoir, who lived at nearby Fort Defiance. The feet-friendly downtown features an outdoor sculpture gallery, friendly storefronts, and quaint dining opportunities.

getting there

Lenoir is 20 minutes beyond Hickory on US 321 north, taking you to the edge of Pisgah National Forest.

where to go

Caldwell Arts Council. 601 College Ave. Southwest; (828) 754-2486; caldwellarts.com. Easily the most impressive accomplishment of the Caldwell Arts Council to date is an outdoor sculpture tour that has grown to more than 75 pieces since 1985. An annual event, held the first Saturday after Labor Day, celebrates the acquisition of new works that are added to a walking tour. A metal pig, one of the first pieces acquired, sits atop the arts council building, while the others populate downtown and J.E. Broyhill Park. Works in metal, stone, found objects, and more are part of this exhibit. Download a walking map of the exhibit from the arts council website or pick one up at the office.

Fort Defiance. 1792 Fort Defiance Dr.; (828) 758-1671; historicfortdefiancenc.org. General William Lenoir was a self-educated man who could read and write four languages and made his mark through his role and account of the Battle of Kings Mountain. It would take him four years, beginning in 1788, to build this home. It is restored and furnished with hundreds of items as it was in the 18th century. Admission is $7 for adults and $5 for children. Open Thurs through Sat 10 a.m. to 5 p.m., Sun 1 to 5 p.m. Apr through Oct and on weekends Nov through Mar.

J.E. Broyhill Civic Center. 1913 Hickory Blvd. Southeast; (828) 726-2407; broyhillcenter .com. Operated by Caldwell Community College and Technical Institute, the civic center features a 1,000-seat state-of-the-art auditorium that serves as a venue for student per-formances, the Western Piedmont Symphony, community theater groups, and other local performers. It's named for James Edgar Broyhill, who along with his brother established the furniture company.

where to shop

Twenty Miles of Furniture. US 321, Hickory to Blowing. The marketers with the Caldwell County Furniture Dealers Association found a way to direct shoppers to some of the best discounts on furniture and slapped this clever moniker on it. Most of the outlets are concen-trated in the city limits of Lenoir and feature all the famous brands.

where to eat

1841 Cafe. 117 Main St. Southeast; (828) 572-4145; 1841cafelenoir.com. This bustling restaurant with indoor and patio seating offers a broad menu of sandwiches and burgers, steak, and pasta as well as homestyle meals. Save room for banner pudding. Open Tues through Sat 11 a.m. to 9 p.m. $$.

Piccolo's Italian Restaurant. 915 West Ave. Northwest; (828) 757-3554; piccolospizza.com. Before Octavio Martinez and his wife opened Piccolo's in Lenoir in 2001, they served pizza on Archer Avenue in Chicago. Appropriately they still serve Chicago-style pizza along with wood-fired offerings and pasta. $$.

Sims Country BBQ. 6160 Petra Mill Rd., Granite Falls; (828) 396-5811; simscountrybbq.com. Dinner and dancing are on tap every Fri and Sat night at this old barn in a small com-munity between Lenoir and Hickory. Barbecue and all the fixin's are served in a buffet. Then the live music and Sims Country Cloggers crank up. You can get your toes to tapping, too. Open Sat and Sun 5 to 9 p.m. $$.

day trip 02

northwest

>>> **south mountains:**
valdese, morganton

The view from the car just keeps getting better the closer you get to the Blue Ridge, and the history here is all the more intriguing. In Valdese day-trippers learn about a pocket in the population that includes the Waldenses, who carved out a life and community after being forced from their homes in the Italian Alps. Today that community includes a winery and one of North Carolina's longest-running outdoor dramas.

Nearby, the South Mountains offer just a taste of things to come at higher elevations—hiking, trout fishing, and other outdoor activities. This day trip also offers a taste of apple cider, views of a table Mother Nature set, and more.

valdese

Eleven families, persecuted by French and Italian armies in their Northern Italy homes, founded the town of Valdese in 1893. More members of this small religious sect, called Waldenses, joined them, and Valdese incorporated in 1920. First trying to carve out an agrarian "life in common" economy, the settlers soon discovered they would have to turn to manufacturing and other enterprises to survive. They harvested timber initially and then developed other industry and eventually a small, heritage-based tourist attraction. The town now has fewer than 5,000 residents.

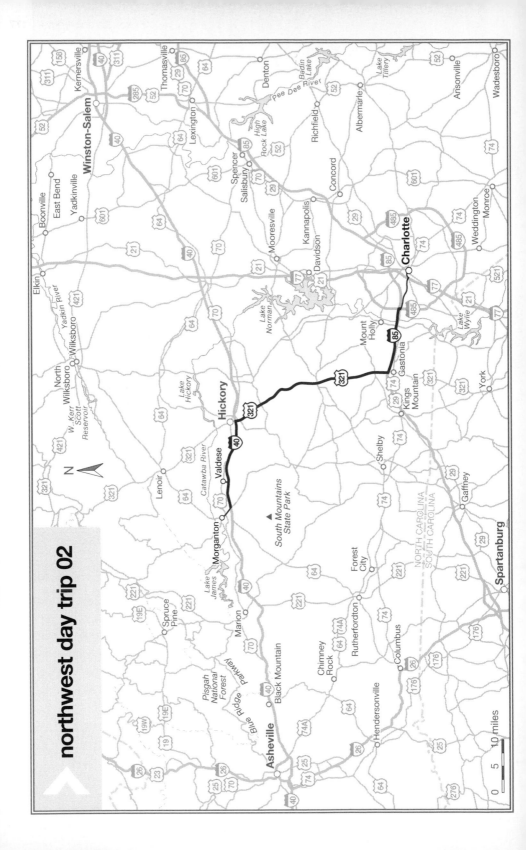

getting there

It is about an hour and 15 minutes to Valdese from the center of Charlotte heading west on I-85 to US 321 North. From US 321 take I-40 West to exit 11 to Valdese.

where to go

From This Day Forward. Old Colony Players Ampitheatre on Church Street; (828) 522-1150; oldcolonyplayers.com. The most memorable way to learn about Waldensian life and struggles is through the outdoor drama *From This Day Forward,* which this band of actors has portrayed here for a half century. The Old Colony Players perform the play that follows the emigrants who more than 100 years ago crowded into steamship steerage quarters and traveled to America for a new life. Tickets are $18 for adults, $16 for students and seniors; preschool students are admitted free. Presented Fri and Sat mid-July through mid-Aug.

Old Rock School. 400 Main St. West; (828) 879-2126; visitvaldese.com. The Valdese tourism office is located here, so it is a good place to begin your visit. An HO scale model train from the Piedmont & Western Railroad Club depicts a route through the region. You'll also find two small exhibit galleries that typically house local artwork. You can also purchase theater tickets for *From This Day Forward* here. Open Mon through Fri 9 a.m. to 5 p.m., 11 a.m. to 3 p.m. Sat.

Waldensian Heritage Museum. Corner of Rodoret Street and St. Germain Avenue; (828) 874-1111; waldensianheritagemuseum.com. Owned by the Waldensian Presbyterian Church, this museum has the obvious mission of collecting and preserving the history of these people, who trace their heritage back to the time of Christ. Most important it reflects more than 100 years of life in America through photos, tools, furnishings, clothes, and other objects. Open for tours Tues through Fri 11 a.m. and 2 p.m.

Waldensian Trail of Faith. 401 Church St.; (828) 874-1893; waldensiantrailoffaith.org. This trail includes a series of buildings and other exhibits that tell the story of the Waldenses and centuries of religious persecution. Among them is a replica of a cave where a group of Waldenses worshipped in secret, a 16th-century bible that was the first full bible translated into French, a community oven, and a memorial to their 1848 emancipation. Free. Open Sat and Sun 2 to 5 p.m.

Waldensian Winery. 4940 Villar Lane Northeast; waldensian.com; (828) 879-3202. The climate and soil in the Blue Ridge foothills are similar to those of the Alpine Valley from which the Waldenses came, so it made sense that they would have success in growing grapes and making wine here, too. They opened this winery in 1930, and now the products from it are widely marketed. Visitors can tour the winery that functions largely in a manual mode solely by volunteers. There are no paid employees here, but volunteering at a winery has its benefits. Open Thurs through Sun 1 to 6 p.m.

where to shop

Dolls & Designs by Sandi. 122 Main St. West; (828) 893-0640; dollsanddesigns.webs .com. Artist Sandi Walker can look at a photo of a loved one and craft a porcelain doll to resemble them in exacting detail. This unique shop also sells ornaments and other figurines. Sandi offers classes in doll making, too. Shop hours vary according to the class schedule.

Downtown Valdese. 100 and 200 blocks of Main Street. Located along this stretch are a dozen or so locally owned shops. Among them are consignment stores, a used record store, classic toys and collectibles as well as clothing, jewelry, and housewares.

where to eat

Myra's. 212 Main St. West; (828) 879-8049; myrasofvaldese.com. Right out of the 1950s comes this fun diner with burgers and ice cream. Classic cars cruise in every Friday night in spring, summer, and fall. Open Tues through Thurs 8 a.m. to 9 p.m., Sat. 9 a.m. to 9 p.m., and Sun 10:30 a.m. to 9 p.m. $.

Myra's Little Italy. 155 Bobo Ave. Northwest; (828) 874-7086. This Italian restaurant offers good pizza and typical Italian fare, all served on classic red-checkered tablecloths. $$.

morganton

Most of this area is relatively new, with settlements and incorporation of municipalities that date back a little more than 100 years. Morganton's story begins in the 1500s, however, with the Spanish settlement of Fort San Juan some 40 years before Jamestown was settled on the coast. There is some archeological evidence of Spanish conflict with the native Joara culture that lived here. The site is still being excavated. Much more recent history brings Morganton significance as the birthplace of the late Senator Sam Ervin Jr., who presided over the 1970s Watergate hearings. The day-tripper can explore that history, but abundant opportunities to explore nature are also here. Appropriately named Table Rock is visible from Morganton between Lake James and the Blue Ridge Parkway and offers a quick hike from the parking area at its base. A nearby state park offers a bit more.

getting there

Morganton is a mere 15 minutes from Valdese on I-40 West.

where to go

The History Museum of Burke County. 201 W. Meeting St.; (828) 437-1777; thehistory museumofburke.org. Located in the old city hall, this small history museum presents rotating exhibits on area history, including artifacts from the Berry Archeological Site, where remains of a 16th-century Spanish fort are being unearthed; photos that date to the turn of the 20th century; and maps and other documents that date to the Revolutionary War. Free. Open Tues through Fri 10 a.m. to 4 p.m., Sat 10 a.m. to 2 p.m. The 1916 Western North Carolina Railroad Depot is open Sat 2 to 4 p.m.

McDowell House at Quaker Meadows. 119 St. Marys Church Rd.; (828) 437-4104; historicburke.org. Researchers believe this Federal-style home is the oldest brick structure in Burke County. It was built by Captain Charles McDowell Jr. in 1812 and is now on the National Register of Historic Places. The good captain's father, General Charles McDowell, was here in 1780 to plan his strategy for the Battle of Kings Mountain at what is known as the Council Oak. Open for tours Sun 2 to 4 p.m. Apr through Oct.

Historic Burke County Courthouse. Courthouse Square; (828) 433-6793; historicburke .org. This courthouse, on the National Register of Historic Places, is the oldest in the western part of the state and served as the state supreme court from 1847 to 1861. The Historic Burke Foundation and Visitor Information Center are located here, so it's a good first stop on a day trip. Noted architectural facets are its ancient Greek porticos and Baroque cupola. It was remodeled in 1903 with neoclassical elements. Among the stories discovered through the few exhibits and the audiovisual presentation is the shooting of Samuel Flemming in 1851 by lawyer William Waightstill Avery. Free. Open Mon through Fri 10 a.m. to 4 p.m.

Quaker Meadows Cemetery. 127 Branstrom Dr.; (828) 437-4104; historicburke.org. In 1767 Joseph McDowell created this cemetery when his grandson, David, died. The cemetery is the earliest identified site associated with white settlement in western North Carolina. During the next 100 years, 59 members of McDowell's family and other prominent Burke County citizens and Revolutionary War soldiers were buried here.

Senator Sam J. Ervin Jr. Library & Museum. 1001 Burkemont Ave.; (828) 448-6195; samervin.wpcc.edu. Located on the campus of Western Piedmont Community College, this museum includes Ervin's furniture from his Washington, D.C., office. He served in public office from 1935 to 1975 and was selected to serve as chairman of the Senate Watergate hearings due to the huge respect he garnered from his colleagues. The collection is extensive with hundreds of books, documents, and memorabilia. Free. Hours vary according to college hours.

South Mountains State Park. 3001 South Mountains Park Ave., Connelly Springs; (828) 433-4772; ncparks.gov. The postal address for this great state park is Connelly Springs, but it is easily accessible from Morganton. It's the largest state park in North Carolina and has more than 40 miles of well-maintained hiking trails. While the 3,000-foot elevation is dwarfed by nearby Blue Ridge elevations, the fishing in trout-stocked waters is ample. A moderately difficult one-mile trail leads to the 80-foot High Shoals Falls. An easier three-quarter-mile trail begins near the park office. Displays along this trail explain the area ecology and describe the flora and fauna that inhabit the park. The area is also popular among area horseback riders. Fees are charged for camping facilities. Generally open during daylight hours.

where to shop

Apple Hill Orchard & Cider Mill. 2075 Pleasant Hill Ave.; (828) 419-7955; applehillorchard .com. Orchard employees start picking apples here in late July. By late August the country store opens for business, and in September the fields are opened for public picking. Nine varieties of apples plus jams, jellies, honey, cider spices, apple-related products, and home-made cider are available seasonally. The orchard also offers wagon tours Sat from 11 a.m. to 3 p.m. early Sept through mid-Nov. Orchard hours vary according to crops.

where to eat

Mountain Burrito. 408 W. Fleming Dr.; (828) 438-5008; mountainburrito.com. Mexico meets Appalachia at what seems to have become a Morganton institution. Build your own burrito, tacos, or nacho bowl with locally sourced items. Roast pork or seasonal veggies seem to work well on any of them. Open daily 10:30 a.m. to 9 p.m. $$.

root & vine. 139 W. Union St.; (828) 433-1540; rootandvinerestaurant.com. If the 42 draft beer taps or the extensive wine list don't draw you into root & vine, perhaps the unusual menu items will. Chilean salmon, pork chop with pimento cheese grits, and jerk roasted oyster mushrooms are just an example of the creative recipes you'll enjoy here. $$$.

where to stay

Fairway Oaks Bed & Breakfast. 4640 Plantation Dr.; (828) 584-7677. Located on the fifth green at Silver Creek Plantation Golf Course, the inn has no shortage of amenities. Guests have access to the golf course's clubhouse and Papa's Bar and Grill, as well as beautiful views from the rocking-chair front porch and gazebo. $$.

worth more time

With pleasant weather nine or ten months out of the year, Morganton is a great place for overnight camping. **South Mountains State Park** accommodates tent campers for a mod-est fee, but there are also a handful of privately owned operations dotting the landscape. Try one of these:

Daniel Boone Family Campground. 7360 SR 181; (828) 433-1200.

Optimistic RV Resort & Campground. 6618 SR 181 North; (828) 438-0550.

Riverside Family Golf & RV Park. 611 Independence Blvd.; (828) 433-6464; riverside golfrvpark.com.

Rose Creek Family Campground. 3471 Rose Creek Rd.; (828) 438-7162; rosecreekfamily campground.com.

Steele Creek Park & Campground. 7081 SR 181; (828) 433-5660; steelecreekpark.com.

day trip 03

northwest

>>> **international travel:**
marion, old fort, little switzerland

You are well advised in this region to put away the GPS, to allow yourself to be diverted, to explore nature, and to discover the towns that surround Lake James. A bike rack duly loaded or a sturdy pair of hiking boots will do nicely for a jaunt down a shady trail or an interesting sidewalk.

This day trip runs along I-40, through a portion of Pisgah National Forest south of the Blue Ridge Parkway. It includes the small mountain communities of Marion and Old Fort that come with easy access provided by modern modes of transportation and mountain charm that has attracted travelers for decades. Little Switzerland looks a little different from those small towns and perhaps a little less European than its name might lead you to believe. Still, a visit isn't likely to leave you disappointed.

marion

Marion itself is a walkable town of nearly 8,000 people. It was founded in 1844, but a sweeping fire in 1894 burned the town to the ground. Its citizens persevered, and the mountain town was rebuilt soon enough. Today it's on the National Register of Historic Places.

getting there

Marion is less than 100 miles from Charlotte using I-85 West, US 321 North, and I-40 West. From I-40 take the exit for SR 226/US 221 North. Lake James is accessible from a number

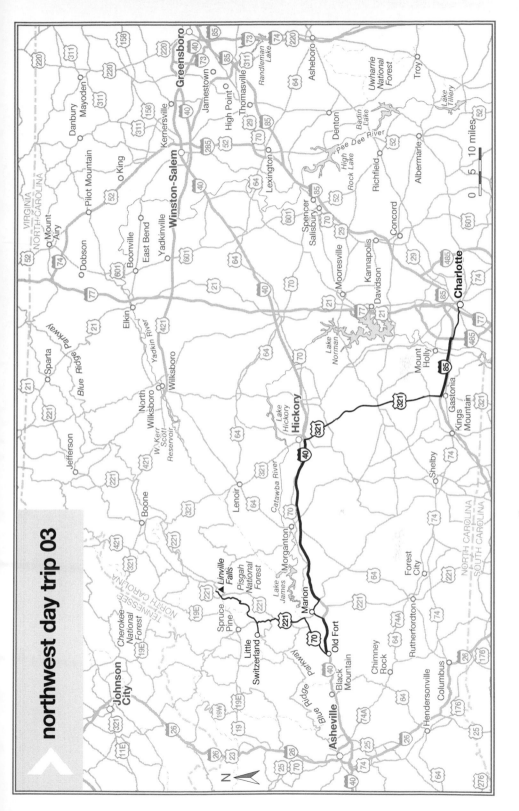

northwest day trip 03

of points in and around Morganton, Marion, Glen Alpine, and Nebo, which is the official address of the state park.

where to go

Historic Carson House. 1805 US 70 West; (828) 724-4948; historiccarsonhouse.com. Built in 1793 before the town of Marion was established, the Carson house offers stories that touch much of American history. It was built by Colonel John Carson, who served in state government when North Carolina ratified the Constitution. Historians also say that Davy Crockett and Andrew Jackson visited here. It withstood several sieges during the Civil War and is on the North Carolina Civil War Trail. The three-story house that started as a log cabin has been maintained with historical furnishings and artifacts since the 1960s. Admission is $10 for adults and free for children. Open Wed through Sat 10 a.m. to 4 p.m. and Sun 2 to 5 p.m. Apr through Dec. In December the home is filled with period Christmas decorations.

Lake James State Park. SR 126; (828) 544-6800; ncparks.gov. Since 2004 Lake James has been an incorporated community on and around the reservoir of 10 square miles that straddles the McDowell and Burke County lines. Duke Power created the lake on the Catawba River between 1916 and 1923, and since then its 150 miles of shoreline have become a much-desired place for residents and tourists. The picturesque state park, which is North Carolina's largest waterfront state park, offers 565 glorious acres for picnicking, swimming, canoeing, camping, hiking, boating, and more. Lounging on the lake could be a day trip in itself. Large- and smallmouth bass, walleye, bluegill, and a host of other fish offer the angler more than enough challenge. Several trails of varying levels of difficulty (up to moderate) offer mountain laurel, azalea, rhododendron, and opportunities to view a variety of birds and other animals. A sandy beach near the park office permits sunbathing and swimming. Generally open during daylight hours. Swimming permitted daily 10 a.m. to 6 p.m. in summer. Fees charged for campsites, canoe rentals, and some other attractions.

Linville Caverns. 19929 US 221 North; (828) 756-4171; linvillecaverns.com. A trip deep inside Humpback Mountain allows the day-tripper to see beautiful stalactites, stalagmites, and blind fish, and to experience total darkness. This is North Carolina's only public cavern, in operation since 1937. Admission is $12 for adults, $11 for seniors, and $10 for children under age 13. Open Thurs through Mon 9 a.m. to 5:30 p.m.

where to shop

Marion Tailgate Market. 67 W. Henderson St.; (828) 652-2215. Fresh local produce for this market comes from area family farms. Vendors also offer handmade quilts, baked goods, crafts, and personal care items. It's become a big social event over its 15 years. Open Tues 3 to 6 p.m. in summer and fall.

McDowell Arts Council Association. 50 S. Main St.; (828) 652-8610; mcdowellarts
.org. The Artisan Shop located here represents as many as 60 artists who produce jewelry,
woodwork, paintings, handcrafted soaps, and more. Open Tues through Sat noon to 5 p.m.

where to eat

Bruce's Fabulous Foods. 63 S. Main St.; (828) 659-8023; brucesfabulousfoods.com.
Whatever you eat at Bruce's make sure you save room for one of his fabulous cheese-
cakes, which he ships across the country. First enjoy any number of his alliterative selections from awesome appetizers, spectacular sandwiches or bodacious burgers. Open
daily 11 a.m. to 3 p.m. $.

Countryside BBQ. 2070 Rutherford Rd.; (828) 652-4885; countrysidebbq.net. This barbecue house always appears to be a favorite of locals. Within the red-barn walls, barbecue of
standard fare is offered alongside down-home favorites plus a buffet. Open Tues through
Sat for breakfast, lunch, and dinner. $.

where to stay

Catawba River Inn. 17677 Hwy 221 North; (828) 756-7001; catawbariverinn.com. Located
just off the Blue Ridge Parkway is this cozy inn along the Catawba River. Rooms all have gas
fireplaces and private balconies. $$.

Hidden Creek Campground Resort. 1210 Deacon Dr.; (828) 652-7208; https://spacious
skiescampgrounds.com/hidden-creek. In addition to RV and tent camping sites, there are
lakeview cabins and yurts with all the comforts of home. $$.

worth more time

Linville Falls. Located in the Jonas Ridge community, Linville Falls (not to be confused
with the town of Linville) is the most-visited waterfall in the Blue Ridge with easy access
at milepost 316.3 on the Blue Ridge Parkway. You can also access the falls from Marion
via US 221—a 30-minute drive. Two trails lead to the falls that plunge on three levels into
Linville Gorge.

old fort

Old Fort is one of the area's smaller towns. A 12-foot-tall granite arrowhead monument
stands at the center of town as a symbol of peace between the European settlers and
the Cherokee who originally inhabited the area. It's named for Davidson Fort, built during
the Revolutionary War. Andrews Geyser, located in a grassy municipal park on Mill Creek
Road, is a second roadside attraction here. This is a man-made geyser that was originally a

fountain built in 1879 at Round Knob Hotel. It was later moved and preserved as a tribute to the some 120 men who died during the construction of this stretch of the Southern Railroad.

getting there

Take I-40 west out of Marion by using Sugar Hill Road. Old Fort is 15 minutes away.

where to go

Davidson's Fort Historic Park. 140 Lackey Town Road; (828) 407-8300; davidsonsfort historicpark.com. In Colonial America this was the western frontier. Davidson's Fort was, at that time, the westernmost outpost in the new world, originally constructed in 1776 to protect settlers against Cherokee attacks. With the assistance of troops provided by General Griffith Rutherford, a group of volunteers began to build a replica of the fort in 2004. Frequent re-enactments and other events are held at the site. Hours vary according to events.

Mountain Gateway Museum. 24 Water St.; (828) 668-9259; mgmnc.org. This small museum located in a historic stone building is operated by the North Carolina Museum of History based in Raleigh. Its exhibits focus appropriately on mountain life and pioneer history. Exhibits on agrarian life include displays on how pioneers created water systems, tools, and other early implements. A seasonal garden exhibit is also interpreted. Free. Open Tues through Sat 9 a.m. to 5 p.m., Sun 2 to 5 p.m.

Old Fort Depot, Railroad Museum & Visitor Center. 25 W. Main St.; (828) 668-4244. Located behind the arrowhead monument, the visitor center is a good first stop in Old Fort. Pick up area brochures, chat with staff, and browse the small railroad exhibit. Free. Open Mon through Sat 9 a.m. to 5 p.m.

where to shop

Old Fort Ride House. 59 Commerce St.; (828) 412-4244. The Ride House has become a gathering spot for biking enthusiasts and others. There's repair shop for bikes and related outdoor apparel as well as a coffee shop.

where to eat

Hillman Beer. 78 Catawba Ave.; (828) 688-6372; hillmanbeer.com. With the original restaurant in Asheville, Hillman opened here in 2020 along Mill Creek. It features 32 taps and pub-style food such as sandwiches and wraps. Open daily at 11 a.m. $.

Whistle Stop Pizza & Subs. 27 E. Main St.; (828) 668-7676. The locals really turn out at this downtown pizzeria, especially for lunchtime sandwiches and salads. Specials on pasta dishes are also offered on a daily basis. Open Tues through Sat for lunch and dinner. $.

where to stay

Curtis Creek Campground. Curtis Creek Road; (828) 652-2144. The US Forest Service operates this 10,000-acre site within the Pisgah National Forest. It includes a black bear sanctuary and a campground. Most of the private sites are for tents, but there are several RV sites. $.

Inn on Mill Creek. 3895 Mill Creek Rd.; (828) 668-1115; innonmillcreek.com. This expansive bed-and-breakfast is close to I-40, giving good access to Asheville, Black Mountain, and other attractions, yet it is rather serene. The grounds, surrounded by nearby hills and forest, include a trout pond, orchards, and trails. Breakfast is often served in the sunroom overlooking the pond. $$.

Sky Island Retreat and Campground. 88 Flatlander Dr.; (828) 668-4928; skyisland retreatandcampground.com. This campground is well-suited for families. It has a miniature golf course, running streams, and private campsites. It also offers several small cabins for rent. $–$$.

little switzerland

Little Switzerland is an unincorporated community founded by a North Carolina Supreme Court justice in 1909 on Grassy Mountain. It was so named for the landscape's resemblance to the Swiss Alps. Its 4,000-foot elevation affords views of the North Carolina Mountains' most notable landmarks: Mount Mitchell, Table Rock, and Grandfather Mountain. Today it is part country club, part western frontier town offering a variety of attractions, accommodations, restaurants, and shopping experiences.

getting there

You could just as easily stop off in Little Switzerland from the Blue Ridge Parkway, but from Old Fort take US 70 to SR 226/US 221 North, which cuts through the Pisgah National Forest in what only a few years ago was a somewhat arduous ride. Today it's a rather pleasant jaunt of 30 minutes or so.

where to go

Emerald Village. 331 McKinney Mine Rd.; (828) 765-6463; emeraldvillage.com. The North Carolina Mining Museum is located in this retired underground mining operation. After touring the mine and the museum buildings that include tools and displays on old mountain mining life, visitors have the opportunity to mine for gems or gold at several of the mining sites located on the property. Open daily 10 a.m. to 5 p.m. Apr, May, Sept, and Oct, and 9 a.m. to 6 p.m. Memorial Day weekend through Labor Day weekend. Museum admission is

$10 for adults, $8 for students kindergarten through high school, free for preschool children. Mining costs an additional fee.

The Orchard at Altapass. 1025 Orchard Rd., Spruce Pine; (828) 765-9531; altapass orchard.org. This century-old orchard is especially fun for families. It's a fascinating and entertaining way to learn about regional history and culture. The history of the orchard is fascinating itself. Sliced in two by the construction of the Blue Ridge Parkway, it was beginning to deteriorate, until the early 1990s when Kit Trubey, her brother Bill Carson, and his wife bought the land. Since that time, they have developed the southern half into a fun attraction that includes hayrides, music, storytelling, a monarch butterfly program, and a store that offers ice cream, fudge, country products, local crafts, and of course, apples in every imaginable form. Open seasonally.

where to shop

Little Switzerland Books & Beans. 9426 US 226-A; (828) 766-2601; lsbooksandbeans .webs.com. This is a bookworm's dream. The store is stuffed with used books and unusual finds. It's located in a three-story building topped by the Mountain Arts and Crafts Gallery. A fireplace reading room makes it easy to take a midday break. Open daily 8 a.m. to 5 p.m.

Switzerland General Store. 9441 US 226-A; (828) 765-5289. This fun store is at the heart of Little Switzerland and is a gathering spot for all. It offers souvenirs, local crafts, and food items. A nice deli with a selection of domestic and imported cheeses as well as wines and hand-crafted beer serves lunch or an early dinner. Open daily 9 a.m. to 6 p.m.

Trillium Gallery. 101 High Ridge Road; (828) 765-0024. Trillium carries handmade arts and crafts, jewelry, and home decor from local and nationally known artists. Shoppers will also find display-quality pottery and other similar items. Open Sun through Thurs 9 a.m. to 5 p.m., Fri and Sat 9 a.m. to 7 p.m. mid-Apr through mid-Nov.

where to eat

Switzerland Cafe. 9440 US 226-A; (828) 765-5289; switzerlandcafe.com. Located in the same building as the Switzerland General Store, the cafe offers soups, salads, sandwiches, and full meals with smoked meats, trout, and salmon. Zackery's Pub, located here, offers music on Fri and Sat nights. Open 10 a.m. to 4 p.m. mid-Apr through Oct. Dinner is typically served Fri and Sat from 5 to 9 p.m. $.

where to stay

Switzerland Inn. 86 High Ridge Rd.; (828) 385-4500; switzerlandinn.com. The views at this inn are why this town is named Little Switzerland. Open since 1909, it offers a variety of rooms and suites, some with balconies. Chalet Restaurant is also located here. Next door, the Geneva Hall holds square dances on Saturday nights during the summer. $$–$$$.

day trip 04

northwest

tale of two cities:
black mountain, asheville

Asheville is home to one of North Carolina's premier attractions: Biltmore Estate. But this, the largest city in western North Carolina, has been influenced by a Bohemian flair that comes from its dynamic arts culture and by students from the University of North Carolina at Asheville. You can't really take a single day trip to Asheville without feeling like you missed something. There's so much to explore, it would take a dozen days of trips to put a dent in your travel appetite. But here's to trying.

Black Mountain immediately begins to whet the appetite of the artist lurking in us all. If not the artist, then it's likely to spark something in the shopper. Black Mountain is a friendly mountain town settled originally by the Cherokee thousands of years ago. The story of its settlement by Europeans begins to unfold with a walk down the streets of this historic town, where you might discover the dulcimer in production or performance, or a place to claim a piece of jewelry that can be found nowhere else on earth. Just beyond Black Mountain, the Swannanoa Valley sets the table for your entrée into Asheville.

black mountain

The Black Mountains range is the tallest in the eastern US. The town of Black Mountain was a pathway for settlers for decades, but now provides tourism opportunities for people who visit nearby conference centers, including Billy Graham's Montreat. Its downtown is as

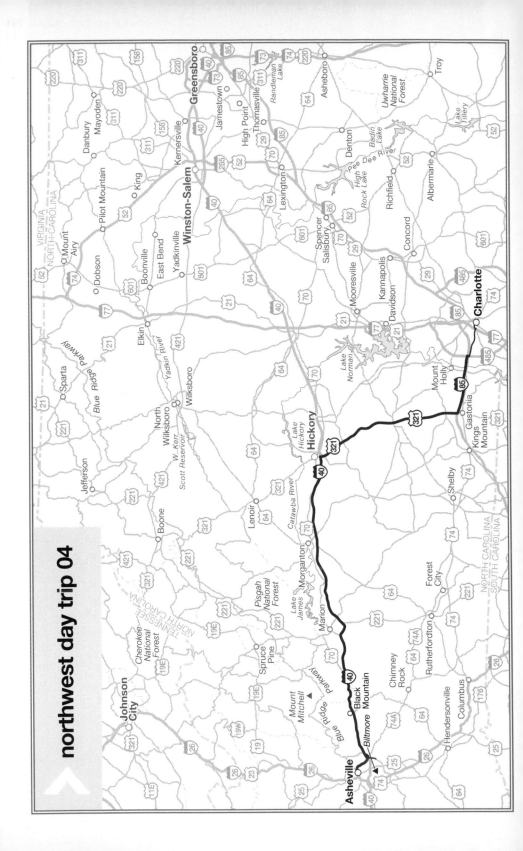

northwest day trip 04

friendly and walkable as they come. If you are looking for a mountain retreat and the big city of Asheville doesn't appeal to you, this is the place to come.

getting there

Black Mountain is located on I-40 a little more than 100 miles and a little less than two hours from Charlotte. Get there via I-85 West to US 321 North to I-40 West.

where to go

Black Mountain Center for the Arts. 225 W. State St.; (828) 669-0930; blackmoun tainarts.org. Located in the former city hall, this center includes gallery, performance, and classroom space. It frequently has author readings, films, and musical events. Exhibits typically feature regional artists and works that tell the story of the Southern Appalachians. Open Mon through Fri 10 a.m. to 5 p.m. and for special events.

Swannanoa Valley Museum & History Center. 223 W. State St.; (828) 669-9566; swan nanoavalleymuseum.org. Even the Cherokee used the Swannanoa Valley as a passage from the western Blue Ridge over the Catawba River headwaters or through the Swannanoa Gap. It is also said that noted frontiersman Davy Crockett passed through here. So the Swannanoa museum remains to tell those stories and others through photos and earlier artifacts. They also offer walking tours monthly. Free. Open Wed through Sat 10 a.m. to 5 p.m.,

White Horse. 105C Montreat Rd.; (828) 669-0816; whitehorseblackmountain.com. This different sort of performance venue brings regional musicians to the areas but also features storytelling, puppetry, poetry, film, and other events. It has seating for 140, creating an intimate atmosphere and superb acoustics produced by the high ceilings of this old auto dealership.

where to shop

Seven Sisters Gallery. 119 Broadway Ave.; (828) 669-5107; sevensistersgallery.com. This gallery carries upscale arts and crafts from literally hundreds of artists. Many potters, jewelry makers, woodworkers, and others come from the local area, but the store has made an effort to engage other, more distant artists who produce pieces that are reflective of the region. Open Mon through Sat 10 a.m. to 6 p.m., Sun noon to 5 p.m.

Town Hardware & General Store. 103 W. State St.; (828) 669-7723; townhardware.com. Of course, no respectable guidebook would recommend a hardware store as a destination, unless it was something special. This is still a working hardware store, but it qualifies as a destination because of its fun selection of old-time toys, humorous signs, novelty items, and even old-time housewares such as hand-crank ice cream freezers. Open Mon through Sat 8 a.m. to 6 p.m., Sun noon to 5 p.m.

where to eat

Berliner Kindl German Restaurant. 121 Broadway; (828) 669-5255; berlinerkindlgerman restaurant.com. A young visiting German gave this restaurant a tremendously positive review for being "authentic German." The menu supports those claims with lots of sausages, brats, schnitzel, and strudels for dessert. Open Mon through Sat 11 a.m. to 8 p.m. $.

Red Rocker Inn. 136 N. Dougherty St.; (828) 669-5991; redrockerinn.com. The restaurant at the Red Rocker Inn has received rave reviews from national media, including the *New York Times* and *Atlanta Journal Constitution*. Well-prepared comfort food like roasted stuffed chicken, prime rib, local vegetables, and buttermilk biscuits served with apple butter are ready for the table. Open Mon through Thurs 5 to 7:30 p.m., Fri and Sat 5 to 8 p.m. $$$.

where to stay

Black Mountain Inn. 1186 Old US 70 West; (828) 669-6528; blackmountaininn.com. This inn has as storied a past as you will find. Perched on a hill overlooking beautiful old trees and lawns, it began as a stagecoach stop, was a sanatorium for a period, and served as an artist's retreat. Ernest Hemingway, John Steinbeck, and Helen Keller are all said to have stayed here. Today it includes seven rooms with private baths. $$–$$$.

Inn Around the Corner. 109 Church St.; (828) 669-6005. The name simply doesn't do this 1915 Victorian inn justice. It is just around the corner from Black Mountain's downtown, but it is set amongst a variety of heirloom plants and has two levels of front porch just right for rocking. $$.

Red Rocker Inn. 136 N. Dougherty St.; (828) 669-5991; redrockerinn.com. Yes, there are red rockers and even a red porch swing at the Red Rocker Inn. Dining at this inn was duly recommended in the previous section, but this is also one of the best places to stay in Black Mountain. The 17 rooms are varied, but all are cozy and comfortable. $$–$$$.

asheville

Asheville is the kind of place where painters, sculptors, writers, musicians, and other creative types yearn to live and work. The Art Deco architecture that remains from the turn of the 20th century combines with an energetic arts cultural, and culinary scene to create an experience you won't find in other North Carolina cities. Here indie rock meets mountain music and country crafts meet fine art. Engaging opportunities are readily available throughout Asheville's downtown, which offers dozens of art galleries, clubs, breweries, restaurants, and other fun and funky places to visit by day or night.

Although frontiersmen like Daniel Boone and Davy Crockett would pass over this plateau in the days of fur trading, it wasn't until the railroad was run through here in the late

1800s that the city got its real start. Though it was founded and named Asheville by the late 1700s, it would take 100 years for the city to come into its own. By 1890 30,000 people were coming to Asheville each summer to escape the heat wherever they lived. Temperatures at these elevations are typically about 10 degrees cooler than in Charlotte, so summers are comfortable with highs that usually top out at 90 degrees. Early spring and fall can be blustery, so Mom would want you to bring a jacket.

About the same time vacationers were discovering Asheville, George Vanderbilt, whose family had gained a fortune in the transportation business, purchased 120,000 acres in Asheville where he would build what would become one of North Carolina's most popular tourist attractions. More than a million people visit Biltmore Estate, the largest private residence in America, each year. Nearby Biltmore Village in the southern and more upscale part of the city adds a host of other points of interest, restaurants, and shopping.

If you want to get more information about Asheville before you head out, contact the **Asheville Convention & Visitor Bureau** (36 Montford Ave.; 828-258-6129; exploreashe ville.com). There you will find a useful interactive maps and other tips to help you plan your route; plus it lists a handful of tour companies that take visitors on themed tours from historic to haunted. They depart from the visitor center, hotels, and other easy-to-find starting points.

getting there

Asheville is about 15 minutes from Black Mountain traveling on I-40 west.

where to go

Asheville Museum of Science. 43 Patton Ave.; (828) 254-7162; asheveillscience.org. Sparkling gemstones, ancient fossils, and common Carolina minerals once made up most of the exhibits at a well-done earth science museum that mades rocks and plate tectonics engaging. Once known as the Colburn Science Earth Science Museum, AMOS still includes those standard collections of rocks and minerals, but other hands-on exhibits make weather, volcanoes, earthquakes, and other scientific phenomena more fun and, more important, understandable. Admission is $8.50 for adults, $7.50 for students and seniors. Open Mon 10 a.m. to 5 p.m., Wed 10 a.m. to 3 p.m., Thurs 11 a.m. to 5 p.m., Fri and Sat 10 a.m. to 5 p.m., and Sun 1 to 5 p.m.

Asheville Area Arts Council Galleries. 11 Biltmore Ave.; (828) 222-0436; artsavl.com. The Asheville arts community is massive, and it may be difficult for day-trippers to get their arms around it. One place to start navigating is the Asheville Area Arts Council, renamed ArtsAVL in early 2023. It's centrally located in downtown and has exhibition spaces for local and emerging artists, produces an event calendar, and has plans for a trolley system and other ways to connect Asheville's dozens of galleries. Free. Open Tues through Sat 10 a.m. to 7 p.m., Sun 1 to 6 p.m.

Asheville Art Museum. 2 S. Pack Sq; (828) 253-3227; ashevilleart.org. Featuring exhibitions primarily of 20th- and 21st-century American art, the museum focuses on art of the region, but also includes works of artists who simply have a connection to the Asheville area. While some of the work can be classified as contemporary and some regional craft, the collection is more diverse than at some of the art museums in the state. Admission is $8 for adults, $7 for students and seniors. The Holden Community Gallery on the first floor of the museum is free. Open Tues through Sat 10 a.m. to 5 p.m., Sun 1 to 5 p.m.

Asheville Balloon Company. 1572 Sand Hill Rd.; (828) 707-2992; ashevillebalooncompany.com. If you want to splurge on a tour of Asheville, this is probably the way to go. Balloon flights take passengers up to 200 feet over the Great Smoky Mountains and include sites like Cold Mountain—the basis for the popular Charles Frazier novel—Mount Mitchell, and more. Trips depart from Westridge Shopping Center and take about two and a half hours. Flights are $225 per person.

Asheville Adventure Company. 99 Riverside Dr.; (828) 417-7109; ashevilleadventure company.com. Visitors will certainly find no shortage of outdoor opportunities in and around Asheville, and one of the easiest ways to experience them is with a reliable guide. Ashville Adventure Company offers a host of services, including flat water float trips on the French Broad River. The center also offers canoe, kayak, tube, and bike rentals from its riverside location. It also operates a public gem mining operation. Hours are seasonal.

Asheville Urban Trail. Downtown Asheville; (828) 259-5815; exploreasheville.com. Part of the city's parks system is a trail that includes a tour of bronze sculptures related to its history and the notable people who have lived in the city, including authors O. Henry and Thomas Wolfe. The tour begins at Pack Place, and it takes about two hours to walk to each of the 30 stations. Download a map and podcasts for the self-guided tour at the city's website.

Basilica of St. Lawrence. 97 Haywood St.; (828) 252-6042; saintlawrencebasilica.org. This architectural gem was designed by the same architects who worked on Biltmore House, including nationally renowned architect Rafael Guastavino, designer of Grant's Tomb, Grand Central Station, and Carnegie Hall. The Catholic church was built in a Spanish Renaissance style in 1909. Amazingly there are no beams in the entire building, making its dome the largest freestanding dome in the country. The basilica is chock-full of intricate details and artwork from the vestibule to the altar and windows. Open daily 9 a.m. to 6 p.m.

Biltmore. 1 Lodge St.; (800) 411-3812; biltmore.com. An astonishing 250 rooms, extensive gardens, a winery, and more make up the largest private home in America. On the grounds visitors can hike, ride horses, raft, and sling mud in a four-wheel-drive vehicle. Experiencing all that Biltmore has to offer simply cannot be done in a day or even two, so make plans to return often.

Completed in 1895 as a summer retreat for George and Edith Vanderbilt, the home is the spectacular backdrop for furniture, clothing, tapestry, and other items that reveal their lavish lifestyle. Among the most significant items you will see here are Napoleon Bonaparte's chess set, dozens of fireplaces, and trim detailed in gold lamé and silk. In addition to the living areas, tours of the home include the bowling alley, indoor pool, banquet hall with 75-foot ceilings, and servants' quarters.

Fredrick Law Olmsted, the country's foremost landscape architect, designed the seemingly endless gardens on the 8,000-acre property. An azalea garden, English walled garden, and rose garden are just the beginning. The estate's trees and gardens highlight Vanderbilt's interest in horticulture. His estate essentially sold the US government the property that is now Pisgah National Forest for $5 an acre at his bequest. While the winery has been a part of Biltmore estate for decades, that area has been expanded to include Antler Hill Village, which has a farm exhibit, a vintage car exhibit, a pub, and village green, where music and storytelling are regularly presented.

Beyond these traditional tours, an outdoor adventure area offers a rambunctious ride in a Land Rover, sport clay shooting, fly fishing, and Segway tours. The estate also offers no less than seven options for dining, from snacks to fine dining. Want to shop? Find nearly a dozen opportunities to purchase everything from toys to wine. The Inn at Biltmore is acclaimed by practically every travel publication, coming in at number 11 on the *Condé Nast Traveler* list of the best US hotels, and receiving top ratings by AAA, *Forbes Travel Guide,* and others.

Tickets to tour the home and grounds start at $89. Additional fees are charged for a variety of other attractions and activities. Biltmore is open 365 days a year, hours vary by attraction and by season. Things typically open by 9 a.m. and close by 5 p.m., except during the holidays when a candlelight tour is offered.

Blue Ridge Parkway Visitor Center. 195 Hemphill Knob Rd.; (828) 298-5330; blueridge parkway.org. While there are many points of access in North Carolina to the Blue Ridge Parkway's 469 miles, this is one of the more interesting ones, and this visitor center is a good place to pick up brochures and learn more about the area. There is a small exhibit hall, a 22-foot-tall interactive map wall, and a film about the parkway and regional heritage. Along the parkway drivers find scenic overlooks, trail heads, grassy dales, and picnic areas. The speed limit is 45 miles per hour, so using the road for quick travel isn't wise. The parkway intersects Asheville at US 25, US 70, US 74, and SR 191.

Botanical Gardens at Asheville. 151 W.T. Weaver Blvd.; (828) 252-5190; ashevillebotani calgardens.org. Though this garden is located on the campus of the University of North Carolina, an unaffiliated nonprofit organization maintains these serene 10 acres. The garden specializes in native plantings of Southern Appalachia. A half-mile trail along a stream, meadow, and woodland holds some expected and unexpected treasures. The garden's collection includes rare and endangered species such as broad-leaved coreopsis and pale yellow trillium. Free. Generally open during daylight hours.

Center for Craft. 67 Broadway St.; (828) 785-1357; centerforcraft.org. The center features rotating exhibitions of professional artists that focus on the craft heritage of the region, including pottery, jewelry, wood works, and more. It's run by the University of North Carolina at Asheville at its Kellogg Conference Center. The center also sponsors workshops and lectures throughout the year. Free. Open Mon though Sat 1 to 5 p.m.

Wortham Center for the Performing Arts. (828) 257-4530; worthamarts.org. This theater is another of Asheville's intimate presentation spaces, with 500 seats. Productions run the gamut from musicals to dramas to dance theater from professional touring groups and some of the city's own cultural groups.

Folk Art Center. Blue Ridge Parkway Milepost 382; (828) 298-7928; southernhighland guild.org. This center is the home of the Southern Highland Craft Guild, which represents generations of hundreds of craft artists from nine states of Southern Appalachia. Their work, sold here at the Allanstand Craft Shop, is nothing less than exquisite. You'll be able to interact with artists producing their wares. Open daily 9 a.m. to 6 p.m. Apr through Dec, 9 a.m. to 5 p.m. Jan through Mar.

Grovewood Gallery. 111 Grovewood Rd.; (828) 253-7651; grovewood.com. The Grovewood property includes the Estes-Winn Memorial Automobile Museum, the North Carolina Homespun Museum, a small display garden, and a working artist studio. The automobile museum holds horse-drawn carriages as well as vintage automobiles, and the city's 1922 American La France fire engine is on display. The Homespun Museum tells the story of Biltmore Industries' wool weaving business at the early part of the 20th century. The studios have a dozen or so artists in residence. Free. Open Mon through Sat 10 a.m. to 5 p.m., Sun 11 a.m. to 5 p.m. Apr through Dec.

cruisin' for brews

A new society is brewing in Asheville . . . or should we say a brew society is dawning. According the North Carolina Department of Tourism, Asheville now has more breweries per capita than any other city in the nation, even taking on and beating beer mecca Portland, Oregon, in a national online poll. Cozy tasting rooms have popped up in the city over the past decade and so have beer-centric events There's even a way to take a brews cruise through the city, sampling these sometimes lacy, robust, and (on occasion) downright freaky-tasting concoctions. One brewery even serves a banana beer.

Oscar Wong, a retired nuclear waste engineer, started it all when he opened **Highland Brewing Company** *(12 Old Charlotte Hwy.; 828-299-3370; highland brewing.com) Asheville's first and now largest brewery, in 1994 in the basement of Barley's Taproom. It's now located in a much larger facility east of downtown. Others of note include the* **French Broad Brewing Company** *(101 Fairview Rd.; 828-277-0222; frenchbroadbrewery.com) and the* **Asheville Brewing Company** *(77 Coxe Ave.; 828-255-4077; ashevillebrewing.com), which also runs a pizza joint here.*

For about $65 per person, **Brews Cruise** *takes drinkers on a tour of several breweries in an afternoon or evening. Tours even include a meal and tastings. Learn more at www.brewscruise.com. The Asheville Convention & Visitor Bureau has created an online guide to help you make plans yourself, or avoid the middle man and log straight on to www.brewtopiansociety.com.*

Hazel Robinson Amphitheatre. 92 Gay St.; (828) 254-5146; montfordparkplayers.org. Year after year the Montford Park Players produce North Carolina's longest-running and most acclaimed Shakespeare festival. The free productions are staged in the outdoor theater throughout the summer, Fri, Sat, and Sun 7:30 p.m.

Mount Mitchell. Milepost 355, Blue Ridge Parkway; (828) 675-4611; ncparks.gov. Mount Mitchell, at 6,684 feet above sea level, is the highest point on the East Coast. A small visitor center has exhibits on the peak and its plant and animal inhabitants. Behind the center is an observation platform and the grave of Dr. Elisha Mitchell, who fell to his death while trying to confirm the mountain's height. Picnicking is welcome, but there is also a restaurant here. Typically open during daylight hours.

The North Carolina Arboretum. 100 Frederick Law Olmsted Way; (828) 665-2492; ncar boretum.org. Art and cultivated gardens are parts of the exhibit that help guests understand the importance of plants to our world. Among the most prominent exhibits is a display of bonsai, an exhibit greenhouse, an azalea collection, and a heritage garden. In all there are more than 400 acres on which to enjoy reconnecting to the natural world. Guided outdoor walks are held Sat in warm weather months. The Baker Exhibit Center allows the garden ample opportunity to display art- and nature-based exhibits on a regular basis. It also hosts an orchid show early in the year and other events of horticultural interest later in the year. Admission is $8 per vehicle. Open daily 8 a.m. to 9 p.m. Apr through Oct, 8 a.m. to 7 p.m. Nov through Mar.

The Orange Peel. 101 Biltmore Ave.; (828) 398-1837; theorangepeel.net. Nothing better characterizes the Asheville music scene better than this venue. Featured in national media since reopening in this old skating rink in 2002, it is listed in *Rolling Stone*'s top five rock clubs in the country. Accommodating only 1,000 people even for national acts such as Bob Dylan and Ziggy Marley, this venue is intimate by comparison to other venues. When major acts aren't in town, the club caters to regional and up-and-coming artists.

Pinball Museum. 1 Battle Sq.; (828) 776-5671; ashevillepinball.com. If these flashing, dinging, tilting, bell-ringing machines were part of your past, you absolutely have to play the Adams Family Game. This Asheville museum doesn't have anything to do with art, history, science, or any of that—it's just for fun. The pinball museum has more than 30 machines— from the 1960s through the '90s—at any given time. Admission is $15 for adults and $13 for children under age 10. Play all you like for one low price. Open Wed through Fri 2 to 9 p.m., Sat noon to 9 p.m., and Sun 1 to 6 p.m.

Smith-McDowell House Museum. 283 Victoria Rd.; (828) 253-9231; wnchistory.org. This stunning brick home, built when bricks were rare, is meticulously maintained by the Western North Carolina Historical Association. The circa 1840 Victorian home is a clear window into the Antebellum South, and was built by James McConnell Smith, the son of a Revolutionary War colonel. Smith acquired great wealth, became mayor of Asheville for a period, and owned a number of businesses. Two other families and the Catholic diocese would own the home during its history, so today the home and exhibits trace that history through period rooms, clothing, and other items. The Historical Society renovated the home in winter 2023 with plans to reopen by summer. Admission is $7 for adults, $3 for ages 5 to 18. Open Wed through Sat 10 a.m. to 4 p.m., Sun noon to 4 p.m.

Thomas Wolfe Auditorium. 87 Haywood St.; (828) 259-5736; harrahscherokeecenter asheville.com. Located in the city's civic center, this auditorium is host to most of Asheville's performing arts groups, including the ballet and symphony.

Thomas Wolfe Memorial State Historic Site. 52 N. Market St.; (828) 253-8304; wolfe memorial.com. This is the boyhood home of someone who can reasonably be called one of America's great 20th-century novelists. Thomas Wolfe's home and life here were the basis of his novel *Look Homeward, Angel.* The home was tragically and significantly damaged by arson in 1998, and although restoration took six years, it reopened with artifacts that give a glimpse of life in this boarding house operated by Wolfe's mother. A visitor center located behind "old Kentucky Home," as Wolfe called it, includes slick audiovisual exhibits and other artifacts from his short life and stoic work. Admission is $5 for adults and $2 for students. Guided house tours are offered daily beginning at the bottom of each hour. Open Tues through Sat 9 a.m. to 5 p.m.

Whitewater Sportsman. Various locations around the Asheville area; (828) 216-1336; white watersportsman.com. Whitewater Sportsman offers guided raft fishing trips on the French Broad River even for anglers with little or no experience. This is one of the state's best rivers for smallmouth bass. Full-day trips take seven to eight hours, while half-day trips take four to five hours.

WNC Nature Center. 75 Gashes Creek Rd.; (828) 259-8080; wildwnc.org. This small and well-done zoo is located in a wooded area between downtown and the Blue Ridge Parkway. Gray wolves, bobcats, cougars, and coyotes are among the species represented along a hilly but navigable trail. It also has a farm exhibit with a petting zoo as well as indoor exhibits of spiders, snakes, and other small critters. Admission is $13.95 for adults, $12.95 for seniors, and $13.95 for children ages 3 to 15. Open daily 10 a.m. to 4:30 p.m., with reduced hours in winter.

The YMI Cultural Center (Young Men's Institute). 39 S. Market St.; (828) 257-4540; ymiculturalcenter.org. The YMI is the central part of "The Block," the center of Asheville's African-American commerce and culture. The center located in Pack Place conducts events and programs and hosts performances based on the African-American experience here and throughout the country. Hours vary according to programming.

where to shop

Grove Arcade. 1 Page Ave.; (828) 252-7799; grovearcade.com. The Grove building originally opened in 1929. It was a thriving public market until World War II when the federal government took it over as part of the war effort. The government maintained control of the building until the 1980s, when an effort began to renovate it for its original use. Today its tenants include apartment residents, offices, restaurants, and shops. It has dozens of fun, boutique stores with everything from gifts to clothing to bed and bath. Open Mon through Sat 10 a.m. to 6 p.m.; hours on Sun vary by store.

Historic Biltmore Village. 7 All Souls Crescent; (828) 274-8788; historicbiltmorevillage .com. Developed as part of George Vanderbilt's estate, Biltmore Village includes several dozen shops, galleries, and restaurants located in historic homes on tree-lined streets. Toy stores, antiques shops, craft galleries, hobby shops, and others make up this area. Hours vary by merchant.

River Arts District. Clingman Avenue at Lyman Street; (828) 552-4723; riverartsdistrict .com. Located along the French Broad River and the railroad, dozens of artists' studios are open in one of Asheville's coolest neighborhoods. An old depot, warehouses, and once-deteriorating buildings are vibrant works of art themselves.

Western North Carolina Farmers Market. 570 Brevard Rd.; (828) 253-1691; ncagr.gov. Don't slip out of Asheville without taking home some of the local delicacies. Fresh fruits and vegetables, jams, cheese, bakery items, honey, homemade fudge, handmade crafts, flowers, and plants are all offered. A deli, full-service restaurant and complete garden center are also on the site. Open daily 8 a.m. to 5 p.m.

where to eat

Barley's Taproom & Pizzeria. 42 Biltmore Ave.; (828) 255-0504; barleystaproom.com. One of the most popular places for locals to listen to music, Barley's Taproom & Pizzeria is in a renovated 1920s appliance store, and it's been here since 1994. A restaurant that serves pizza and sandwiches is located on the main floor with a music stage. Open daily at 11 a.m. $.

French Broad Chocolate Lounge. 10 S. Pack Sq.; (828) 252-4181; frenchbroad chocolates.com. The Liquid Truffle is the specialty of the house at this sweet spot in down-town Asheville. The handcrafted chocolates and other desserts are made largely from local and organic ingredients. Staff will even help pair chocolate desserts with the perfect wine. Open Sun through Thurs 11 a.m. to 11 p.m., Fri and Sat 11 a.m. to midnight. $.

Homegrown. 371 Merrimon Ave.; (828) 232-4340; slowfoodrightquick.com. Located near UNCA, Homegrown is as advertised—fresh local ingredients turned into great menu items like buttermilk fried chicken, smoked pork tacos, or redneck potpie that includes barbecue chicken and cheesy grits. Open Thurs through Mon 11 a.m. to 9 p.m. $$.

Jack of the Wood. 95 Patton Ave.; (828) 252-5445; jackofthewood.com. Play a game of darts, listen to music, drink a pint of ale, or get a plate of fish and chips at this warm and friendly Celtic pub downtown. Also try the specialties like shepherd's pie or Guinness stew along with burgers and salads. Open Mon through Sat 11:30 a.m. to 2 a.m., Sun 3 p.m. to 2 a.m. $$.

Sunny Point Café. 626 Haywood Rd.; (828) 252-0055; sunnypointcafe.com. A bright, cheery spot in West Asheville, Sunny Point, with its indoor and patio seating along a beauti-ful garden, is a great spot for brunch. Carrot hotcakes, Praline French Toast, and the MLT (mushroom, lettuce, and tomato) are just a few of the more unusual selections. Open daily at 8:30 a.m. $$.

Table. 18 N. Lexington Ave.; (828) 254-8980; tableasheville.com. Table is regarded as one of Asheville's best fine-dining experiences, but it's not traditional fine dining. Local meats and produce are used to produce exotic dishes. A simple rib eye, for example, is honey roasted with parsnip, and pork chops are combined with cranberry and Russian kale. The decor is clean and simple, the owner and chef Jacob Sessoms says, to "keep the focus on the food." Open for lunch 11:30 a.m. to 2:30 p.m., dinner 5:30 to 10 p.m., Sunday brunch 10:30 a.m. to 2:30 p.m. $$$.

where to stay

Asheville Bed & Breakfast Association. (877) 262-6867; ashevillebba.com. Asheville has almost 100 inns and bed-and-breakfasts, so the local association can help you work your way through the selections.

Biltmore Village Inn. 119 Dodge St.; (828) 274-8707; biltmorevillageinn.com. Not to be confused with properties at Biltmore Estate, this luxury inn is close to the estate but is run independently. Located on a hill overlooking the village and Swannanoa Valley, the 1892 Queen Anne Victorian has been restored to its original opulence. Unusually large rooms are located in the inn's two buildings. $$.

The Omni Grove Park Inn. 290 Macon Ave.; (800) 438-5800; groveparkinn.com. This well-known resort is more than a place to stay. It offers restaurants, a spa, golf, great views, a spectacular lobby known as the Great Hall, and more. The stone structure was built by a St. Louis entrepreneur in 1912 and 1913, in less than 12 months, using local stone. $$$.

Sourwood Inn. 810 Elk Mountain Scenic Hwy.; (828) 255-0690; sourwoodinn.com. Located outside Asheville near the parkway, this cedar and stone structure sits at an elevation overlooking Reams Creek. A private balcony offers great views in warm months, while a woodburning fireplace in each room offers a cozy atmosphere in cooler months. Rockers and quiet places scattered about the property beg for a little reading. $$$.

day trip 05

northwest

>>> **the high country:**
blowing rock, boone, banner elk

Elevations of around 3,500 feet keep this area blustery in winter, and winter sports enthusiasts take advantage of a climate that can bring 100 inches of natural snow to area peaks and their corresponding ski areas each year. An average high summertime temperature of less than 80 degrees creates the same enthusiasm for fair weather outdoor activities.

While Blowing Rock is named from a Cherokee legend that says a warrior was blown back up into the arms of his maiden from the strong winds rising out of Johns River Gorge, Boone gets its name from the legendary Daniel Boone, who is believed to have camped in the area that is now the city of Boone. It was incorporated in 1872, while Blowing Rock followed with incorporation in 1889 as the region was becoming a tourist destination with the opening of several hotels. Even as far back as the Civil War, soldiers would join their families here, and the wealthy from southern cities found their way here to beat the heat of summer.

Appalachian State University was founded in Boone as a teaching school in 1899 and became part of the state university system in 1967. Concurrently, clever entrepreneurs discovered they could draw skiers to the area, and the first of the region's three ski areas opened. Another popular 1960s attraction, Tweetsie Railroad, became the state's premier theme park for many years.

High Country Host (6370 US 321 South, Boone; 800-438-7500; highcountryhost .com) has become a central clearinghouse for information that even extends beyond Boone. You can stop at its visitor centers, call ahead, or check out the website for information or road conditions. Both Boone and Blowing Rock have visitor centers, too: **Boone Convention & Visitor Bureau** (331 Queen St., Ste. 101, Boone; 828-266-1345; explore

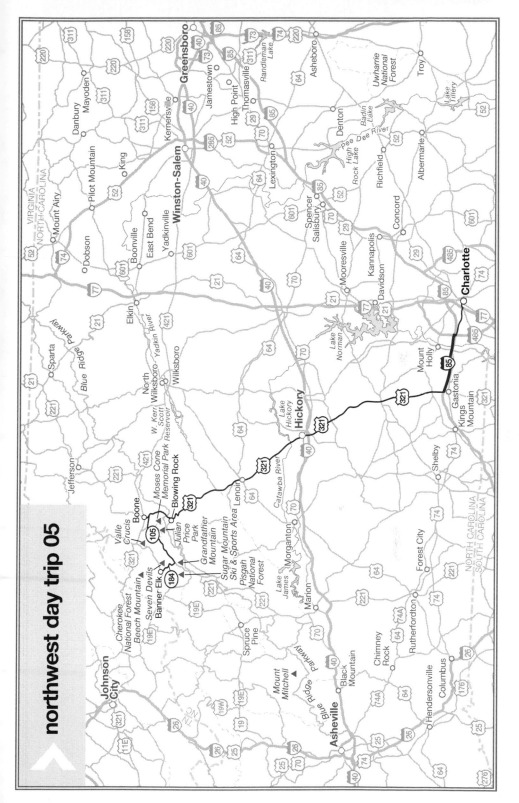

boone.com); and **Blowing Rock Tourism Development Authority** (132 Park Ave., Blowing Rock; 877-750-4636; blowingrock.com).

blowing rock

Blowing Rock is named after an outcropping that juts more than 1,000 feet from the surrounding landscape. Strong winds coming out of the gorge 1,500 feet below will be blown back up. It's a small town with a winter population of 1,400 and a summer population of 10,000 that depends heavily on tourism. Easy access to the Blue Ridge Parkway helps in that respect.

getting there

From Charlotte travel west on I-85 to US 321 North. Instead of taking I-40 near Hickory, continue on US 321. Blowing Rock is less than two hours away.

where to go

Appalachian Ski Mountain. 940 Ski Mountain Rd.; (828) 295-7828; appskimtn.com. Twelve slopes, an ice rink, and two terrain parks are included at this popular slope. It's smaller and at a lower elevation (4,000-foot peaks) than others, but it's also more easily accessed. The season typically runs mid-November through March. The facility includes a nice lodge with restaurant and ski shop. Lift tickets start at $34 weekdays in late season and go up to $77 weekends in season. Rentals start at around $20.

The Blowing Rock. 432 The Rock Rd.; (828) 295-7111; theblowingrock.com. Learn the legend of The Blowing Rock as you take in the views of Grandfather Mountain and Table Rock, all while breathing deeply the fresh mountain air. The Blowing Rock has been a tourist attraction since 1933 and includes a short scenic walk with a waterfall, garden, and observation tower. Admission is $9 for adults, $7 for seniors, and $3 for children ages 4 to 11. Open daily Apr through Dec, and Sat and Sun Jan through Mar.

Mystery Hill. 129 Mystery Hill Ln.; (828) 264-2792; mysteryhill.com. This small, non-traditional science center features a gravity-related phenomenon apparently related to its location. Balls appear to roll uphill, water flows differently than it does at your house, and walking down a sloped floor is a struggle akin to walking uphill. Other exhibits allow guests to enclose themselves in bubbles and experiment with other phenomena. An American Heritage Museum, American Indian artifact display, and several other attractions are also located at the same site. Open daily 9 a.m. to 5 p.m. with extended hours in summer. A variety of ticket packages start at $12.95.

Tweetsie Railroad. 300 Tweetsie Railroad Ln.; (800) 526-5740; tweetsie.com. The main attraction at this Wild West family theme park is a ride on ol' Number 12, a steam-powered train that takes a three-mile jaunt around the park's wooded acreage. Careful . . . outlaws are likely to hop aboard at any time. Other traditional theme park rides have a county fair feel. Shopping, restaurants, a saloon, and live entertainment populate the western board-walk town. It's especially good for families traveling with young children. Tickets are $58 for adults and $39 for children ages 3 to 12. Open 9 a.m. to 6 p.m. Fri through Sun in May, daily Memorial Day weekend through mid-Aug, and Fri to Sun mid-Aug through Oct. A Ghost Train Halloween Festival runs weekend evenings in Oct. Thomas the Tank Engine typically visits in summer.

where to shop

Historic Downtown Blowing Rock. Main Street; (877) 750-4696. A dozen or so shops are interspersed with restaurants and inns throughout downtown in the Village of Blowing Rock. A Bob Timberlake gallery, handcrafted jewelry, dulcimer makers, and other artists represent the range of offerings. All are in a shady, amicable downtown.

Parkway Craft Center. 6570 Blue Ridge Pkwy.; (828) 295-7938; southernhighlandguild .org. Located at Moses Cone Manor in Moses H. Cone Memorial Park, this shop is oper-ated by Southern Highland Craft Guild. Demonstrations are conducted on the big porch overlooking the farm, equestrian trails, and carriage paths. Handmade items from guild members are available for purchase. Open daily 9 a.m. to 5 p.m. mid-Mar through Nov.

Tanger Outlet. 278 Shoppes on the Parkway Rd.; (828) 295-4444; tangeroutlet.com. Located just off the parkway, this outlet offers 30 retailers. It has less personality than shop-ping districts in downtown Boone and Blowing Rock, but its location and layout are conve-nient. It includes outlets from the Gap to Ralph Lauren.

where to eat

Blowing Rock Brewing. 152 Sunset Dr.; (828) 414-9600; blowingrockbrewing.com. The convenient downtown location makes Blowing Rock Brewery an easy choice for lunch. Their well-done craft brews make it an even easier choice. While you will find traditional pub fare, you can also try the bison burger or a creative portobello melt. $$

Wheelie's Refresher. 8960 Valley Blvd.; (828) 295-7661; wheeliesrefresher.com. Beautiful views make good, casual food a little better. Located at the edge of a valley in the former Canyons Restaurant is a new casual restaurant serving a substantial selection of American food that ranges from Southwestern to salads and burgers. Open daily 11 a.m. until. $$

The Woodlands Barbecue Restaurant. 8304 Valley Blvd.; (828) 295-3651; wood landsbbq.com. Live, local entertainment plays nightly at this restaurant that serves a good plate of barbecue. Plates with hush puppies and slaw are served in a rustic atmosphere that includes picnic tables indoors. Open Sun through Thurs 11a.m. to 9 p.m., Fri and Sat 11 a.m. to 10 p.m. $–$$.

where to stay

Chetola Resort. 185 Chetola Lake Dr.; (800) 243-8652; chetola.com. This spectacular resort, whose name in Cherokee means "Haven to Rest," was first developed as an estate after the Civil War. It changed hands and developed through the years, until 1982, when a group of businessmen decided to open it as a luxury resort. Recreational activities include a spa, fishing, boating, hiking, swimming, a fitness center, and tennis. $$$.

Green Park Inn. 9239 Valley Blvd.; (828) 414-9230; greenparkinn.com. This sprawling Victorian hotel, built in 1882, was among the first in the High Country, making it the second-oldest operating hotel in the state. It's listed on the National Register of Historic Places. Continental breakfast is served each morning and tea each afternoon. Guests have included Eleanor Roosevelt, John Rockefeller, Annie Oakley, and Henry Fonda. Its trademark green shingle roof and shutters give it a stately place in the landscape. $$$.

Hemlock Inn. 134 Morris St.; (828) 295-7987; hemlockinn.net. Located in the heart of the village, the Hemlock is the perfect location for the day-tripper. Rooms in the main building offer a rustic, mountain setting with hardwood floors and antique decor. A new building that opened in 1999 has a more contemporary feel with vaulted ceilings and carpet. $$.

boone

Boone is a college town with a twist. While it has its share of traditional college attractions—pizza joints, music halls, team stores, and pubs—it is situated at one of the highest points east of the Mississippi for a city its size (population about 13,000). Appalachian State University, part of the state college system, is a central part of the city's energy and life. Winters can be long, snowy, and cold, but that doesn't stop vacationers from coming here year-round. Not only does it offer easily accessible winter sports, but also a spring and summer that are warm and temperate.

getting here

US 321 North turns seamlessly from Blowing Rock to Boone during the 15-minute drive almost as if they were one.

where to go

Daniel Boone Native Gardens. 651 Horn in the West Dr.; (828) 964-1815; danielboone nativegardens.org. North Carolina native trees, shrubs, and wildflowers are presented in an informal landscape design. With only three acres, the major objective is preserving native species and educating visitors about them. Admission is $5 for ages 16 and up. Open Mon 1 to 4 p.m., Thurs 9 a.m. to noon, and Sat. 11 a.m. to 1 p.m.

Hickory Ridge Living History Museum. 591 Horn in the West Dr.; (828) 264-2120; horn inthewest.com. Several original log cabins, one dating to the last quarter of the 1700s, afford an opportunity to observe antique dwellings, tools, and lifestyles. Docents in authentic 18th-century dress demonstrate various trades and tasks like weaving and hearthside cooking in this carefully curated facility. Free. The museum is open for guided tours seasonally, from 5:30 to 7:30 p.m. on the evenings of the outdoor drama *Horn in the West* performed here, and Sat mornings during the on-site farmers' market May through Oct.

Horn in the West. 591 Horn in the West Dr.; (828) 264-2120; horninthewest.com. Written by Kermit Hunter, this is a Revolutionary War period story of the families that settled the Blue Ridge in an effort to escape the British. Since 1952 a cast of 50 has presented the outdoor drama on a natural stage. Tickets are $30 for adults and $20 for children ages 12 and under. Shows nightly 8 p.m. late June to mid-Aug.

River & Earth Adventures. 1655 SR 105 South; (828) 355-9797; raftcavehike.com. Guided whitewater rafting, caving, hiking, and canoeing trips start from this base in Boone. Lunches and snacks are typically included. Offerings are seasonal and costs vary widely.

where to shop

Mast General Store. 3565 SR 194, Valle Crucis; (828) 963-6511; mastgeneralstore.com. Although there is a Mast General Store in downtown Boone and several other areas in the North Carolina mountains, this is the original store, founded in 1883 between Boone and Banner Elk. Candy, outdoor clothing, crafts, and specialty packaged food are for sale. This location offers an opportunity to warm up by the pot-bellied stove and see an era bygone. Open Mon through Sat 7 a.m. to 6:30 p.m., Sun noon to 6 p.m.

where to eat

Dan'l Boone Inn Restaurant. 130 Hardin St.; (828) 264-8657; danlbooneinn.com. Go ahead and make plans for a nap! Big, filling, home-cooked meals are served family-style in this restaurant. Open Mon through Fri 11:30 a.m. to 9 p.m., Sat and Sun 8 a.m. to 9 p.m. $$.

The Gamekeeper. 3005 Shulls Mill Rd.; (828) 963-7400; gamekeeper-nc.com. Buffalo, ostrich, and pheasant on the menu let diners know right away why this is called the Game-keeper. Adventurous diners can bring more conservative companions, who will find more traditional fine dining options on the menu. Dinner is served beginning at 5 p.m. Days of operation vary seasonally. $$$.

the grandfather of grandfather mountain

*Because of **Hugh Morton,** there are no buildings taller than three stories along the Blue Ridge Parkway, the air in North Carolina is a littler cleaner, and the parkway doesn't slice through Grandfather Mountain. Morton, a lifelong resident of the Old North State, inherited Grandfather Mountain from his grandfather in 1952 and began to develop it as an attraction where travelers could study nature. It now is the home of the mile-high swinging bridge and sick or injured animals that can't be returned to the wild.*

*But his legacy goes much further. At the top of a long list of Morton's accomplishments is facilitating a compromise with the US Park Service after 12 years of controversy to route the Blue Ridge Parkway around his mountain instead of through it. The result was the **Linn Cove Viaduct,** an engineering marvel and one of the most popular sections of the parkway. He helped spur the passing of **North Carolina's Clean Air Bill** that makes the state's air pollution laws tougher than federal mandates. And he helped push through a measure called the **Ridge Law** that excludes tall buildings in the pristine landscape along the parkway.*

*Principled, persuasive, and passionate is how Morton's friend and right-hand man of 33 years, Harris Prevost, described him. "He never, ever gave up. He would fight for what he believed in to the end." Morton died in 2006, but that's nowhere near the end of his story. It crosses county lines throughout the state. He was the unofficial, official photographer of the UNC Tar Heels basketball team for seven decades and is credited with the mooring of the USS Battleship North Carolina, another of the state's major attractions in Wilmington. But when they wanted to name SR 105 after him, he said no. There is plenty by which to remember him. An exhibit on Morton's life is open at **Grandfather Mountain** (Milepost 305, Blue Ridge Parkway, Linville; 828-733-4337; grandfather.com).*

where to stay

Lovill House Inn. 404 Old Bristol Rd.; (828) 270-0831; lovillhouseinn.com. This inn received a four-diamond rating from AAA for its seven spectacular rooms and well-appointed landscaped 11 acres. Rockers stand ready on the wraparound porch, and a hammock beneath maple trees beckons. Inside, natural woodwork and impeccable hardwood floors cast a warm glow along with the numerous fireplaces. $$$.

banner elk

The elevation in Banner Elk is slightly higher at 3,700 feet, and the population slightly sparser at fewer than 1,000 people. But height has its benefits. The highest ski slope in this part of the country is here, making Banner Elk an apt candidate for a day trip.

getting there

Banner Elk is west of Blowing Rock, just over two hours from Charlotte, but you'll want to get to it through Boone via US 321. Take a left on SR 105 South and a right on SR 184 North. The trip will take just about 30 minutes.

where to go

Hawksnest Tubing & Zip Line. 2058 Skyland Dr., Seven Devils; (828) 963-6561; hawks nesttubing.com. Those who want to avoid the high cost of skiing can head to this ski-slope-turned-tubing-park. The park is especially good for families, even those with younger children. Weekday tubing tickets are $35, and weekend tickets are $45. A four-cable zip-line tour around the park is $45. Hours vary seasonally.

Beech Mountain Resort. 1007 Beech Mountain Pkwy.; (828) 387-2011; beechmountain resort.com. Beech Mountain Resort is the highest ski area in the East with a peak of 5,506 feet. It has 15 slopes and a variety of terrain for skiing and snowboarding. There's a skating rink here, too. Weekday lift tickets start at $26 and top out at $87. Rentals start at $22 for a half day. Hours vary seasonally.

Sugar Mountain Resort. 1009 Sugar Mountain Dr.; (828) 898-4521, (800) 784-2768; skisugar.com. This is the area's largest ski area with 20 slopes and a terrain park. There is also an area for snow tubing and an outdoor ice skating rink. A snowshoe hiking program on Sugar Mountain has caught on in recent years. Sugar has two restaurants and a ski shop. The season usually runs from the first week in Nov to late Mar. Lift tickets start at $21 a night during the week and top out at $66 for a full holiday. Rentals start at $20. Hours vary seasonally.

ashe county frescoes

As drivers begin their descent from the High Country on scenic US 421, they are well advised to detour north on US 221 to the county of Ashe. Not only will this detour reveal New River State Park and the confluence of what some geologists believe is one of the world's oldest rivers, it's an opportunity to view the earliest work of North Carolina's most prestigious artist.

*Ben Long's frescoes in two old local churches make this county a destination not to be missed. Long, who grew up in Statesville not far from here, studied in Italy and brought his remarkable talent for painting on wet plaster back to the Carolinas. His first frescoes were Mary Great with Child, John the Baptist, and The Mystery of Faith at Saint Mary's Episcopal Church in West Jefferson. A few years later he painted a life-size depiction of The Last Supper at Holy Trinity Episcopal in Glendale Springs. He now has more than 10 other murals in North Carolina, including office buildings in downtown Charlotte. For more information contact the **Ashe County Frescoes Foundation** (201 River Knoll Dr., Jefferson, NC; 336-982-3261; ashefrescoes.org).*

where to stay

Banner Elk Winery & Villa. 60 Deer Run Ln.; (828) 898-9090; blueberryvilla.com. This spectacular countryside villa overlooks rolling landscapes, a vineyard, and winery as well as a trout pond. Named for the blueberries cultivated here, it has eight rooms. The winery is open for tours and tastings every day except Monday. $$$.

Inn at Elk River. 875 Main St. West; (828) 898-9669. This Williamsburg-style inn appears to be historic, but in fact has only been here since the mid-1990s. Private treetop decks with spectacular mountain views overlooking Elk River are only part of the amenities offered at this conveniently located inn. Four of the eight rooms have wood-burning fireplaces. $$.

festivals & celebrations

january

Battle of Cowpens Anniversary Celebration. Chesnee; (864) 461-2828; nps.gov/cowp. Living history encampments, tactical demonstrations, and lantern walks highlight the anniversary of the Battle of Cowpens, a key fight in the American Revolution.

Winterfest. Blowing Rock; (828) 295-7851; blowingrockwinterfest.com. This four-day festival begins with the Fire on the Rock cooking competition, then hayrides, bonfires, children's activities, music, a chili cook-off, and an ice carving completion. A polar plunge at Chetola Lake is one of the event highlights.

march

African-American Arts Festival. Greensboro; (336) 373-2044; greensboro-nc.gov. The City of Greensboro and a variety of cultural organizations celebrate African and African-American cultures during this one-day event at Festival Park. Music, demonstrations, storytelling, and craft activities make up the celebration.

april

Carolina First Carolina Cup. Camden; (803) 432-6513; carolinacup.org. Fans from across the Southeast break out big, fancy hats for this popular event at Springdale Race Course. This steeplechase racing tradition, called the "rites of spring," dates back to the 1920s.

Come See Me Festival. Rock Hill; (803) 329-7625; comeseeme.org. For 10 days each spring, the city of Rock Hill rolls out the red carpet for visitors. Virtually all the local attractions, arts organizations, and merchants participate in the festival. Highlights are concerts, a fun run, a parade, fireworks, and other festivities.

MerleFest. Wilkesboro; (336) 838-6267; merlefest.org. Held on the campus of Wilkes Community College, this is one of North Carolina's biggest musical events of the year. It brings out big-name national acts and gives a bigger stage to lesser-known regional acts. Named in memory of the late son of bluegrass legend Doc Watson, the show is renowned for the big-name acts taking the stage with virtual unknowns.

Pickens Azalea Festival. Pickens; (864) 878-3258; pickensazaleafestival.org. In North Carolina one of the largest and longest-running events is the Azalea Festival—but its site in Wilmington falls outside the purview of this guide. To pay homage to the flowering shrub in this region, you must travel only as far as upstate South Carolina. This two-day festival features music, tours of the historic town, arts and crafts, and other entertainment.

Spring Kiln Opening. Seagrove; discoverseagrove.com. More than 50 area potters participate in this bi-annual event in which each studio unloads its kilns of hundreds of pieces. They offer the pottery for sale either by lottery or by placing the pieces in the yard and offering them for sale in a method more typically associated with Black Friday.

may

Artisphere. Greenville; (864) 271-9398; artisphere.org. Greenville stakes a claim as a regional arts force with this event that brings nationally and internationally acclaimed artists to the city. It also provides a stage for local performers, youth groups, and artists.

NC Wine Festival. Clemmons; ncwinefestival.com. Tanglewood Park is the host of this event that features nearly 50 wineries. In addition to wine tasting, the event includes musical entertainment, food, and North Carolina crafts.

South Carolina Book Festival. Columbia; (803) 771-2477; huimanities.org. Nationally known authors, booksellers, and local cultural organizations come together for this weekend-long event. Writing workshops, lectures, and book signings comprise the event.

Yadkin Valley Wine Festival. Elkin; (336) 526-1111; yvwf.com. Crafts, music, and food are mixed with wines from more than two dozen wineries in the Yadkin Valley Area. Family-friendly events are also added to the festival.

june

43rd Annual Lumbee Homecoming. Pembroke; (910) 521-1311; lumbeehomecoming .com. A beauty pageant, golf tournament, and fishing tournament the week of the event lead up to a weekend of fireworks, games, and other events that help highlight the Lumbee tribe.

july

Highland Games. Linville; (828) 733-1333; gmhg.org. Grandfather Mountain has hosted these games for more than 50 years. There are serious competitions, bagpipes, and plenty of guys in kilts.

Pageland Watermelon Festival. Pageland; (843) 672-6400; pagelandchamber.com. Northing says summer in the South quite like watermelon, and they say summer loud and clear in Pageland, known far and wide for its watermelon. A parade, rodeo, music, and seed spittin' and watermelon eatin' contests create a fun down-home atmosphere.

august

Annual Mountain Dance & Folk Festival. Asheville; (828) 258-6101; folkheritage.org. Asheville has hosted this event for 80 years, and organizers say that makes it the nation's longest-running folk festival. The three-day event showcases the best of the region's traditional and old-time musicians, mountain dance groups, cloggers, ballad singers, and storytellers.

NC Gem and Mineral Festival. Spruce Pine; (828) 765-9033; ncgemfest.com. Since the 1950s this area has held a festival to celebrate the value of gems and minerals. They have been a big part of this area's production and tourist economy ever since it was settled. The festival includes gem sales, mine tours, and a variety of activities at local attractions.

september

Irmo Okra Strut Festival. Irmo; (803) 781-6122; okrastrut.com. What began as a little fundraiser for a local women's organization in the 1970s has become a two-day event that brings tens of thousands of people to downtown Irmo each year. The event contains all the typical festival ingredients, plus lots of fried okra. You might also find recipes for pickled okra, ham and okra pilaf, okra gumbo, etc.

NC Apple Festival. Hendersonville; (828) 697-4557; ncapplefestival.org. People fill the friendly streets of Hendersonville every Labor Day weekend for the state's official apple festival. A parade, children's activities, music, and other entertainment are planned. Of course, there are apples, applesauce, apple cider . . . you get the picture.

october

The Barbecue Festival. Lexington; thebarbecuefestival.com. The Barbecue Festival is held in downtown Lexington the third Sat in October, but make no mistake about it, October is barbecue month. It includes promotional events, singing competitions, a tennis tournament, a golf tournament, and more. On festival day, though, it's all about the 'cue.

South Carolina Jazz Festival. Cheraw; (843) 537-8422; scjazzfestival.com. The festival is held in honor of jazz legend Dizzy Gillespie, who was born here. In addition to a host of jazz performances, it includes restaurant crawls, art events, a bebop parade, and Sunday jazz Mass.

South Carolina State Fair. Columbia; (803) 799-3387; scstatefair.org. For 12 days people come from across the Carolinas for rides, games, exhibits, a petting zoo, barrel racing, grandstand entertainment, bands, dancers, and local entertainment.

Woolly Worm Festival. Banner Elk; (828) 898-5605; woollyworm.com. Fuzzy caterpillars provide the entertainment and predict the weather at this festival that's been going on in downtown Banner Elk since 1973. In addition to food, crafts, and entertainment, the festival holds a 5K for humans and slightly shorter races for woolly worms.

november

Festival of Lights. Clemmons; (336) 778-6300; forsyth.cc/parks. Drive through storybook scenes from Christmas past and present in one of North Carolina's biggest displays of more than one million lights. The transformation of Tanglewood Park runs from mid-November through January 1.

Holiday Lights at the Garden. Belmont; (704) 825-4490; dsbg.org. Daniel Stowe Botanical Garden begins a month-long celebration of the holiday with a walking light experience that focuses on the natural elements of the holiday. The event runs through December 31.

Holiday Lights on the River. Columbia; (803) 772-1228; icrc.net. This two-mile drive through Saluda Shoals Park along the Saluda River includes light displays that are presented from late November through December.

december

Christmastown USA. McAdenville; mcadenville-christmastown.com. After more than a half century of putting on this show, this mill town located between Belmont and Gastonia has earned the name of Christmastown USA. It's a traditional drive-through experience with green, red, and white lights that adorn trees and buildings throughout town.

index